The Genres
of *Gulliver's Travels*

The Genres of *Gulliver's Travels*

EDITED BY
Frederik N. Smith

DELAWARE

Newark: University of Delaware Press
London and Toronto: Associated University Presses

Associated University Presses
440 Forsgate Drive
Cranbury, NJ 08512

Associated University Presses
25 Sicilian Avenue
London WC1A 2QH, England

Associated University Presses
P.O. Box 488, Port Credit
Mississauga, Ontario
Canada L5G 4M2

The paper used in this publication meets the requirements of the American National Standard for Permanence of Paper for Printed Library Materials Z39.48-1984.

Library of Congress Cataloging-in-Publication Data

The Genres of Gulliver's travels.

Includes bibliographies and index.
1. Swift, Jonathan, 1667–1745.   Gulliver's travels.
2. Literary form.   I. Smith, Frederik N., 1940–
PR3724.G8G46   1990   823'.5   88-40261
ISBN 0-87413-359-9 (alk. paper)

PRINTED IN THE UNITED STATES OF AMERICA

To the memory of

Irvin Ehrenpreis

(1920–1985)

I think this, however, to be a plain proof that we act altogether by chance; and that the game, such as it is, plays itself.

Swift to the Earl of Peterborough
18 May 1714

Contents

8   Contents

Preface

The idea for this collection of essays grew out of a session I devised and chaired at a meeting some years ago of the American Society for Eighteenth-Century Studies. The positive response to the panel led me to consider putting together a collection of essays on *Gulliver's Travels*, each essay interpreting Swift's masterpiece from the standpoint of a different literary genre. Although the original idea has evolved over the years and although many genres have been added to the original four (only two contributors were part of the ASECS session), the idea with which I began has not changed.

What follows is a collection of previously unpublished essays that accomplish, I believe, two things at once: (1) they serve as a series of fresh interpretations of *Gulliver's Travels*, something that has not been done in book form for more than twenty years; and (2) they serve as a test case for recent thinking about the function of genre in the eighteenth century—not as a set of prescriptive conventions but as a malleable array of literary expectations. Those who read this volume will be in a position to judge the effectiveness of genre criticism in approaching works in the genre-conscious age of Swift. Such readers will also be able to recognize the difference between the restrictive sense of genre applied by previous generations of critics and the much wider, more flexible sense of genre applied by the contributors to this book.

I cannot thank everyone who should be thanked. I do wish, however, to express my appreciation to the University of Akron for awarding me a year's leave at a crucial stage of the development of the project, and while I no longer teach there, I recall with fondness the moral support of many colleagues in the Department of English. I likewise wish to express my appreciation to my present colleagues at the University of North Carolina at Charlotte, many of whom have encouraged me to pursue this project to its conclusion, and some of whom have heard about its progress more often than they deserved. More specifically, I wish to thank John Sena, Professor of English at Ohio State University and a contributor, a friend, and one who has all along felt sure of the ultimate success of this book and offered a number of helpful suggestions to guarantee that success. I want as well to thank Paula Wissing, our copyeditor at Associated University Presses; although I have never met her, I have seen the results of her careful, sensitive editing on every page of the manuscript.

I cannot thank enough my wife Jane, who has believed from the beginning in the value of this project (most forcefully when I wavered), has made time in our busy schedules for me to work on it, and has on innumerable occasions made suggestions for improvement from the sharpening of a sentence to the clarification of an idea. Although this book is not dedicated to Jane, this is only because it seems more timely to dedicate it to another.

Irvin Ehrenpreis has been the major influence on my career. His seriousness about his own scholarship was coupled with a deep respect for serious scholars; and he instilled in me, his student at the University of Virginia, a sense of the importance of the scholarly life. Equally important to me, however, was Irvin's teaching in a seminar on Swift and Pope—a course that compelled me to defend (if I could) all my critical assumptions, demanded of me imaginative, supportable responses, and never let me get away with a flimsy explanation of anything. His directing of my dissertation on Swift continued my tutorial on how to think and how to write. Tough-minded yet humane, Irvin continues to serve as a model in my teaching as well as my scholarship.

As a graduate student, when I once cited one of his published essays in a note, Irvin made me delete the reference; it was to be expected, he said, that a teacher would have had an influence on a student. When I sent him a copy of my first book, inscribed with a note saying that he could undoubtedly sense his influence on every page, he quickly wrote back that what he sensed most were the ways I had outgrown his ideas. I remember one other time that he told me never to dedicate a book to him. He believed strongly in the now somewhat lost sense of generations of scholar-teachers, each influenced by their mentors of the previous generation, all working toward a better, fuller understanding of their eighteenth-century subjects. Irvin would be embarrassed by these words, but he would understand, I hope, my deep appreciation of his profound effect on my life.

Notes on Contributors

JANET E. AIKINS is Associate Professor of English at the University of New Hampshire. She has published articles on *Clarissa, Venice Preserv'd, Roxana, The Tragedy of Jane Shore,* and other Restoration and eighteenth-century literature.

PAUL K. ALKON is Leo S. Bing Professor of English at the University of Southern California. In addition to various articles on eighteenth-century topics, he is the author of *Samuel Johnson and Moral Discipline* (1967), *Defoe and Fictional Time* (1979), and *Origins of Futuristic Fiction* (1987).

LOUISE K. BARNETT is Associate Professor of English at Rutgers University, New Brunswick, N.J. She has published widely on eighteenth-century subjects, and is the author of *Swift's Poetic Worlds* (1981) and editor of Pier Paolo Pasolini's *Heretical Empiricism* (1988).

J. PAUL HUNTER, Professor of English, University of Chicago, is the author of *The Reluctant Pilgrim: Defoe's Emblematic Methods and Quest for Form in "Robinson Crusoe"* (1966) and *Occasional Form: Henry Fielding and the Chains of Circumstance* (1975). His new book is titled *Before Novels* (1989).

MAXIMILLAN E. NOVAK is Professor of English at the University of California, Los Angeles. He is the author of *Defoe and the Nature of Man* (1963), *Realism, Myth, and History in Defoe's Fiction* (1983), and numerous articles on eighteenth-century fiction.

WILLIAM BOWMAN PIPER is Professor of English at Rice University in Houston, Texas. He has published articles on Berkeley, Swift, Pope, Gay, Johnson, Goldsmith, and others, and is the author of *Laurence Sterne* (1965), *The Heroic Couplet* (1969), *Evaluating Shakespeare's Sonnets* (1979), and a forthcoming book, *Immaterialist Aesthetics.*

JOHN F. SENA is Professor of English at Ohio State University. He has published on a range of eighteenth-century subjects and is the author of *A Bibliography of Melancholy* (1970) and *The Best-Natured Man: Sir Samuel Garth, Physician and Poet* (1986). He is interested in the relationship between medicine and literature as well as in illustrations for literary texts.

M. SARAH SMEDMAN is Associate Professor of English at the University of North Carolina at Charlotte. She has a wide reputation as a specialist in the field of children's literature and literature for adolescents and is currently at work on a critical biography of Katherine Paterson.

FREDERIK N. SMITH is Professor of English at the University of North Carolina at Charlotte. He has published numerous articles on Swift and on modern fiction, and is the author of *Language and Reality in Swift's "A Tale of a Tub"* (1979). He is now working on a book titled "Beckett's Eighteenth Century."

SIMON VAREY is currently a Lecturer at the University of California, Los Angeles. He is the author of a number of articles on eighteenth-century subjects and has published *Henry St John, Viscount Bolingbroke* (1984) and *Henry Fielding* (1986). He is working on an edition of the correspondence of Lord Bolingbroke.

The Genres
of *Gulliver's Travels*

Introduction

Frederik N. Smith

The eighteenth century's preoccupation with traditions, conventions, and classical models is a problem for newcomers to the literature of this period; although its formal self-consciousness strikes a sympathetic chord in readers of our day, ignorance of the historical and literary background makes it difficult for fledgling readers. Our own century seems to have a fascination with writers who do *not* respect conventions. Of course many of us have discovered that the eighteenth century's reputation for being rigidly rule-bound is about as apt as the label "Age of Reason." Certainly the fact that twentieth-century writers such as Joyce, Beckett, Barth, and Borges have discovered a kinship and an inspiration in the earlier period suggests that there may well be a common denominator here; but that's another story.

It is true that critics have for some time understood that eighteenth-century practice differed from its theory: although distinctions among genres was so much a part of the prevailing aesthetic, there were numerous works that deliberately jeopardized these distinctions. Almost thirty-five years ago, René Wellek wrote in *A History of Modern Criticism*: "In practice hybrids of genres or ruleless new genres outside the table of categories arose and were at least tolerated."[1] About the same time, in his introduction to the anthology of *Eighteenth Century Poetry and Prose*, Louis Bredvold said of the prose writers of the period:

> They transform or even create literary genres to suit their purpose; we talk so much of the uniformity and conventionality of the age that we do not always stop to admire the plasticity and originality of Dryden's critical essays, of Defoe's pamphlets and prose narratives, of the *Spectator's* various performances, of the plain prose of Franklin, Paine, and Corbett, of Swift's unique satires, of the narrative prose of Field, Smollett, and Jane Austen.[2]

Undoubtedly due in part to James Sutherland's conservative, highly influential *Preface to Eighteenth Century Poetry* (1948), the stereotype of a genre-bound eighteenth-century poetry held on a good while longer. Recently, however, Margaret Anne Doody has brought to light the experimental attitude that characterized both Restoration and eighteenth-century poetry:

> The [Restoration] poets dismantle genres, and dissect all poetic effects. . . . The Augustan poets who followed continued that enterprise and built their own poetry up from that shattered and re-modelled foundation. The whole period exhibits extreme generic self-consciousness, and a constant search for new and mixed genres, as well as an extreme stylistic self-consciousness born out of seeing the possibilities of parody, burlesque or alienation in every poetic idiom or voice.[3]

Paradoxically, the critical insistence on generic categories during the eighteenth century created opportunities for generic and stylistic experimentation and for humor, irony, and pathos that did not exist a century before or a century after. The initial reaction to such works as *A Tale of a Tub*, *The Dunciad*, and *Tristram Shandy* must have been enhanced by their appearance in an age that at least nominally saw itself as protector of the principles of classicism.

New Criticism dealt with genre as a given and thus made the subject if not off-limits, then at least an arid prospect for consideration. E. D. Hirsch's *Validity in Interpretation* (1967), however, with its emphasis on the premises of critical reading, including the reader's sense of genre, spawned a fresh (although sometimes antagonistic) interest in the subject.[4] In eighteenth-century circles, this interest was fed by three important theoretical statements on the subject that appeared in the 1970s: Ralph Cohen's "On the Interrelations of Eighteenth-Century Literary Forms" (1974), Ralph Rader's "The Concept of Genre and Eighteenth-Century Studies" (1974), and Murray Cohen's "Eighteenth-Century English Literature and Modern Critical Methodologies" (1979).[5] Renewed concern for the historical context of literature, plus a new focus on the response of readers to texts, have spurred on the reinvestigation of this principle of eighteenth-century criticism. Just as we have given up our relatively neat, novelistic interpretations of Augustan satire based on the New Critical concept of the persona, so we are being urged to surrender the idealistic (and potentially false) notion of readings based on singular conceptions of genre; indeed what appears to be emerging is a far more complex, subtle concept of eighteenth-century form than we have heretofore possessed. Of Rochester's "To a Lady in a Letter," Doody observes that after his treatment of the lyric, "no writer—and no reader—could be confident that genre had saving power, that genre was going to maintain stability so that meaning could be carried by it." Of Dryden's *The Hind and the Panther*, she comments that "the poem incorporates many styles and genres since it wants the reader to remain sceptical about all styles and genres—for all, even narrative fables, obscure the truth, and raise questions not answerable on earth." Speaking more generally, Doody says: "Generic trust had been lost. The Augustans had to work at creating new kinds of poetry that would not depend for support on formal expectations and restrictions."[6]

This is the atmosphere in which Dryden, Swift, Pope, and Fielding were writing. Note, however, that distrust of genre is not the same as debasement of genre; although genre *qua* genre may no longer be possible, and although writers and readers may no longer believe in the values assumed by genres conceived purely and simply, echoes of ancient genres could still be heard and could still be utilized as an interpretative mechanism. In fact the new and hybrid genres depend for their fullest effect on the presence of older genres that have contributed to their evolution. Thus Swift's and Pope's Horatian imitations ask that we remember the subject matter and tone of the originals; Swift's description poems depend on our recalling the traditional Georgic poem; Pope's *Rape of the Lock* and Fielding's *Joseph Andrews* require our knowledge of the epic tradition, and Homer in particular; Swift's *A Tale of a Tub* necessitates, for maximum effect, our knowing something about the "once upon a time" chapbook, the preface, and the learned footnote, to name only a few of the subgenres he toys with. What makes the Augustan handling of generic predisposition so interesting, however, is the fact that the new is often more than a mere send-up of the original type; the reader, knowing the demands of the original genre, is intended to discover the *ways* in which the work he or she is reading is different from the original, even partly different, or is intended in hybrid works to be able to sense and evaluate the interplay of several genres.

In his earliest odes the young Swift was willing to remain within his chosen genre; however, from "The Ode to Congreve" onward he was attracted to satire, and to a brand of satire that deliberately and overtly scrambles literary type. After his panegyric to Congreve, which repeatedly falls into a satirical mode, Swift turns away from idyllic poetry (not altogether unlike the young Pope) and begins to use genre as a pretense, a nominal frame within which he may unabashedly explore a range of genres, styles, and tones. "Mrs. Frances Harris's Petition" (1712), for example, begins and ends as a legal petition but is in essence a sort of working-class epistle—a far cry, of course, from Horace. "The Progress of Beauty" (1719) mocks the conventions of the pastoral, but as its title suggests, it plays on the idea of the conventional progress poem, and Celia ends up serving a much larger function, becoming a metaphor for original sin, the weakness of human nature, and the fragility of life itself. "Verses on the Death of Dr. Swift" (1731) was occasioned, Swift tells us in a headnote, by a maxim of La Rochefoucauld, and itself contains elements of *momento mori*, apologia, panegyric, and, of course, satire directed at the author as well as others. "Cassinus and Peter" (1734) ironically mocks the Petrarchan love poem and its descendants, and in doing so ridicules poetry that imitates not life but other poetry. Just reading a list of the titles of Swift's poems makes it clear how attentive he is (and wants his reader to be) to the presumed genres of these pieces: apology, ode, description, epigram, ballad, letter, libel, history, progress, dialogue, pastoral dialogue, elegy, satirical elegy, etc. Or it is possible to see the mix of genres implied in a title like "A Character, Panegyric, and Description of The Legion Club" (1736).

The Mechanical Operation of the Spirit and *A Tale of a Tub* (published together in 1704) demonstrate prior to *Gulliver's Travels* (1726) Swift's freedom, paraded before the reader, with prose genres. Although *The Mechanical Operation* is on its title page referred to as a "Discourse," the narrator admits to being perplexed as to "the most proper Form to send it abroad in," says he has settled on the epistle, and then within two pages announces that he is abandoning his chosen genre for allegory.[7] Similarly, in *A Tale of a Tub* Swift explicitly draws on the genres of apology, history, allegory, sermon, critical essay, and philosophical tract, and yet his satire breaks all such forms. Like so many other modernist works, it is a compound, "consisting in *Soups* and *Ollio's, Fricasées* and *Ragousts*."[8] In the eighteenth century there seems to be abroad a desire to question, invert, and mock genres and the assumptions that underpin them: "Almost every major poem," says Doody, "questions within itself the nature of its art and its undertaking. . . . Each poem makes room for differences, for various voices, various tones. The poets do

not shy away from, but rather welcome, discord and disso-
nance."[9] Ralph Cohen, commenting on Swift's mixing of genres,
observes that he "seems obsessed with the transformations of
norms to abnorms, of diversions to deviations."[10]

Swift's reference in the *Tale* to a writer's cultural memory is
relevant to any discussion of his habitual iconoclasm:

> Here the severe Reader may justly tax me as a Writer of short Memory,
> a Deficiency to which a true *Modern* cannot but be a little subject:
> Because, *Memory* being an Employment of the Mind upon things
> past, is a Faculty, for which the Learned, in our Illustrious Age, have
> no manner of Occasion, who deal entirely with *Invention*, and strike
> all Things out of themselves, or at least, by Collision, from each other.
> (pp. 134–35)

For a literary genre to function reliably for writer as well as
reader, memory plays an important role in embracing the particulars of convention; in the absence of memory, convention
does not exist, and all things must be spun anew and dealt with
by the reader as isolated instances of this or that. Swift's insight
into literary convention is suggested in the above passage: a
memory-only approach to the composition and reading of a text
would lead to an unoriginal, unchallenging, and all-too-expected
experience for a reader; on the other hand, literature without
memory (if one can imagine such a thing) eliminates resonance
with other texts as well as that within the text itself. Swift's
humorous punch line is not merely an elaboration of the modernist position but a third possibility: he suggests here a manner of
proceeding that neither surrenders to memory nor denies it, but
that sets genres on a collision course, then depends on the
reader's awareness of established forms as well as his or her
willingness to abandon them. This is Swift's method. It is not the
subversion of genre that characterizes his prose and poetry so
much as it is his deliberate mingling of genres. Implicit in this
technique is a relationship to his fictionalized reader (whom he
typically mocks) as well as to his actual reader (whom he tremen-
dously respects).

Although its underplayed style makes it appear as if *Gulliver's
Travels* remains more firmly committed to its genre—the travel
book—than the earlier prose works, the effects here are only
more subtle. In the final chapter of part 4 Gulliver distinguishes
between his own travel book, a vehicle for truth, and the "strange
improbable Tales" now passing for truth.[11] Elsewhere he refers to
his book as a "Treatise," a term Swift himself uses, along with

"Travels," in his well-known letter to Pope of 29 September 1725. Gulliver likewise alludes in the course of his travels to numerous other genres and subgenres: histories, accounts of manners and customs, translations, holy books, panegyrics, scientific essays, moral treatises, laws, inventories, articles of impeachment, and his own journal, the basis of his published travelogue. It is worth observing, however, that the age's skepticism toward genre is hinted at within the book itself; in almost every instance where a specific genre is mentioned (referring either to the *Travels* itself or to a textual type in one of the lands Gulliver visits), it is questioned in some way, said to be spurious, accused of being incorrect or potentially misleading. Thus the Lilliputian inventory of Gulliver's possessions is incomplete because the authors miss his secret pocket. The Lilliputian palace is burned as a result of the carelessness of a maid of honor lost in a romance. Glumdaclitch uses a small religious book she carries with her to teach Gulliver not religion but the Brobdingnagian alphabet. Gulliver fears a translation of his voyages will offend the Brobdingnagians because he has written in such an understated way. Genres are not respected or are used for purposes for which they were not intended. Even travel books can no longer be trusted— improbablities abound, statements cannot be verified, there are so many imposters!

Gulliver's Travels does not admit to easy categorization. Lord Orrery, one of its first commentators, described it variously as a satire, an allegory, a series of voyages, a "moral political romance," a "philosophical romance," and an "irregular essay."[12] In our own day, it has been described as a narrative satire, a picaresque tale, a novel, a political allegory, a travel book, a parody of the travel book, an imaginary voyage, a philosophic voyage, and as both a utopian and antiutopian romance. It has been read as both comic and tragic. It has been looked at as the fictional memoirs of a misanthropic sea captain and as Swift's "pseudo-memoirs."[13] Part 3 has a clear relationship to the history of science fiction. Part 4 suggests the beast fable. The book has been called a moral allegory drawn by its own length into the realm of mimetic fiction, becoming in part 4 a sort of "palimpsest" of allegory and fiction.[14] Since the eighteenth century, of course, it has been a popular children's book and has been illustrated by some of the best illustrators on both sides of the Atlantic; several film versions have been made. Indeed, a rough count shows that within the last five or six years alone there have been three new editions for adults (including one reprinting J. J.

Grandville's marvelous nineteenth-century illustrations), a dozen retellings for children of various ages, at least two *Gulliver* coloring books, and a filming for the BBC (*Gulliver in Lilliput*); the book has even inspired a symphony by Patrick Williams, with Sir John Gielgud narrating. *Gulliver's Travels* is one of those rare literary works—like *Alice in Wonderland*, for example—that endlessly fascinates new generations of children and adults, ordinary readers and critics. Perhaps it has survived precisely because it is so malleable to our evolving needs and tastes. Paradoxically, part of the attraction of a book like *Gulliver* may in fact be its tendency to break out of any category in which we attempt to cage it.

Our new willingness to recognize the instability of genre in the eighteenth century, plus its problematic usefulness in interpreting texts, makes the time right for a reevaluation of *Gulliver's Travels* from this perspective. The first eight of the following essays explore Swift's masterpiece from the standpoint of one or more genres: picaresque, history, novel, children's literature, illustrated book, scientific discourse, science fiction, philosophical treatise. Assumed throughout the volume, of course, is the membership of the book in the category "satire," but assumed also is the fact that "satire," a loose category at best, is not capable of identifying the text that is *Gulliver*. Moreover, it is interesting to note that the contributors to this volume all seem to view genre as a flexible construct, as a critical tool that cannot determine any reading, much less a reading of an eighteenth-century work such as this one. Indeed the very willingness of scholars to contribute to the present collection stems, I believe, from a realization that no single genre is a sufficient label for *Gulliver* and is a tacit acknowledgment that our concept of genre in the eighteenth century is no longer as absolute, as prescriptive as we used to take it to be.

One other emphasis in this collection that would set it apart from a hypothetical collection on the same subject published a decade or more ago is its emphasis on the reader. Each essay stresses the way Swift's reader responds to the text, the way he or she utilizes genre to arrive at meaning, handles conflicting generic cues, and escapes, finally, the temptation to apply genre in an overly rigid fashion. The three final contributions show how Swift's reader is repeatedly fooled but learns at last to walk steadily without the aid of any one genre; my afterword is an attempt to suggest in specific terms how that reader makes his or her way through the shifting generic styles that make up the text. There is throughout this volume an assumption regarding the basic indeterminancy of texts, and there is likewise implicit a certain (I would call it healthy) skepticism regarding the act of reading itself. The reader of the essays included here, like Swift's reader, would seem to be not passive but a willing, active participant in the process of building up meanings from Swift's frequently inconsistent words on the page.

Notes

1. *A History of Modern Criticism* (New Haven: Yale University Press, 1955), 1:20.

2. *Eighteenth Century Poetry and Prose* (New York: Ronald Press, 1956), p. xxii.

3. *The Daring Muse: Augustan Poetry Reconsidered* (London: Cambridge University Press, 1985), p. 56.

4. *Validity in Interpretation* (New Haven: Yale University Press, 1967). Hirsch does not mean "genre" in the altogether traditional way, but refers to a work's so-called intrinsic genres, or "that sense of the whole by means of which an interpreter can correctly understand any part in its determinacy" (p. 86).

5. Ralph Cohen and Ralph W. Rader, in *New Approaches to Eighteenth-Century Literature: Selected Papers from the English Institute*, ed. Phillip Harth (New York: Columbia University Press, 1974), pp. 33–77 and 79–115; and Murray Cohen, *The Eighteenth Century: Theory and Interpretation* 20 (1979): 5–23.

6. Doody, *The Daring Muse*, pp. 61, 78, and 61.

7. In *A Tale of a Tub, etc.*, ed. A. C. Guthkelch and D. Nichol Smith, 2d ed. (1920; Oxford: Clarendon Press, 1958), pp. 262 and 265.

8. *A Tale of a Tub*, p. 143.

9. Doody, *The Daring Muse*, p. 82.

10. Cohen, "On the Interrelations of Eighteenth-Century Literary Forms," in *New Approaches to Eighteenth-Century Literature*, p. 70.

11. *Gulliver's Travels*, ed. Herbert Davis (Oxford: Basil Blackwell, 1965), p. 291. The term "Treatise," mentioned in my next sentence, appears on p. 115.

12. *Remarks on the Life and Writing of Dr. Jonathan Swift*, rpt. in *Swift: The Critical Heritage*, ed. Kathleen Williams (New York: Barnes and Noble, 1970), pp. 121–23.

13. Irvin Ehrenpreis, *Swift: The Man, his Works, and the Age*, vol. 3: *Dean Swift* (Cambridge: Harvard University Press, 1983), p. 446.

14. Robert Scholes and Robert Kellogg, *The Nature of Narrative* (New York: Oxford University Press, 1966), pp. 112–15.

Gulliver's Travels and the Picaresque Voyage: Some Reflections on the Hazards of Genre Criticism

Maximillian E. Novak

1

In Jorge Luis Borges's sketch called "Utopia of a Tired Man," a wanderer stumbles into the world of the future where he encounters a man named "Someone." The narrator introduces himself as Eudoro Acevedo, a writer of "imaginative tales." Someone responds, "I remember having read, not without pleasure, two tales of an imaginative nature, . . . Travels of a Lemuel Gulliver, which many people take to be true, and the *Summa Theologica*. But let us not speak of facts."[1] Someone clearly regards speculations about genre as a fanciful exercise, and in a future world in which the inhabitants prefer to "shun pointless details," it is hardly surprising that he should want to leave such a subject as quickly as possible. Nevertheless, Someone has underscored a number of points for the reader. He has suggested that the concept of genre shifts with different times and places, and he has also put into our heads, as surely as might the narrator of *Tristram Shandy*, the notion that we can find some kind of system which will unite the productions of Swift and Saint Thomas Aquinas.

With the possible exception of Jonathan Swift, no one is more adept at reminding us of our propensity to construct systems and of their futility than Borges, whose stories dramatize this situation again and again. Most of us are probably familiar with his account of the wonderful cataloguing system that a Chinese library prepared for animals. In addition to such mismatches as "embalmed ones," "those that have just broken a flower vase," and "those that resemble flies from a distance," the system contains the useful but disorganized category, "others."[2] The effort to save the literature of the eighteenth century from the chaos in so loose a grouping as "others" has in the last two decades led to an unprecedented critical interest in genre. The real motivation behind modern efforts to establish the basis of genres appears to be that recently suggested by Jacques Derrida—a fear of contagion and a desire to keep things unmixed.[3] As Mary Douglas shows, however, this is an important aspect of primitive psychology, and any parent who has observed a similar pattern in the eating habits of his or her children might be more likely to locate our quest for rigidly defined genres in such a primitive mind-set than in the ability to detect specific genres.[4]

My own interest in fictional genres dates from my reading of E. D. Hirsch's *Validity in Interpretation* (1967), and I suspect that many of those not already under the influence of R. S. Crane and his followers may date their involvement from that time. I was convinced by Hirsch's argument that we cannot start to speak about a work until we know that particular type of literature we are about to discuss.[5] Although this still seems sensible enough, I am not sure that certainty in such matters is either crucial or attainable. On the other hand, I must confess that I have always been suspicious of the approach taken by the late Sheldon Sacks. Important as certain sections of *Fiction and the Shape of Belief* are, the notion of what may be considered Platonic ideas of genre and of an ideal form toward which works should aspire never appeared to me to be a helpful approach to the problem.[6] Some time after the appearance of Sacks's book, I heard him present a paper in which he suggested that genre might well be programmed into the human psyche and that our recognition of the signals given off by a work might be part of the inner working of the brain; using an analogy drawn from Chomsky's theories of an innate capacity to understand grammar, he argued that we may be able to distinguish among tragedy, comedy, and satire by similar means.[7] But a retreat to psychobiological interpretation seldom suggests confidence.

Sacks argued that *Gulliver's Travels* was a satire and that it was the nature of satire to focus on externals; to the extent that *Gulliver* involved the reader in any genuine concern for the titular character, Swift's work would have to be regarded as a failure. As evidence, he offered the shifting nature of Gulliver's character. The reader could hardly be involved with Gulliver as a character in the same way he or she becomes involved with a Pip or a Dorothea Brooke.[8] Sacks of course was not the first critic to remind us that *Gulliver* does not fit the usual pattern of modern fiction, or else we would have to stop and explain how the disturbed misanthrope of the fourth part and of the "Letter from Capt. Gulliver to his Cousin Sympson" could have written the first three parts.[9] But Sacks's seemingly acute argument, acute at least from the standpoint of the modern novel and modern psychology, failed to take into account the degree to which all narrative methods are based upon convention: the conventions of eighteenth-century fiction permitted a narrator to approximate the mental and psychological state of a person at the point in time when the narrative begins, without necessarily intervening along the way to explain the shifting nature of the narrator's character. And we must remember that prose fiction itself shares with satire the condition of being a mixed form; to expect generic purity from a combination of the two is to hope for too much. No wonder then that critics have returned to following the gradual decay of Gulliver's sanity from the cheerful young surgeon of the opening to the maniacal misanthrope of the conclusion.[10]

2

A concern with genre has the benefit of organizing our thoughts, but when we come to regard the systems we create as anything but convenient or compulsive man-made structures, we fall not only into the traps suggested by Borges, we are ensnared by those laid for us by Swift. "Where," asks a modern critic of fantasy, "did one place Rabelais, or Swift, before the term " 'Menippean satire' was rediscovered?"[11] Perhaps the critic most responsible for popularizing Menippean satire as an important category for fiction was Northrop Frye, and his starting point was *Gulliver's Travels*:

> Is *Gulliver's Travels* a novel? Here most would demur, including the Dewey decimal system, which puts it under "Satire and Humour." But surely everyone would call it fiction, and if it is fiction, a distinction appears between fiction as a genus and the novel as a species of that genus. It must then be another form of fiction, as it certainly has a form, and we feel that we are turning from the novel to this form, whatever it is, when we turn from Rousseau's *Emile* to Voltaire's *Candide*, or from Huxley's *Point Counterpoint* to *Brave New World*. The form thus has its own Traditions and . . . integrity.[12]

But before Frye has finished his discussion, he has changed the name of the category to that of the "anatomy" after Burton's

Anatomy of Melancholy. And by the time he has included such works as Walton's *Complete Angler,* on the grounds that it contains both poetry and prose, we might well wonder whether Frye has forgotten that he began with *Gulliver's Travels.* Tzvetan Todorov devoted part of the opening chapter of his book on the literature of the fantastic to demonstrating the inconsistency of Frye's taxonomy, and without wishing to replace Frye's categories with Todorov's "hollow structures" that seem so irrelevant to the discussion of great literature, we can rest with the observation that Frye's "anatomy" or "Menippean satire" is little different from something like "all the rest" or the "others" of Borges's Chinese library.[13]

If we are to use such a broad category we might as well focus on both the voyage aspect of *Gulliver's Travels* and its status as a first-person narrative. Both genuine and fictitious voyage accounts were common enough in Swift's time and bore some relationship to a number of other forms, particularly to the memoir, which was often considered to be indistinguishable from fiction. Some voyage accounts turned inward and followed the model of spiritual autobiography, and we know that to some extent Swift considered his work just that. In 1721 he wrote of his work-in-progress as "a History of my Travells."[14] Again, two years later he wrote to Charles Ford, "I have left the Country of Horses, and am in the flying Island. Where I shall not stay long, and my two last Journeys will soon be over."[15] Swift was not merely speaking of the journeys in the book. He was referring to the writing as a psychological voyage of discovery. In differentiating his own interests from those of his friend, Alexander Pope was fully aware of this. "Your Travels I hear much of," he wrote, "my own I promise you shall never more be in a strange land, but a diligent I hope useful, investigation of my own Territories."[16] I would not want to make too much of the autobiographical aspect of *Gulliver's Travels,* but we need to pay attention to the differences between the third-person narratives of Rabelais's *Gargantua* and the intense involvement of Gulliver in his experiences. Swift could write to Sheridan: "contract your Friendships, and expect no more from Man than such an Animal is capable of, and you will every day find my Description of Yahos more resembling. You should think and deal with every Man as a Villain."[17] There are plainly some ways in which *Gulliver's Travels,* with its conversion to misanthropy and its progressive and intensified movement from seeming thoughtlessness to awareness, bears an odd resemblance to those not uncommon fictional and genuine nautical versions of spiritual autobiography.[18]

But it was the sense of the outward voyage that seemed most apparent to Swift's contemporaries and to early critics. Hence the comparison between *Gulliver's Travels* and *Robinson Crusoe* that appears in works as far apart in time as Jonathan Smedley's *Gulliveriana* in 1728 and in Dunlop's *History of Fiction* in 1814. Smedley's reference to *Gulliver's Travels* as an "unnatural romance" is similar to the kind of insult hurled at Defoe's work by Charles Gildon, but when Smedley comes to a closer examination of the two works, he finds a similarity in their circumstantial detail and their use of voyaging, traits that Dunlop also selected.[19] That the obvious distinctions were not apparent to these critics must seem odd to us. Defoe has his utopian and antiutopian visions, particularly in the second part, but aside from the events of dream and vision, he keeps the marvelous within the arena of human hopes and fears. Swift's exploitation of the fantastic seems to us sufficiently dominant to make the two different in kind, and when Peterborough wrote Swift a letter calling him a "Magician" or "Wizard," he, at least, appears to have been fully aware of that distinction.[20]

We have to recognize that during the seventeenth and early eighteenth centuries, works of fiction, particularly those written in the first person, tended to mix all kinds of elements that we might prefer to believe ought not to be there. Baltasar Gracián's *El Criticón*, translated in 1681 as *The Critick*, commences as a philosophical Robinsonade, if I may be forgiven the anachronism, and gradually turns into a mixture of *Pilgrim's Progress* and *Gulliver's Travels*. Similarly, the mode that we usually consider to be related to an early attempt at fictional realism, the picaresque, usually contains both an imaginary voyage and considerable elements of the supernatural. One version of the second part of *Lazarillo de Tormes* saw the quintessential picaro thrown into the sea to dwell with mermaids for a period of time. In the fifth section of *The Adventures of Simplicissimus*, Grimmelshausen's hero descends to the center of the earth to indulge in lengthy conversations about the condition of the world with the ruler of the sylphs, gnomes, and nymphs; in the sixth section, however, Simplicissimus ends his life on a desert island much in the manner of *Robinson Crusoe*.[21] Frye argued with some assurance that there could be no ghosts in the realistic, low mimetic form—he even offers this as a test case of his classifications.[22] But ghosts are as common in early picaresque works as they are on the island of Glubbdubdrib.

Admittedly, to genre-conscious critics and translators of the nineteenth and twentieth centuries, such seeming aberrations

have been regarded with dismay. Vincente Espinel's fall from
"realism" is so startling that his translator steps from behind the
customary anonymity of that role to wonder aloud to the reader
about the wisdom of rendering into English the visit to the land
of the giants with which *La Vida de Marcos de Obregón* concludes.[23] Espinel's one-eyed giants, despite their fairly neutral
source in Homer's cyclops, have at least one foot in utopia. The
giants believe that worth and valor of mind is more important
than bulk and strength and base their behavior on reason. As a
result, for many of the same reasons that the Houyhnhnms decide to banish Gulliver, they agree to expel the Europeans from
their community:

> For that People, who had all their Members double, were likely to
> possess a spirit of Double-dealing; and as to the Preservation of Peace,
> which they had always professed, they would not be able to continue
> it if Foreigners were allowed to come and take Possession of their
> Territory in this Way. For, that if there should be any Disturbance in
> the Country, the Mischief would be greatly increased, by those being
> at Hand, who would be apt to assist and foment it:—That there would
> be a much better Chance of preserving Peace, if the Turbulent should
> have not to favour and encourage them; for that when Inferiors have
> once lost a proper Sense of Submission to their Superiors, there is no
> Possibility of Maintaining Peace; and if the Disturbers of the Publick
> Quiet meet with no one to unite with them, they remain in a State of
> Tranquility and Repose.[24]

The commander of these giants also argues that since the Europeans are of a different species, they will find peace impossible,
since quarrels are inevitable between such groups. Their presence, he argues, would hinder the giants' ability to "administer
justice with Impartiality."[25]

If, by the proper reading of literary history, the imaginary
voyage is allowed as a de facto extension of the picaresque, then
some other aspects of the picaresque may be seen as having
affinities with *Gulliver's Travels*. Although scatological references are certainly the province of satire, in the fiction of this
period scatological scenes and references were almost exclusively associated with the picaresque. Guzman de Alfarache
is led into a "Jakes" by a maid whom he believes he is about to
seduce, and on another occasion he is struck by a hog as he
pleads his master's cause to a lady and laid sprawling in a pit of
excrement.[26] The effect of such moments in the picaresque is
intense embarrassment and humiliation at the subsequent public

exposure. And in the ironic versions of the picaresque, such as Francisco de Quevedo Villegas's *La Vida del Buscón,* the method of excusing the telling of such accounts is much like Gulliver's way of aplogizing to the reader for what might seem like excessively detailed accounts of his evacuations and of those adventures that finish with him covered by ordure. On one occasion, when he is thrown into a privy by a rearing horse, Quevedo's Paul the Sharper asks the reader's "pardon" for his "plain speech."[27]

In addition to the various types of scatological details that connect *Gulliver's Travels* to the picaresque, the exploitation of the grotesque in the second and occasionally in the third parts draw some of their effects from the kind of exaggeration of the real with which these works abound. And many of the adventures are also similar. In his travels, the picaresque hero is likely to encounter mad projectors of the kind Gulliver meets in the academy of Lagado. Quevedo's rascal meets a man who wants to aid the Spaniards in attacking the Netherlands by using sponges to dry up the bays in the area, and shortly thereafter Paul meets with a projector who has developed a method of swordplay based entirely on mathematics.[28] Estevenillo Gonzales has a similar adventure with a mathematician about whom he comments sarcastically, "what he wanted in Experience, he could more than make amends for in Theory." So involved is this projector in his theories and so divorced from reality that without any concern for bloodshed, he is engrossed in perfecting new fortifications and an original use of gunpowder that he hopes will be employed in the destruction of a peaceful agricultural community.[29]

Although such adventures are common to satirical works of the time, they are especially a part of those in which satire is directed at contemporary society from the seemingly safe harbor of an imaginary land, and as we have seen, the picaro may eventually take a ship to such places. If it be objected that Gulliver is no rogue, we should realize that he is much closer to the picaresque hero than he is to those in Rabelais's *Gargantua* who accompany Panurge on his quest to find the secret of marriage and cuckoldom. Modern critics have too often elevated Gulliver to the status that a great heart surgeon might have in our society.[30] In fact, as a ship surgeon he is a good candidate for a picaresque tale. Marcos de Obregón begins with the picaresque narrator as an old man and famous physician, and part of his narrative involves the adventures of Doctor Sangredo. James Massey, the narrator of Simon Tyssot de Patot's *The Travels and Adventures of James Massey,* a work with a linear structure similar to that of the picaresque, practices as a doctor in France before going to sea as a ship surgeon.[31] Even before Le Sage published *Gil Blas* in 1715, picaresque heroes were by no means limited to low-born rascals. And picaresques such as Richard Head's *The English Rogue* tend to extol freedom, even if others, like Quevedo's *Paul the Sharper*, show the rogue seizing a prohibited and illusory freedom and ending disastrously.

Derrida has warned that genres are neither natural, logical, nor historical, and I would be the first to admit that this argument drawn from literary history is, to a degree, illogical if not unhistorical.[32] My aim in making this comparison between *Gulliver's Travels* and contemporary picaresque fiction has not been to suggest a final category into which Swift's work might be placed so much as to throw the matter open to discussion. While the reader of seventeenth-century romances, with their stylized rendering of landscape and allegorized historical figures, might have had little difficulty in recognizing their genre, even within these long tales they would have encountered numerous interpolated "novels" that would have been as various as a short tale of sensibility or the adventures of a clever rogue.[33] *Gulliver's Travels* is at once a pure (if tongue in cheek) imaginary voyage, written, as Swift has Richard Sympson say, for the benefit of seamen; a journey to utopia and dystopia; a spiritual autobiography; a picaresque narrative; and a parody of all of these forms. It is also a work that shares with the *Arabian Nights* and other popular oriental tales a pleasure in fantasy. The reader was to be surprised by the variety of effects rather than comforted by the fulfillment of expectation. Philip Gove, in his 1941 study of the imaginary voyage, had to clear away some of the problems of terminology in an effort to define the limits of his subject. In the process, he gave a good account of the difficulties encountered by various taxonomists over the centuries in their efforts to establish a definite category for *Gulliver's Travels*. He also expressed some sympathy for William Eddy's inability to decide whether Swift's work was a "Philosophic Voyage," a "Fantastic Voyage," or a "Realistic Voyage." Interestingly enough, in 1734 Nicholas Lengelet du Fresnoy placed both *Robinson Crusoe* and *Gulliver's Travels* in his fourteenth and last category for fiction, "Romans divers qui ne se raportent à aucune des classes précédentes," or that category that has already been discussed, "everything else."[34] The main objection to such a useful classification is that it undoes the very idea of taxonomy. And it is hardly beyond possibility that Swift, who detested all kinds of systems, gave some thought to creating a puzzle for the critic who liked to place his literary works in neat categories.

3

Gulliver's Travels is far from being unique in mixing so many fictional forms. Tyssot's *The Travels and Adventures of James Massey* has long been considered one of Swift's sources, and there is something to be gained by examining the texture of this work, particularly those sections that Swift apparently knew and used, in relationship to Swift's *Travels*.[35]

Tyssot's protagonist, as we have seen, is trained as a surgeon. This decision is made after his father is killed by an explosion on his ship. Interestingly enough, Massey's mother decides that he must become a doctor on the basis of his known delight in travel. From the very beginning of the work, Tyssot works to achieve a sense of authenticity by the circumstantial use of dates and names. His father dies in 1639, and the physicians to whom he is apprenticed are first a Monsieur Rousseau and then a Monsieur La Croix at Dieppe, whom he describes as "a very able Master."[36] While at Dieppe, he has an experience that might have come out of a Gothic romance. He meets Michrob, the Wandering Jew, who informs him that after Christ's death, the saints rose out of their graves and flew up to heaven; Michrob adds the detail that these resurrected spirits had neither teeth nor sexual organs.[37] Massey takes his first post as a ship surgeon on 21 May 1643, but the voyage is unfortunate. The vessel sinks, and they have to be rescued by an Englishman, Captain Davidson, who takes them to Lisbon.

Meanwhile, Tyssot gives the reader a running account of Massey's intellectual development. He loves mathematics and languages, but metaphysics—even that of Descartes and Pascal—leaves him sceptical. When he reads the Bible for the first time, he finds it "an ill-concerted Romance" and Genesis in particular a "meer Fiction."[38] He eventually arrives at a belief in a deity, but in the manner of the Enlightenment's reasonable man he prefers thinkers who swim against the stream—who do not simply accept the ideas of their ancestors. His studies teach him that all sensation comes from without, that humans can have only one perception at a time, and that there is a distinction between internal and external time. His most important discovery is that men need to live according to the laws of nature, but he also informs the reader about his specialty in science. He dissects a black and states that the corpse had a special membrane under the skin to protect the body from the sun; and later in the work, he enters into great detail on the condition of the internal organs of an asthmatic sailor whose body he cuts open.[39] In addition to such accounts, Massey tells a story about a clever rogue who managed to defraud a Dutch merchant named Van Dyke by pretending to be his nephew. Up to this point, Tyssot's book is a fictional memoir with a picaresque plot and the usual realistic detail of that form in combination with an Enlightenment bildungsroman.

After Massey decides to take a ship to the Portuguese East Indies, the work changes direction. The ship is struck by a typhoon off St. Helena, and the crew and passengers are driven ashore in the vicinity of what is probably Argentina. "Curiosity" drives Massey to explore inland, and he sets off with his two companions, Du Puis and Le Foret. They come upon three unexplained pyramidical tombs with Hebrew writing on the outside and upon a terrifying, almost surreal landscape. Du Puis disappears into a great hole in the ground, but after Massey has a dream of "Deliverance," they succeed in crossing a lake and come upon a new civilization that is rich in agricultural products and minerals.[40]

The book turns into a voyage to a limited utopia as they arrive at Austral land. Here there is no death penalty on grounds that are not very different from those to be advanced by Beccaria later in the century—that no man or man-made institution had the right to deprive anyone of his or her life.[41] There are various offices and ranks within the society, but since a revolution overthrew a tyrannical government and a powerful priesthood, a general equality was established among the citizens. Although a monarchy, Austral Land's king rules through the laws. Massey gives a number of examples to illustrate the workings of what appears to be a rather rigid system of justice and also outlines the structure of what seems to be a language based on logical principles of grammar. The nation has apparently never warred with its neighbors, and the king does not understand why men would fight. When Massey tells him that God approves of wars, the king is furious: "I am really charm'd with your Sciences," he remarks, "but your Religion and your Politicks don't please me at all."[42] Massey's explanation of the workings of gunpower and cannons also leave the monarch both puzzled and disturbed:

Fire-Arms were also quite unknown to him, but the bad Use that they were put to, took off his liking to them. Nothing affected him with so much Horror as the Narratives I gave him now and then, of our Wars and bloody Battles. He could not conceive how People could be so silly as to rush into Slaughter, and to the Destruction of their Species, for such trifling Causes, and often only for gratifying the Covetousness, Ambition, or Caprice of one Man.[43]

Le Foret's ability as a watch-maker gives him a certain importance in society, but it also involves him in a disappointing flirtation that makes him want to leave the country.[44] When he and the others finally reach their companions after an arduous journey back to the coast, one of the group wonders why they left "a land of Blessing and Peace, from whence Soldiers are banish'd as much as great Men."[45] Eventually the group is rescued, but before this occurs Massey finds time to continue his scientific experiments and to raise more questions about the myths in the Old Testament.

He is left off at Goa on 13 April 1663 and practices medicine there until 1669, when he is accused before the Inquisition and thrown into prison. Before he is sentenced to be sent back to Portugal to a punishment of hard labor, he has long conversations with a fellow prisoner about the folly of believing in biblical miracles. The ship taking him back to Portugal is captured by pirates, and he is made a slave at Sercelli near Algiers. At this point the work turns into that genre described by G. A. Starr—the narrative of captivity in Barbary.[46] Massey is a slave for fifteen years during which time he has a variety of adventures before managing to contact the English Consul. During his time there he meets Peter Huddle, the man who robbed the Dutchman at the start of his narrative. Huddle's tale is a series of picaresque adventures including an intricate "sting" operation in France that involved his pretended conversion to Judaism, his marriage to the daughter of a wealthy Jew, and his successful theft of vast amounts of gold after having convinced his father-in-law that he had found the secret of the philosopher's stone. Massey leaves Algiers and arrives at London on 4 May 1694. There he finds his brother and a few of the group with whom he had been shipwrecked in South America. He concludes his book with a concern for any omissions and a certain fear for the utopia he has left. "I was afraid lest my Book would excite the Ambition of some insatiable Monarch to conquer the Kingdom I describe, and that he would compel me to serve as a Guide to those who should be employ'd in so difficult an Expedition."[47]

The unity of tone and effect that Swift achieved in *Gulliver's Travels* appears awesome when placed next to Tyssot's work, but certain aspects of the *Travels and Adventures of James Massey* demand our attention. The real land of Japan and the very real pirates in *Gulliver's Travels* have their parallels in Tyssot's picture of Goa and his Algerian pirates. Austral, his utopia, has many of the characteristics of the land of Brobdingnag—a government based on an observation of the law as well as a sense that the present species have deteriorated from what they were in the past. Both are practical utopias. Swift's has beggars and executions; Tyssot's has mining accidents. The passages in Tyssot's narrative that are critical of western religion and of the violations of natural law by the conventional laws of European governments are part of a general pattern of criticism that may be found throughout the work, but the conversations about war, in which Massey suddenly expresses his pleasure in the concept of the God of Battles and seems delighted in the destruction wrought by contemporary weapons, are not prepared for at all. Just as Swift was to insist on providing the grimmest details of the ways in which men are killed during battles on land and at sea, so Massey, long after the king has expressed his strongest disapproval of war, describes how twenty thousand men might be sacrificed to gain five hundred paces and how soldiers often become beggars or outlaws after the war has ended.

From a character who dislikes those who blindly accept the ideas of their ancestors, Massey has suddenly become a defender of the most irrational elements in the life of his society. That he should listen to criticism of the Christian idea of a life after death or of the brief age of the world without commenting is very much in character, since he has earlier expressed his doubts about Christianity and the literal interpretation of biblical texts. That he should suddenly defend the horrors of warfare is not. Yet I doubt if we suddenly feel that we are no longer in the presence of the narrator James Massey. It seems to me that what we do as readers is to take note of this oddity without worrying about it too much. The same kind of situation occurs in *The Adventures of Simplicissmus,* when the narrator, being asked to give a similar account of European life by the king of the underground, suddenly steps entirely out of character to present an idealized picture of the devotion of priests, the mildness of princes, and the happiness of the people under these monarchs.[48] Though it is certainly a lapse in consistency of character, we do not feel that the author has given us a different character to deal with; he is still the man who suffered through the horrors of the Thirty Years' War. All of which may mean that we have made too much of what has been seen as Gulliver's sudden shifts in character or Swift's sudden change in the masks that he wishes Gulliver to wear. There is no reason to posit a different fictional rhetoric for Swift and Tyssot. As readers, we blink at the inconsistencies and then continue to reconstruct a semblance of character. Perhaps at such points the reader tends to perceive character entirely in terms of authorial discourse, and at least momentarily to dismiss the illusion of character.

What I have tried to show is that once we consider *Gulliver's Travels* as a work of fiction, we cannot shunt it off into a meaningless category such as anatomy or Menippean satire. A study of eighteenth-century continuations of *Gulliver's Travels* reveals an even more definite movement in the direction of voyage fiction and the Robinsonade.[49] But to judge Swift's masterpiece by these pitiful imitations would be a grave error. Derrida has advanced the following hypothesis: "A text cannot belong to no genre, it cannot be without or less a genre. Every text participates in one or several genres, there is no genreless text; there is always a genre and genres, yet such participation never amounts to belonging." Taking the novel as an example, he remarks that it "gathers together the corpus and, at the same time, in the same blinking of an eye, keeps it from closing, from identifying itself with itself. This axiom of non-closure or non-fulfillment enfolds within itself the condition for the possibility and the impossibility of taxonomy."[50]

What we need to understand first of all is the degree to which *Gulliver's Travels* participated in the various fictional forms of its time. If we do this, we will be better able to see the various possibilities that Swift explored as well as those that he avoided, and we will not try to impose a unified genre where none was intended and none can exist. Secondly, we have to be aware of the way any great work goes beyond the seemingly established bounds of genre and marks off its own territory. Both *Robinson Crusoe* and *Gulliver's Travels* were new beginnings. To see them too much in terms of genre is to protest too much against their undeniable originality. If *Robinson Crusoe* moved prose fiction in the direction of a realistic portrayal of human nature under extreme circumstances, *Gulliver's Travels* made possible a type of fiction based on artfully constructed systems of fantasy.

Notes

1. Borges, *The Book of Sand*, trans. Norman Thomas di Giovanni (New York: Dutton, 1977), p. 91. Although Borges's work has occasionally been applied to Swift's writings by way of illustrating various methods of entrapment, I am grateful to my student, Annette Leddy, for reminding me of the ways it reflects on the nature of genre.

2. "The Analytical Language of John Wilkins," in *Other Inquistions 1937–1952*, trans. Ruth L. C. Sims (New York: Simon and Schuster, 1965), pp. 103–4. Borges also instances the one thousand subdivisions used by the Bibliographical Institute of Brussels as another example of "arbitrariness" in classification.

3. Jacques Derrida, "The Law of Genre," trans. Avital Ronell, *Glyph 7* (1980): Reprinted in *On Narrative*, ed. W. V. T. Mitchell (Chicago: University of Chicago Press, 1981), pp. 51–77.

4. See Mary Douglas, *Purity and Danger* (New York: Praeger, 1969), pp. 2–3, 41–57.

5. See Hirsch, *Validity in Interpretation* (New Haven: Yale University Press, 1967), p. 113.

6. Although Sacks denied that he was prescribing a particular form, his critical theory leads inevitably to the conclusion that to obtain good artistic results, formal structures must be followed. See Sheldon Sacks, *Fiction and the Shape of Belief* (Chicago: University of Chicago Press, 1964), pp. 10–11.

7. See Sacks, "Psychological Implications of Generic Distinctions," delivered at meeting of the Modern Language Association, 27 December 1967.

8. Sacks, *Fiction and the Shape of Belief*, pp. 16, 34–35.

9. See C. J. Rawson, *Gulliver and the Gentle Reader* (London: Routledge and Kegan Paul, 1973), p. 27.

10. See, for example, Frances D. Louis, *Swift's Anatomy of Misunderstanding* (Totowa, N. J.: Barnes and Noble, 1981), pp. 126–167; and with greater subtlety, Michael Seidel, *Satiric Inheritance* (Princeton: Princeton University Press, 1979), pp. 201–25.

11. Christine Brooke Rose, *A Rhetoric of the Unreal* (Cambridge: Cambridge University Press, 1981), p. 65.

12. Northrop Frye, *The Anatomy of Criticism* (Princeton: Princeton University Press, 1957), p. 303.

13. See Tzvetan Todorov, *The Fantatstic*, trans. Richard Howard (Ithaca: Cornell University Press, 1975), pp. 9–19.

14. Jonathan Swift, *Correspondence*, ed. Harold Williams (Oxford: Clarendon Press, 1963), 2:381.

15. Swift, *Correspondence*, 3:5.

16. Swift, *Correspondence*, 3:96.

17. Swift, *Correspondence*, 3:94.

18. See, for example, Richard Norwood, *The Journal of Richard Norwood*, ed. Wesley Craven and Walter Hayward (New York: Scholars Facsimiles and Reprints, 1945), pp. 31–33, 63–84. For a general discussion of this genre, see G. A. Starr, *Defoe and Spiritual Autobiography* (Princeton: Princeton University Press, 1965), pp. 24, 36–49; and J. Paul Hunter, *The Reluctant Pilgrim* (Baltimore: Johns Hopkins Press, 1966), pp. 76–92.

19. *Gulliveriana* (London, 1728), p. 331; and John Dunlop, *History of Fiction* (London: Longman, 1814), 3:398–402. See also the implicit comparison of the two works in Samuel Taylor Coleridge, *Miscellaneous Criticism*, ed. Thomas Raysor (Cambridge: Harvard University Press, 1936), p. 293.

20. Swift, *Correspondence*, 3:192.

21. See A. T. S. Goodrick, trans., *The Adventurous Simplicissimus*, by Hans Jacob Christoffel von Grimmelshausen (Lincoln: University of Nebraska Press, 1962), p. 357. This comparison is common enough, and Defoe may have known enough German to have read parts of it. But if Defoe gave a boost to island adventures to the extent of appropriating all of these that came before, we need to keep in mind that they were part of the seventeenth- and eighteenth-century mythos long before 1719.

22. *Anatomy of Criticism*, p. 50. In his few comments on the picaresque, Frye treats it as low mimetic.

23. Espinel, *Marcos de Obregón*, trans. Algernon Langton (London: John Booth, 1816), p. 427. Espinel's work was translated into French in 1618.

24. Espinel, *Marcos de Obregón*, pp. 456–57.

25. Espinel, *Marcos de Obregón*, p. 257. Cf. the debate among the Houyhnhnms over the wisdom of allowing Gulliver to remain among them in *Gulliver's Travels*, in *The Prose Works of Jonathan Swift*, ed. Herbert Davis et al. (Oxford: Basil Blackwell, 1939–68), 11:279. Subsequent references will be to this edition.

26. Mateo Alemán, *The Spanish Rogue*, trans. J. Savage, et al. (London, 1708), 2:82–83. I deliberately use this translation with its amplifications by Bremond as part of the tradition of this work rather than the somewhat more accurate translation of James Mabbe.

27. Francisco Gomez de Quevedo, in *The Choice Humorous and Satirical Works*, trans. Sir Roger L'Estrange, John Stevens, et al., ed. Charles Duff (London: Routledge, 1926), p. 27.

28. Quevedo, in *Humorous and Satirical Works*, p. 42.

29. *Estevanillo Gonzales*, in *The Spanish Libertines*, trans. John Stevens (London: S. Bunchley, 1707), pp. 504–7.

30. See especially Louis, *Swift's Anatomy of Misunderstanding*, p. 125.

31. Tyssot, *The Travels and Adventures of James Massey*, trans. Stephen Whately (London, 1733), pp. 4–8. Tyssot's work was originally published in French in 1710. Although the 1733 translation omits a few of Massey's more iconoclastic comments, I have, for convenience, used this edition while checking it against the original.

32. Derrida, "The Law of Genre," pp. 207 and 209.

33. The opposite might be said about *The Spanish Rogue*, which contains interpolated romances.

34. Gove, *The Imaginary Voyage* (London: Holland Press, 1961), pp. 20–25, 36.

35. See William Eddy, *Gulliver's Travels* (Princeton: Princeton University Press, 1923; rpt. 1963), p. 207.

36. Tyssot, *Travels and Adventures of James Massey*, p. 8. Cf. Swift's "my very good Master Mr. Bates," *Gulliver's Travels*, p. 19.

37. Although David McKee in his monograph on Tyssot argues that passages of this kind should be seen entirely in the light of furthering the Enlightenment's attack upon miracles, Massey states that the man claiming to be the Wandering Jew fueled his imagination and desire to travel. This was one of the passages that was excised slightly in the 1733 translation. See Tyssot, *Travels 2nd Adventures of James Massey*, pp. 9–11; and McKee, *Simon Tyssot de Patot and the Seventeenth-Century Background of Critical Deism*, Johns Hopkins Studies in Romance Literatures and Languages, Vol. 40 (Baltimore: Johns Hopkins University Press, 1941), p. 43.

38. Tyssot, *Travels and Adventures of James Massey*, p. 15.

39. One reason for the account of the autopsy on the black slave is to suggest that the biblical account of the sons of Ham was a fable. See McKee, *Simon Tyssot de Patot*, pp. 41–42. For a fuller rendition into English of this passage, see the 1743 translation, Tyssot, *The Travels and Adventures of James Massey* (London: J. Watts, 1743), p. 24.

40. Tyssot, *Travels and Adventures of James Massey*, p. 68. "Deliverance" is a major theme in *Robinson Crusoe*, which like Swift's work may have been influenced by the realism of Tyssot's voyage account. See Hunter, *The Reluctant Pilgrim*, pp. 168–201.

41. See Cesare Beccaria, *An Essay on Crimes and Punishments* (Stanford: Stanford University Press, 1953), pp. 97–98. Unlike Tyssot, Swift had no objection to capital punishment. There is nothing in the grotesque description of an execution among the Brogdignagians to suggest an objection to such punishments, though he certainly disliked having the victims make speeches before being dispatched.

42. Tyssot, *Travels and Adventures of James Massey*, p. 140.

43. Tyssot, *Travels and Adventures of James Massey*, p. 138.

44. This adventure leads to a typical picaresque adventure with the consequent humiliation of the roguish hero. Le Foret has to escape through a privy to avoid being discovered in the apartment of one of the queens.

45. Tyssot, *Travels and Adventures of James Massey*, p. 232. Swift would certainly have appreciated this attack upon war and military greatness, but what must have amounted to a fascination with the imaginary voyages of his time has to raise some questions about his willingness to read through so much of the questioning of traditional religious doctrine and practice that was endemic to the form.

46. "Escape from Barbary: A Seventeenth-Century Genre," *Huntington Library Quarterly* 24 (1965): 35–52.

47. Tyssot, *Travels and Adventures of James Massey*, pp. 317–18. Cf. *Gulliver's Travels*, pp. 292–94.

48. Grimmelshausen, *Der Abenteuerliche Simplicissimus* (Stuttgart: Riederer Verlag, 1963), pp. 502–5.

49. For example, see Pierre François Guyot Desfontaines, *The Travels of Mr. John Gulliver*, trans. J. Lockman (London, 1731), 1:110 and 168.

50. Derrida, "Law of Genre," p. 212.

Exemplary History and the Political Satire of *Gulliver's Travels*

Simon Varey

If Swift, Pope, Gay, and Bolingbroke satirized any one political system in the late 1720s, that system was obviously Walpole's. The satirists continually contrasted the key vice of corruption with that rare and elusive commodity, virtue. One way in which the opposition literature vexed the Walpolean world was to present examples of vicious men who resembled Walpole, or virtuous men who did not. Gulliver in Glubbdubdrib contents himself with "beholding the Destroyers of Tyrants and Usurpers, and the Restorers of Liberty to oppressed and injured Nations."[1] Pope went a little further, and occasionally named names; Gay was hardly more circumspect, and in an openly defiant campaign Bolingbroke pointedly likened specific destroyers and usurpers from the past to the first minister. In the case of *Gulliver's Travels* the parallels and contrasts have caused a well-known critical problem, for although the characters seem in some places to represent real people from among Swift's contemporaries, they do not do in others, so that consistent identifications of the fictional characters with real public figures are simply not to be found.

The political significance of *Gulliver's Travels* has been widely recognized since Sir Charles Firth identified individual characters with real people.[2] Then in a famous and influential essay on *Gulliver's Travels*, Arthur E. Case put forward an extensive series of identifications of Swift's characters: in Case's scenario, "Lilliput represents the joint political fortunes of Oxford and Bolingbroke during the latter half of Queen Anne's reign"; Swift can "make use of the most dramatic incidents from the life of each man," yet "avoid too close a parallel with the life of either."[3] Case made Gulliver in Lilliput a composite of two men and the emperor of Lilliput becomes George I because he does *not* resemble him; Skyresh Bolgolam is the Earl of Nottingham; Blefuscu is

France, Lilliput England; High-Heels are Tories, Low-Heels Whigs; Flimnap is Walpole; Limnac, Lalcon, and Balmuff are identified by the offices they hold as Stanhope, the Duke of Devonshire, and Lord Cowper respectively. And so it goes. As long as *Gulliver's Travels* is taken to be allegorical, such identifications may lead to impossible parallels. Case therefore had to explain some of them away: "Flimnap is represented from the beginning of the story as Prime Minister and Gulliver's most potent enemy, though Walpole did not become head of the government until 1720. Swift is careful, however, not to attribute to Walpole any act of hostility to the Tory administration for which he was not responsible."[4] Flimnap is a prime minister but he is not always Walpole. J. A. Downie has demonstrated the "unhistorical" nature of Case's interpretation of the voyage to Lilliput as a political allegory of England between 1708 and 1715.[5]

Case also found that the first and third voyages are "primarily satiric in tone," but that the second and fourth (with a few exceptions) "are in differing degrees Utopian commonwealths" and that Swift "has no desire to identify their ruling classes with those of his own country."[6] Yet, as Downie has convincingly shown, the king of Brobdingnag exposes the shortcomings of the Walpole administration with a counterblast of the "most potent and deliberate" satire.[7] Similarly, Gulliver ironically condemns "a *First* or *Chief Minister of State*," and his Houyhnhnm master releases a satirical attack on the irrational, corrupt state of British government and law (11:255, 259–64). The second and fourth voyages may seem less satiric because the satire is more general, less obviously directed at named characters, apparently involving fewer individuals.

Although some early readers saw in *Gulliver's Travels* only a general satire, others were quick to make individual identifications, which Swift seems to have veiled intentionally. In a much-quoted (and variously interpreted) letter of 16 November 1726, Pope told Swift: "I find no considerable man very angry at the book: some indeed think it rather too bold, and too general a Satire: but none, that I hear of, accuse it of particular reflections (I mean no persons of consequence, or good judgment; the mob of Critics, you know, always are desirous to apply Satire to those they envy for being above them) so that you needed not to have been so secret upon this head."[8] It is a fact that almost none of Swift's contemporaries recorded identifications of the kind put forward by Case.

Opposed to Firth and Case, F. P. Lock's recent study of

Gulliver's Travels is extreme in denying virtually any allusions to specific people and events, even though the opposition literature to which the *Travels* belonged was developing a system of ironic allusion (in part to avoid attracting prosecutions for libel) in order to point to Walpole. In overthrowing the very kind of approach used by Firth, Case, and their many followers, Lock pleads for an entirely general satire, whose aid is "to attack not particular Whigs or Whig policies, nor even Whiggism, but the perennial political disease of which Whiggery was only a contemporary manifestation."[9] Lock's argument is important, even if many are unconvinced by it. All good satires have a generalizing tendency: very few present exact portraits of real individuals, where every detail in the fictional portrait corresponds to a detail in a real person. But a political satire so general that it presents no recognizable individuals would have very little bite; it could too easily read like philosophy. One of the great strengths of Augustan satire is its very specificity: satiric characters such as Peachum, Sporus, and Timon have a definite presence as individuals, who may yet suggest a general type. In Augustan satire, particularly in the atmosphere of the late 1720s, general implications lay behind specific allusions, prompting alert readers to recognize a reference to Walpole when they saw one.

To the expert allusion-hunters who were Swift's readers, "disposed," as Lock points out, "to find veiled hints and allusions almost everywhere," the specific example gave satiric life to the general idea.[10] It was a commonplace of the age that examples work more forcibly on the mind than precepts.[11] One of the many allusive comparisons used by the opposition to Walpole contrasted the example of the stable, prosperous state of Britain under Queen Anne's last ministry with the national decline over which "a certain *Great Man*" had presided since 1721. Indeed, a conspicuous example of this contrast is a passage, later deleted, in Benjamin Motte's first edition of *Gulliver's Travels*, part 4, chapter 6.[12] Phillip Harth has argued persuasively that the period from 1710 to 1714 is unlikely to have provided the model for political activities and relationships in Lilliput, especially because contemporary readers do not seem to have made any such allegorical identification.[13] While *Gulliver* contains, in my view, many allusions to specific people and events from the period of the queen's last ministry and other periods, it is not a political allegory in which every character, action, and motive contributes to a portrait of a single period.

Gulliver's Travels is analogical rather than allegorical, and its

generality emerges only through specific allusions. I shall argue
that it is simultaneously a satire and a species of history: so
rather than search for alternative identifications, I shall consider
the analogical technique of Swift's political satire in *Gulliver's
Travels* in light of his conception of historiography. In common
with so many of his contemporaries, Swift accepted that human
nature was generally uniform and therefore did not change fundamentally from one age to the next or from one European
culture to another. He also subscribed to the concomitant theory
that history is cyclical. The major classical influences on Swift's
conception of history were Tacitus, Polybius, and Dionysius of
Halicarnassus, although Swift learned much from Sir William
Temple, as A. C. Elias has ably shown; Elias, Lock, and others
have argued that Swift also learned his politics from Temple.[14]
Swift's principles of history and politics had been long established by the time he came into contact with the leaders of
Queen Anne's last ministry: Oxford and Bolingbroke.

Herbert Davis has pointed out the main features of what he
calls "the Augustan Conception of History."[15] This conception,
which Swift certainly shared, requires wisdom, virtue, and judgment in the historian. Like his friends, Swift hoped that an
objective history of Britain could one day be written, and he
hoped in particular that the four last years of the queen would be
the subject of an objective history, whether written by himself or
by Bolingbroke. The objective historian is a judge, a public wit-
ness whose task is to praise the virtuous and punish the vicious.
Now Swift knew very well that praise and blame belonged appropriately to the domain of the rhetorician, and that objectivity
could be distorted—or discarded altogether—by any historian.
The historian who sits in judgment on the grand designs of
politics and wars is close, as Davis saw, to the satirist who
comments "on the contemporary scene."[16] This essentially
moral conception of historiography becomes an important part
of the foundation on which the political satire of *Gulliver's
Travels* is built and should help explain why a consistent pattern
of allegorical identification is so elusive.

In his memorial to the queen dated 15 April 1714, Swift peti-
tioned for the post of historiographer (and for the necessary
documents) in order to write an official history of Anne's reign.
The reason why such a history should be written, he said, was
that "The change of ministry about four years ago, the fall of the
Duke of Marlborough, and the proceedings since, in relation to

the peace and treaties, are all capable of being very maliciously represented to posterity, if they should fall under the pen of some writer of the opposite party, as they probably may," and therefore "some able hand" should be employed, to ensure "that the truth of things may be transmitted to future ages, and bear down the falsehood of malicious pens" (8:200). Two things strike me about this brief document: first, only the last four years—not the whole reign—interest Swift; and second, as historiographer, Swift would aim to combine the preservation of truth with the business of vindication—against malice—for the benefit of posterity.

The failure of Swift's application for the post did not stop him from writing five historical works about the period from 1710 to 1714. That this was an unusually important period for Britain cannot be doubted. Swift thought so, perhaps because he had found in Harley a minister whose "Old Whig" principles agreed so well with his own. J. W. Johnson thinks that so much ostensibly historical writing about these important and eventful years shows Swift's "obsession with preserving facts, setting the historical record 'straight.'"[17] But Johnson's judgment takes at face value Swift's claims to justify men's actions to posterity and therefore makes the historical writing seem much more objective than it really is. Swift's editors, Herbert Davis and Irvin Ehrenpreis, call these histories "valid" despite their being "the work of one whose party and personal loyalties are never disguised, and who seems to write with the intention of pursuing his enemies and witnessing against them to later generations" (8:xxxix). The only one of these works that even pretends to be objective is the *History of the Four Last Years of the Queen.*

The *History* is certainly less personal than the shorter *Memoirs, Relating to That Change Which Happened in the Queen's Ministry in the Year 1710*, or *Some Free Thoughts upon the Present State of Affairs*, and, as one should expect, it lacks the immediacy of such a controversial pamphlet as *The Publick Spirit of the Whigs*. The pamphlets are partisan pieces, obviously full of bias and distortion. Although their author is a judge, he is certainly not objective. But Swift's *History* justifies the ministry and its one great achievement, the Treaty of Utrecht of 1713, in a tone that is on the whole sober and detached.

Yet I think that Swift's few departures from that tone are the most revealing parts of the *History*. His professed aims in the *History* are close to those of his petition for the post of historiographer:

> Although in an Age like ours I can expect very few impartial Readers;
> yet I shall strictly follow Truth, or what reasonably appeared to me to
> be such, after the most impartial Inquiries I could make, and the best
> Opportunityes of being informed by those who were the principal
> Actors or Advisers. Neither shall I mingle Panegyrick or Satire with
> an History intended to inform Posterity, as well as to instruct those of
> the present Age, who may be Ignorant or Misled: Since Facts truly
> related are the best Applauses, or most lasting Reproaches. (7:1–2)

In the customary formulation of the time, panegyric is associated
with applause, satire with reproach. But the historian, it seems,
should stand impartially between these two extremes, allowing
"Facts" to distribute praise and blame. To present the truth—
those facts which he proposes to relate truly—this historian is
obliged to confess that his portraits of the principal characters
are incomplete: "I do not pretend to draw their Characters entire,
which would be tedious, and little to the purpose; but shall only
single out those Passions, Acquirements and Habits, which the
Owners were most likely to transferr into their Political Schemes;
and which were most subservient to the Designs they seemed to
have in View" (7:5). Although a minor confession like this may
be designed to establish an image of an impartial narrator, it
actually has the opposite effect, since Swift lays himself open to
an accusation that such an incomplete account must be biased,
as the first editor of the *History* complained: "What writing, what
sentence, what character can stand this torture?—What extreme
perversion may not, let me say, does not, this produce?—Yet thus
does he choose to treat all men that were not favorers of the *latest*
measures of the QUEEN."[18] The whole truth, therefore, can
scarcely be obtained.

Sometimes Swift is an impartial narrator who gives credit
where it is due to an opponent—for instance, the French foreign
minister, Torcy (7:160). At other times Swift casts himself in the
role of moral judge. For example, referring to the incomplete and
misleading accounts of peace negotiations before 1710, Swift
dismisses one such negotiation as "a Piece of Management altogether Absurd, and without Example; contrived only to deceive our People into a Belief, that a Peace was intended; and to
shew what great Things the Ministry designed to do" (7:33).
There is nothing impartial about this explosive intrusion. Where
the narrator of the *History* speaks directly to his reader, he often
appeals either to reason or to the superior knowledge he has
gained by his insider's access to authoritative sources. But here,
or later where the historian presumes (without citing evidence)

to identify the concealed intentions of Monsieur Buys, Swift is not relating facts dispassionately at all (7:56–57).

Of such instances of his partiality, the most emphatically partisan and striking is his commentary on the rapid rise of the new system of public credit. Here, Swift attacks England's adoption since 1688 of Dutch financial practices. With William III needing money for his wars, funds were raised

> upon the Security of Taxes, that were only sufficient to pay a large Interest. The Motives which prevailed on People to fall in with this Project, were many and plausible. For supposing, as the Ministers industriously gave out, That the War could not last above One or Two Campagnes at most, it might be carryed on with very moderate Taxes, and the Debts accrueing would in process of Time be easily cleared after a Peace. (7:68)

The effect of this arrangement was to attract money from those involved in trade that was now insecure. "It was," Swift continues, "the Business of such as were then in Power to cultivate a money'd Interest" because the gentry cared little for William's Dutch "Notions in Government" based on unrepayable debts (7:69). Swift had established some of his argument in *The Conduct of the Allies*. Here, though, he holds William himself partly responsible for Britain's large debts because although Dutch financial practices might work effectively in the Netherlands, they do not work in Britain. Of course, the British themselves should have realized that conditions were different in the two countries and thus should not have adopted those "pernicious Counsels," half-digested and half-understood, which have brought financial—and moral—trouble.

Swift relates how the "artful Men" who exploited this financial system found it "the most fruitful Seminary, not only to establish a Faction they intended to set up for their own Support; but likewise, to raise vast Wealth for themselves in particular, who were to be the Managers and Directors in it" (7:69). It was in their interests then to accumulate national debts, which would tend to impoverish "the Landed Men" and loosen their grip on borough elections: "this was arrived to such a Height, that a very few Years more of War and Funds would have clearly cast the Balance on the Money'd Side" (7:70). This economic system—whose success rested on that baffling network of credit—had thus been introduced and established between 1688 and 1710. Swift therefore attributes the large national debt not to mismanagement by the queen's last ministry but to an imported economic system

inherited as a problem by that ministry. One task facing the
ministry is to resist this new financial system's tendency to
hasten the transfer of political power from land to money—to
resist, therefore, the imposition by "artful Men" of a Dutch economic base for political power. After 1720, Swift and his fellow
satirists opposed Walpole by resisting this system and denounc-
ing corruption among its exponents.[19]

Later in the *History*, Swift attacks the behavior of the Dutch
during the Utrecht negotiations with a rhetorical energy that
recalls not only *The Conduct of the Allies* but also his own
Examiner and Bolingbroke's *Letter to the Examiner*—all of them
partisan in the extreme. The Dutch are said to have been guilty of
"a Strain of the lower Politicks," at which they are the world's
experts, and of lying in wait to take advantage of the poor,
distressed British (7:109). Dutch politicians at the Hague are
portrayed as "daily fed with the vain Hopes of the Queen's
Death" by "their old ejected Friends in *England*" (7:124). The
result of this is litigiousness among the Dutch plenipotentiaries,
"than which nothing could give greater Advantage to the Enemy"
(7:124). By aligning the Dutch explicitly with the disaffected in
England, the partisan historian associates opposition to the ministry with opposition to the national interest; since his most
consistent appeal is to the authority of reason, one might detect a
rhetorical tendency to make opposition to the queen's last ministry irrational, too. And opposition comes from the Dutch-in-
spired moneyed interest, governed by that most discreditable of
motives, greed. Thus the problem facing the new ministry in
1710 was simultaneously financial, political, and moral.

Important to any discussion of *Gulliver's Travels* and history is
Swift's notion of history as exemplary. As he says in the *Memoirs,
Relating to That Change Which Happened in the Queen's Ministry in the Year 1710*: "I am deceived, if in history there can be
found any period more full of passages, which the curious of
another age would be glad to know the secret springs of; or, from
whence more useful instructions may be gathered for directing
the conduct of those, who shall hereafter have the good or ill
fortune to be engaged in business of the state" (8:108). The
period of the Oxford-Bolingbroke ministry therefore claims so
much of Swift's attention because it is exemplary. Exemplary
history is a means of distributing applause and reproach for the
purpose of promoting virtue and discouraging vice. Indeed, such
history does what Swift said at the outset his own *History* would
do, and what he was satisfied it had in fact achieved:

The blackest Characters to be met with in [the *History*], were not drawn with the least Mixture of Malice or ill Will; but meerly to expose the Odiousness of Vice; For I have always held it as a Maxim, that ill Men are placed beyond the Reach of an Historian, who indeed hath it in his Power to reward Virtue, but not punish Vice; Because I never yet saw a profligate Person, who seemed to have the least regard in what manner his Name should be transmitted to Posterity. . . . (8:141–42)

With a characteristically disingenuous twist, Swift at once presents an example of "a profligate Person," the Earl of Wharton. In 1736, when Swift was revising his *History,* Bolingbroke was building his own historical philosophy on the basis of the exemplar theory of history, whose "principal duty," according to Tacitus, "is to erect a tribunal" where men's actions are judged.[20]

Based on Polybius, and on Dionysius's cliché that history is philosophy teaching by examples, the exemplar theory of history had also become the cornerstone of popular opposition satire in *Cato's Letters* (which first appeared in the *London Journal,* 1720–21), in the Duke of Wharton's *True Briton* (1723), and most obviously in Bolingbroke's *Remarks on the History of England* (1730–31) and his other papers for the *Craftsman.* Using the lessons of examples, historian and satirist alike could turn history to an effective moral purpose, as Swift knew. He also knew that history placed before the satirist a temptation to distort. In the *Examiner* he wrote of an "Expedient, frequently practised with great Safety and Success by satyrical Writers: Which is, That of looking into History for some Character bearing a Resemblance to the Person we would describe; and with the absolute Power of altering, adding or suppressing what Circumstances we please, I conceive we must have very bad Luck, or very little Skill to fail" (3:26). And in a well-known *Intelligencer,* Swift distinguished between two satiric purposes, "one of them less noble than the other, as regarding nothing further than the private Satisfaction, and Pleasure of the Writer; but without any View towards *personal Malice:* The other is a *publick Spirit,* prompting Men of Genius and Virtue, to mend the World as far as they are able" (12:34). History and satire, to Swift as to Bolingbroke, are linked by the common aim of promoting virtue at the expense of vice. This function seems to be inevitably bound up with the task of preserving truth: as Gulliver discovers to his disgust in Glubbdubdrib, most modern history conceals and distorts the truth. And, of course, Gulliver confesses that in Brobdingnag he suppressed or altered truth when describing his own country, but

in the light of his experience, "NOTHING but an extreme love
_th could have hindered me from concealing this Part of my
ᴗᴛᴏ._ʃ" (11:133).

To Swift the historian, the period from 1710 to 17,14 is an
example of political virtue faced with malicious opposition, and
his duty is to make history reflect this conflict. In common with
his fellow satirists, Swift renews the theme in the 1720s. Without
being allegorical, *Gulliver's Travels*, like the other contemporary
opposition satires, sometimes alludes to the period of Queen
Anne's last ministry; it also alludes more generally to the struggles of the virtuous to overcome the effects of the economic
system basic to Walpole's power. The system is the same: those
resisting it were ministers under Queen Anne, but are the opposition under King George. Gulliver's descriptions of his native
country persuade the king of Brobdingnag that British political
institutions originally "might have been tolerable; but these half
erased, and the rest wholly blurred and blotted by Corruptions"
(11:132). Gulliver's Houyhnhnm master concludes that British
"Institutions of *Government* and *Law* were plainly owing to our
gross Defects in *Reason*, and by consequence, in *Virtue*": all that
reason has done is "to aggravate our *natural* Corruptions, and to
acquire new ones which Nature had not given us" (11:259). In
parts 2 and 4, Gulliver describes Britain as suffering a decline
brought about by corruption; he thus adheres closely to a cyclical
view of history. Where Gulliver recounts the conflict in his mind
between truth and patriotism, he appeals to the authority of an
ancient historian and identifies himself implicitly as an historian:

> Yet thus much I may be allowed to say in my own Vindication; that I
> artfully eluded many of his Questions; and gave to every Point a more
> favourable turn by many Degrees than the strictness of Truth would
> allow. For, I have always born that laudable Partiality to my own
> Country, which *Dionysius Halicarnassensis* with so much Justice
> recommends to an Historian. I would hide the Frailties and Defor-
> mities of my Political Mother, and place her Virtues and Beauties in
> the most advantageous Light. This was my sincere Endeavour in
> those many Discourses I had with that Monarch, although it unfor-
> tunately failed of Success. (11:133)

The basis of exemplary history is analogy. Satirists and political writers unsympathetic to Walpole often resorted to irony,
allusion, and the analogies of example in order to avoid a repetition of the "Great Man's" harrowing of the press in 1722–23.[21] In

the *True Briton* no. 35 (30 September 1723), the Duk
defines exemplary history, which instructs the pr
imitate or avoid "the Good or Bad Actions of past Ag
goes on to praise Edward III and then to draw the co
whatever the "wicked Favourites" do, "it has, sooner or latter,
pleased the Divine Providence to retribute upon their Heads their
evil Practices; and no Examples are more frequent in History,
than those of Great Men made Sacrifices after the very *same*
Manner, and by the *same* Precedents whereby they have endeavour'd their own Security, and the Destruction of their Adver-
saries." Since Wharton invites his readers to view "the present
Race of Statesmen in Most Nations, when compared with the
Heroes of Old," there can be no doubt that Edward III compares
favourably with George I, and Walpole resembles one of the
"wicked Favourites." Wharton expected his readers to make the
necessary application to convert this essay from an innocent
historical reflection into a satirical commentary on the present.[22]

Of course no exponent of exemplary history expected his examples to be congruent with the present in every respect and in
every detail; not even Bolingbroke, who used exemplary history
more than any other of Walpole's opponents, expected a total
identification of two kings, or two ministers, from different periods of history. Thus in *Gulliver's Travels* some of Swift's examples, such as the emperor of Lilliput or Lord Munodi, do not
match even their most plausible candidates for identification in
every respect. The fictional time scheme of *Gulliver's Travels*
does not allow Flimnap to be Walpole between 1708 and 1715;
nor can the emperor of Lilliput be George I if Lilliput represents
England before George's accession. But like Wharton, Swift expected his readers to make necessary application. The author of
Craftsman no. 374 (1 September 1733) did so: he applied the
example of the academy of political projectors at Lagado to
Walpole's administration. With a customary ironic disclaimer,
that author drew an analogy while denying it: "I shall not presume to make any Application of these Politicks to our own
Country, whose Situation, Laws and Constitution are so different
from Those of *Laputa*."

For all the puzzles it causes, Swift's technique of political
satire makes frequent use of direct allusion. The articles of impeachment against Gulliver in Lilliput surely refer to the impeachment of Bolingbroke and Ormonde, Oxford and Strafford
in 1715, if they refer to any specific impeachment at all. If they
refer only to the idea of impeachment, then it is still up to Swift's

readers to apply the example as they see fit. When the king of Brobdingnag declares that the British "must be a quarrelsome People . . . and that our Generals must needs be richer than our Kings" (11:131), he has never heard of Marlborough, but Swift's readers, who have, make the necessary application and recognize a satirical gibe at the Duke. The same method holds true for the general reflections. The king of Brobdingnag's questions expose corruption among the leaders of Gulliver's Britain: although Gulliver is supposed to be in Brobdingnag from 1702 to 1706, the Britain he describes for the king is Walpole's Britain. Even if the period from 1702 to 1706 were intended as the subject of the king's questions, it is the period of Walpole's ministry to which the satire most pertinently and obviously applies. Opposition satirists often spoke of great men and kings in an apparently general reflection when they meant one great man and the king who appointed him. Gulliver's description of "the management of our Treasury" seems general enough until the king of Brobdingnag's questions expose the inevitable danger of living on credit. The country party's opposition to the growing national debt, which they had condemned in January 1725 and again in January 1726, is likely to lie behind the general reflection; but even if this is only a general comment on the dangers of credit, it still functions as an analogue that readers may apply. And there can be little doubt that Swift expected his reader to make such an application.

Prefixed to the 1735 edition of *Gulliver's Travels* was "A Letter from Capt. Gulliver to his Cousin Sympson," in which Gulliver complained that the printer's timidity had allowed parts of his 1726 text to be distorted, including the description of the Academy of Lagado, which recalls the *Craftsman's* essay:

> When I formerly hinted to you something of this in a Letter, you were pleased to answer, that you were afraid of giving Offence; that People in power were very watchful over the Press; and apt not only to interpret, but to punish every thing which looked like an *Inuendo* (as I think you called it.) But pray, how could that which I spoke so many Years ago, and at above five Thousand Leagues distance, in another Reign, be applied to any of the *Yahoos*, who now are said to govern the Herd; especially, at a time when I little thought on or feared the Unhappiness of living under them [?] (11:5–6)

Such an ironic disclaimer can only instruct Swift's readers to look for innuendo that would give offence to "People in Power" and to seek parallels between Swift's characters and contemporary governors.[23] This, in 1735, meant that Swift intended that his readers should interpret the political satire of *Gulliver's Travels* in precisely the same way as they did that of the *Crafts-man* or any other political journal that satirized Walpole with ironic innuendoes every week. Particular or general, the political analogues in *Gulliver* therefore function in the same way as those of exemplary history.

Gulliver's Travels also fulfills the function of exemplary history in that the ruler of each land puts Gulliver on trial in order to judge men's actions; it also uses exemplary history's pattern of virtue beset by malicious opposition. In Lilliput, Gulliver him-self—already the object of Skyresh Bolgolam's enmity—is the victim of Flimnap's malice, and he must defend his own inno-cence as well by that of the Treasurer's wife against a rumor put about by "the Malice of some evil Tongues" (11:65). In Brob-dingnag, the dwarf, called variously "malicious little Cubb," "malicious Urchin," and "malicious Rogue," conceives a "mali-cious Hatred" of Gulliver (11:107–8, 116). Because of the "mali-cious Reprobate" of a Dutchman, Gulliver is set adrift at the start of part 3, and at the end of the same book, "a malicious Rogue of a Skipper" tries to betray Gulliver (11:155, 217).

Not only is Gulliver himself the victim of malice: when the truth of past history is revealed to him in Glubbdubdrib, he observes innocents confronted by "the Malice of Factions" 11:199), and in each remote nation he sees virtue threatened or overthrown by malice and corruption. In Glubbdubdrib, virtue, patriotism, and the spirit of liberty—all good opposition words in the late 1720s—have been ousted by corruption. Malice caused "a young Lord of great Hopes" (11:205) to be poisoned in Luggnagg, where Gulliver guesses that "the Virtue of those Rever-end Sages," the Struldbruggs, might be "too strict for the corrupt and libertine Manners of a Court" (11:207–8). He mistakenly congratulates the inhabitants for their luck in enjoying "so many living Examples of antient Virtue" (11:208). Indeed, if Gulliver were a Struldbrugg, he thinks

These *Struldbruggs* and I would mutually communicate our Obser-vations and Memorials through the Course of Time; remark the sev-eral Gradations by which Corruption steals into the World, and oppose it in every Step, by giving perpetual Warning and Instruction to Mankind; which, added to the strong Influence of our own Exam-ple, would probably prevent that continual Degeneracy of human Nature, so justly complained of in all Ages (11:210).

Gulliver would write an impartial history of public affairs and mould young men's minds "by convincing them from my own Remembrance, Experience and Observation, fortified by numerous Examples, of the Usefulness of Virtue in public and private Life" (11:209). He would, that is, write Swift's *History*.

Having arrived in Houyhnhnmland the victim of a conspiracy, Gulliver later explains to his virtuous Houyhnhnm master the effects of human "Lust, Intemperance, Malice, and Envy" (11:244). Part 4 clearly contrasts "the many Virtues of those excellent *Quadrupeds*" with "human Corruptions" and the natural malice—mentioned at least three more times—of the Yahoos (11:248, 266, 271). Opposed to the malice of the Yahoos, the virtues of the Houyhnhnms seem to provide Gulliver with an example he should imitate, for he would find it impossible to "think with Temper, of passing my Days among *Yahoos*, and relapsing into my old Corruptions, for want of Examples to lead and keep me within the Paths of Virtue" (11:280). Although there can be no serious question of anyone's imitating the Houyhnhnms, "the Lectures and Example of my noble Master, and the other illustrious *Houyhnhnms*" act as a reminder to Gulliver that his narrative must "*strictly adhere to Truth*" (11:292). In this respect Gulliver admits that he imitates his Houyhnhnm master: "I had likewise learned from his Example an utter Detestation of all Falsehood or Disguise; and *Truth* appeared so amiable to me, that I determined upon sacrificing every thing to it" (11:258). The Houyhnhnms are exemplary:

> For, who can read of the Virtues I have mentioned in the glorious Houyhnhnms, without being ashamed of his own Vices, when he considers himself as the reasoning, governing Animal of his Country? (11:292)

One might well ask who *does* consider himself as "the reasoning, governing Animal of his Country": even if our attention is drawn only momentarily to a possible allusion to Walpole, the general allusion still points to the specific system over which Walpole presides, since it is by following the example of Houyhnhnm virtue that Gulliver is persuaded to expose British political life for what it really is: that is, corrupt.

Eventually, with a supreme irony, a Houyhnhnm utters a "malicious Insinuation" by implicitly likening Yahoos to ministers of state (11:263).[24] The situation is therefore the reverse of Swift's picture of the four last years of the queen, for in this "Insinuation" human governments are normally corrupt and malicious. Decline began at some unspecified time in the past.[25] Swift's *History* places the beginning of recent British political decline soon after the accession of William III and shows that in 1710–14 the ministry was constantly struggling against such forces as malice and corruption. The period of the Oxford-Bolingbroke ministry was then just a brief but glorious respite from a long, general decline of public government.

As W. A. Speck has noted, Gulliver's fourth voyage begins in September 1710, when Queen Anne broke with the Whigs, and ends in February 1715, when the power of the Whigs and the Hanoverian dynasty—a composite symbol of the moneyed interest—was firmly established at a general election.[26] That unholy alliance further entrenched the financial system, which, the satirists argued, damaged the financial, political, and moral health of Britain. In *Verses on the Death of Doctor Swift*, Swift describes how, at the death of the queen the rising Whig faction destroyed "our Weal"; the aim of the Whigs in 1714 was

> To ruin, slaughter, and confound;
> To turn Religion to a Fable,
> And make the Government a *Babel*:
> Pervert the Law, disgrace the Gown,
> Corrupt the Senate, rob the Crown;
> To sacrifice old England's Glory,
> And make her infamous in Story.
> When such a Tempest shook the Land,
> How could unguarded Virtue stand?[27]

Opposition to the ministry of 1710–14 was therefore an attack on virtue, and conversely, the ministry becomes an example of virtue battling to survive in a world menaced since 1688 by an economic system encouraging corruption and self-interest and bringing out men's inherent malice. Examples of this same conflict occur in *Gulliver's Travels*, where so many political and institutional issues are expressed in terms of virtue and malice. There is no consistent set of identifications because—as Swift said of the people in his *History*—he did not "pretend to draw their Characters entire" and because he exercised the power of alteration that he mentioned in the *Examiner*. Above all, the principles of exemplary history render a consistent set of identifications superfluous to the purpose of satirizing the Walpole regime with examples of virtue and malice. Taken together, *Gulliver's Travels* and the *History of the Four Last Years of the*

Queen suggest that the Oxford-Bolingbroke ministry bravely resisted the dark forces of malice and corruption, forces that had gathered strength and momentum since 1688 and flourished particularly under the openly corrupt administration of Walpole.

I would suggest, then, that the political satire of *Gulliver's Travels* is based on Swift's conception of exemplary history. Notoriously difficult to classify or categorize, *Gulliver's Travels* is, after all, "a faithful History," concerned less with "Ornament" than with "Truth" and written for "the PUBLICK GOOD" (11: 291–92).

Notes

1. *Gulliver's Travels*, in *The Prose Works of Jonathan Swift*, ed. Herbert Davis et al. (Oxford: Basil Blackwell, 1939–68), 11:196. Quotations from Swift's prose writings are all taken from this edition; volume and page numbers appear in parentheses after quotations.

2. "The Political Significance of *Gulliver's Travels*," *Proceedings of the British Academy* 9 (1919–20): 237–59.

3. "Personal and Political Satire in *Gulliver's Travels*," in *Four Essays on "Gulliver's Travels"* (Princeton: Princeton University Press, 1945), p. 70.

4. Case, "Personal and Political Satire," pp. 79–80.

5. "Political Characterization in *Gulliver's Travels*," *Yearbook of English Studies* 7 (1977): 108–20.

6. Case, "Personal and Political Satire," p. 69.

7. Downie, "Political Characterization," p. 118.

8. *The Correspondence of Jonathan Swift*, ed. Harold Williams (Oxford: Clarendon Press, 1963–65), 3:181. For contemporary responses to *Gulliver's Travels*, see Bertrand A. Goldgar, "*Gulliver's Travels* and the Opposition to Walpole," in *The Augustan Milieu: Essays Presented to Louis A. Landa*, ed. Henry Knight Miller, Eric Rothstein, and G. S. Rousseau (Oxford: Clarendon Press, 1970), pp. 155–73.

9. F. P. Lock, *The Politics of "Gulliver's Travels"* (Oxford: Clarendon Press, 1980), p. 2.

10. Lock, *The Politics of "Gulliver's Travels,"* p. 111.

11. This particular formulation is Fielding's, from the opening of *Joseph Andrews*, 1.i.

12. *Works*, 11:318. Even when this passage had been omitted, Gulliver drew attention to the contrast between the queen's last ministry and Walpole's administration by declaring his admiration of the queen and his loyalty to her memory in his prefatory letter to his cousin Sympson (first printed in Faulkner's 1735 edition).

13. "The Problem of Political Allegory in *Gulliver's Travels*," *Modern Philology*, Supplement (May 1976): S40–S47.

14. A. C. Elias, *Swift at Moor Park* (Philadelphia: University of Pennsylvania Press, 1982), pp. 55–66.

15. "The Augustan Conception of History," in *Reason and Imagination: Studies in the History of Ideas 1600–1800*, ed. J. A. Mazzeo (New York: Colum-

bia University Press, 1962), pp. 213–30. See also J. R. Moore, "Swift as Historian," *Studies in Philology* 49 (1952): 583–604; Irvin Ehrenpreis, *The Personality of Jonathan Swift* (London: Methuen, 1958), pp. 59–82; Myrddin Jones, "A Living Treasury of Knowledge and Wisdom: Some Comments on Swift's Attitude to the Writing of History," *Durham University Journal*, n.s. 36 (1975): 180–88; and the only study of Swift and history with which I seriously disagree, James William Johnson, "Swift's Historical Outlook," *Journal of British Studies* 4 (1965): 52–77, reprinted in *Swift: Modern Judgments*, ed. Norman A. Jeffares (London: Macmillan, 1968), pp. 96–120.

16. Davis, "The Augustan Conception of History," p. 218.

17. Johnson, "Swift's Historical Outlook," p. 114.

18. *The History of the Four Last Years of the Queen* (London, 1758), p. x. The editor was probably Charles Lucas.

19. See Isaac Kramnick, *Bolingbroke and His Circle: the Politics of Nostalgia in the Age of Walpole 1720–1735* (Cambridge: Harvard University Press, 1968).

20. *The Works of Lord Bolingbroke* (London: Henry G. Bohn, 1844; reprinted by Frank Cass & Co., 1967), 2:185. See also George H. Nadel, "Philosophy of History before Historicism," in *Studies in the Philosophy of History: Selected Essays from "History and Theory,"* ed. George H. Nadel (New York: Harper and Row, 1965), pp. 49–73.

21. In reality, the writers' tactics offered only very limited protection against prosecution. Ironic allusion—not in itself easy to prove libelous—merely encouraged Walpole to seek alternative grounds for prosecuting printers of newspapers and pamphlets. He was not above having printers harassed illegally.

22. Wharton's printer, John Payne, was continually arrested for printing issues of the *True Briton* that Walpole found offensive.

23. Surprisingly, this prefatory letter has been taken literally as evidence of Swift's dissatisfaction with Motte's printing of the 1726 text of *Gulliver's Travels*. For discussion of the merits of the different texts, see Harold Williams, *The Text of "Gulliver's Travels"* (Cambridge: Cambridge University Press, 1952); Arthur E. Case, "The Text of Gulliver's Travels," in *Four Essays*, pp. 1–49; and Lock, *The Politics of "Gulliver's Travels,"* pp. 66–88.

24. The allusion was picked up again in the 1735 "Prefatory Letter," where Gulliver refers to "the Yahoos who now are said to govern the herd" (11:6).

25. The king of Brobdingnag reacts to Gulliver's "historical account . . . of our Affairs during the last Century" (11:132). Cf. J. W. Johnson, "Swift's Historical Outlook," p. 104.

26. "From Principles to Practice: Swift and Party Politics," in *The World of Jonathan Swift: Essays for the Tercentenary*, ed. Brian Vickers (Oxford: Basil Blackwell, 1968), p. 85.

27. *The Poems of Jonathan Swift*, ed. Harold Williams, 2d ed. (Oxford: Clarendon Press, 1958), 2:568. Cf. Robert C. Elliott, "Jonathan Swift: The Presentation of Self in Doggerel Rhyme," in Robert C. Elliott and Arthur H. Scouten, *The Poetry of Jonathan Swift* (Los Angeles: William Andrews Clark Memorial Library, 1981), p. 21.

Gulliver's Travels and the Novel

J. Paul Hunter

Gulliver's Travels is not a novel in any meaningful sense of that slippery term that I know, yet its generic status would be difficult to establish without having the novel in mind. Swift's masterpiece is, in fact, so conceptually dependent upon the novel that it is almost impossible to imagine the existence of the *Travels* outside the context of the developing novelistic tradition. The relationship of *Gulliver's Travels* to the novel has been obscured, however, by two contextual matters, one historical, the other generic. The historical issue involves the fact that the *Travels* appears when the English novel had barely begun, and it is difficult for us to think of it as involved in the tradition. With only Defoe, among major English novelists, having yet tried the waters, with the issue of definition still two decades away from even being broached, and with the great craze for novel-reading and novel-writing also still well in the future, how can it be meaningful to think of there yet being a *tradition* of the novel even though there are some few discernible examples? Unless one regards the *Travels* as a kind of paradigm—positive or negative—for the tradition, how can one think of it as involved in a tradition-to-be? The second issue, although generic, does not involve the genre of the novel; rather it involves parody and the assumptions we make about its strategy of working from, imitating, and trying to tease or embarrass a particular writer or work. Because of the way we define parody, we do not usually think of Swift as a parodist, and I think we miss something about both Swift and the possibilities of parody by the standard definition. I shall, then, first try to suggest in what sense Swift is a parodist and show how some of his parody works; second, I shall try to suggest how his particular type of parody enables him to associate himself with the developing tradition of the novel; finally, and more briefly, I shall try to suggest how the *Travels* works as a kind of parodic answer to the early novel and as a satire of the novelistic consciousness.

1

The many faces of Jonathan Swift often remind us of his contemporaries, and there is seldom a moment in his best satires when he is not helping some fool or knave to stand forth and profess a muddled—but nevertheless distinctive and definable—set of values and opinions. Snoop that he is, Swift spends a lot of time in other people's consciousnesses, trying to organize in some memorable way what he finds there. Whether as tale-teller or voyager, modest economist or befuddled Christian apologist, panegyricist of the world and the number three or putative satirist disappointed that all human folly has not been extirpated in six months, Swift is ever the impersonator, borrowing his voice from someone else. We recognize his antagonists clearly—clearly, that is, until we try to be specific, and then we often discover how very little we know about whom he has personated. About some few, everyone can agree: in *A Tale of a Tub*, William Wotton, Richard Bentley, John Dryden, and Sir Roger L'Estrange, for example, or in *Meditation upon a Broomstick*, Robert Boyle. But agreement is possible only because Swift himself names the originals. How good, then, is Swift as a parodist, or (to put the issue more aptly for my argument) is he the kind of parodist through whom one hears the voice of the original: I wish to examine Swift's strategy of personation in a very simplified form, hoping to sort out how his attention to particular writers blends into a broader concern for style and the implication of style. Two of Swift's short minor works offer interesting test cases of Swift's skill and method, for they are "pure" examples of Swift as a parodist in the sense that both the works—*The Last Speech and Dying Words of Ebenezor Elliston* and *A Meditation upon a Broomstick*—pretend to be real works by a real person.

In *The Last Speech and Dying Words*, Swift alludes to a popular subgenre of an important paraliterary form, the "dying confessional" of a criminal about to be executed. Such confessionals, obviously prepared well in advance of the occasion by prison ordinaries, hacks, and booksellers, were hawked about at the execution itself, and their conventional pieties, tearful abjuration of past crimes, and invocation of God's mercy evidently ministered to the audience's need to feel the public usefulness of the occasion. Swift cuts through the easy pieties and has Elliston forego repentance and dispense with the usual rhetoric. Instead, he substitutes a vivid account of knaves driven by baser motives than poverty or ill luck:

If any Thing in this World be like Hell . . . the truest Picture of it must
be in the Back-Room of one of our Alehouses at Midnight; where a
Crew of Robbers and their Whores are met together after a Booty, and
are beginning to grow drunk; from which Time, until they are past
their Senses, is such a continued horrible Noise of Cursing, Blas-
phemy, Lewdness, Scurrility, and brutish Behaviour; such Roaring
and Confusion, such a Clatter of Mugs and Pots at each other's Heads;
that *Bedlam*, in Comparison, is a sober and orderly Place: At last they
all tumble from their Stools and Benches, . . . and generally the
Landlord or his Wife, or some other Whore . . . , picks their Pockets
before they wake.[1]

And Swift's Elliston offers a particular incentive to reform, one
very different from the high-minded hopes in the usual confessionals.

Now, as I am a dying Man, something I have done which may be of
good Use to the Publick. I have left with an honest Man (and indeed
the only honest Man I was ever acquainted with) the Names of all my
wicked Brethren, the present Places of their Abode, with a short
Account of the chief Crimes they have committed; in many of which I
have been their Accomplice, and heard the rest from their own
Mouths: I have likewise set down the Names of those we call our
Setters, of the wicked Houses we frequent, and of those who receive
and buy our stolen Goods. I have solemnly charged this honest Man
. . . that whenever he hears of any Rogue to be tryed for robbing, or
House-breaking, he will look into his List, and if he finds the Name
there of the Thief concerned, to send the whole Paper to the Government. Of this I here give my Companions fair and publick Warning,
and hope they will take it. (p. 39)

Prince Posterity has luckily preserved for us the "authentic" last
words of Ebenezor Elliston, which, of course, are utterly conventional and predictable. Elliston repents his life of crime,
claims he was framed in the fatal instance, and hopes others will
learn from his bad example. At least one critic has suggested that
Swift's style is "an almost perfect parody" of Elliston's own.[2] But
I find no stylistic resemblance whatever. Unlike the hard, clear
syntax that Swift's Elliston uses to express his smug toughness,
the real Elliston speaks like this:

. . . the Roberies which I was concerned in from October 1719 to
January 1720 were so many that I cannot give a true account of them
all, but leave them aside, and come to acquaint you of my last
misfortunes some small time before Christmas last for some reasons

best known to my self, not for any Roberies that I committed, I left my House and Familly, and took a private Lodging, in which time there was a Roberey committed on the Gravel Walk on a Captain, which robbery, one Elizabeth Gorden I believe by the perswasions of a Man in power in this City went before the Lord-Mayor and as I am informed swore that I and two or three other Persons in my Company committed the said robbery, which I now declare that Neither they or I had any Hand whatsoever in it, for which Mr. H——s made it his Business to haunt Night and Day for me, and also informed several Persons, that there was Twenty Pounds Reward for any one who would Apprehend me, so that I might be brought to Justice, for which Several People as well as himself made it their Business to look for me, but God knows how Innocent I was at that Time of Committing any Manner of Robbery whatsoever, but to avoid Dangers, I made my Case known to several of my Friends, who advised me to leave this Town, whose advice I took, but Unfortunately I was concerned with another person in taking Counsellor Sweeny's Mare.[3]

It is not really surprising that Swift does not closely imitate Elliston's prose style, for his audience would not have known Ebenezor Elliston's style even if there had been one. We need not suppose he would even have cared to see this particular "real" confession; it was enough for his audience to know what kind of thing it was likely to be. *The Last Speech and Dying Words of Ebenezor Elliston* plainly is not an attack upon an individual person or an individual style but rather upon custom, a particular subspecies of literature that grew out of that custom, and a cheap and self-congratulatory morality that was both a cause and result of such "confessions." There must be some idea in the audience's mind of what the "last speech and dying words" tradition is like, but Elliston himself is irrelevant, ultimately, and so is his flaccid, rambling (and possibly genuine) prose.[4]

We might, on the other hand, expect a close verbal imitation in Swift's *Meditation upon a Broomstick,* for there he personates a writer whose style was distinctive and well known to his audience. Thomas Sheridan's anecdote about the occasion of Swift's *Meditation* is well known.[5] Swift, as a guest of Lord and Lady Berkeley in London, was often asked to attend Lady Berkeley's private devotions, and Lady Berkeley's excessive fondness for Boyle's meditations led her to ask Swift to read repeatedly from them. Swift's careful insertion of his own manuscript imitation in the volume, his solemn reading of it, Lady Berkeley's effusive praise of it first in private and then among company who knew Boyle's meditations well enough to know that there was no such meditation—knowledge of these carefully planned steps of the hoax may add to our appreciation of Swift's finely tuned absurdities:

> This single Stick, which you now behold ingloriously lying in that neglected Corner, I once knew in a flourishing State in a Forest: It was full of Sap, full of Leaves, and full of Boughs: But now, in vain does the busy Art of Man pretend to vye with Nature, by tying that withered Bundle of Twigs to its sapless Trunk: It is now at best but the Reverse of what it was; a Tree turned upside down, the Branches on the Earth, and the Root in the Air: It is now handled by every dirty Wench, condemned to do her Drugery; and by a capricious Kind of Fate, destined to make other things clean and be nasty it self.
>
> But a *Broom-stick*, perhaps you will say, is an *Emblem* of a Tree standing on its Head; and pray what is Man but a topsy-turvy Creature?[6]

The "parody" is brilliant, but it is hard to say exactly how it works because it is hard to say exactly what is parodied. A quick reading makes Swift's *Meditation* seem quite like Boyle, except for the distortion crucial to parody, but on detailed comparison the similarities become hard to find. No single Boyle meditation has ever been regarded as the model for Swift's parody, and for a very good reason. None of Boyle's meditations is much like Swift's version, either in subject matter or style. The first meditation in Boyle's 1665 volume is perhaps the closest to Swift:

> *Upon his manner of giving meat to his dog.*
>
> Ignorantly thankful creature, thou beggest in such a way, that by way would appear an antedated gratitude, if it were not a designless action, the manner of thy petitioning before-hand, rewards the grant of thy request; thy addresses and recompence being so made and ordered, that the meat I cast thee may very well feed religion in me. For, but observe this dog, I hold him out meat, and my inviting voice loudly encourages and invites him to take it: it is held indeed higher than he can leap; and yet, if he leap not at it, I do not give it him; but if he do. . . .[7]

But there is not much phraseological or syntactic similarity, and the argument is developed in a very different way. Boyle has favorite words and devices that distinguish him from other meditators (he likes the word "divers" so much, for example, that he once uses it four times in a single paragraph, and many of his meditations are actually dialogues), but Swift pays no attention to these distinctive and easy-to-parody strategies. It is as if he cared not at all for distinctive stylistic devices or even for obvious structural principles. What then makes it a parody of Boyle and not of someone else? The answer, I am afraid, is that one would have a very hard time proving that it *is* a parody of Boyle if it were not for a published subtitle that asserts such a parody and for the fact of Thomas Sheridan's anecdote.[8] If we were to put it beside the meditative effusions of, say John Flavell, we could just as easily think it parodied him. Here is a typical beginning of one of Flavell's meditations in *Husbandry Spiritualized, or The Heavenly Use of Earthly Things* (1669):

Upon the sight of a fair spreading Oak.

What a lofty flourishing Tree is here? It seems rather to be a little Wood, than a single Tree; every limb thereof having the dimensions and branches of a Tree in it; and yet as great as it is, it was once but a little slip, which one might pull up with two fingers; this vast body was contained virtually, and potentially in a small Acorn. Well, then, I will never despise the day of small things, nor despair of arriving to an eminency of grace, though at present it be but as a bruised reed, and the things that are in me, be ready to dye. As things in nature, so the things of the Spirit, grow up to their fulness and perfection, by slow and insensible degrees. The famous and heroical acts of the most renowned believers, were such as themselves could not once perform, or it may be think they ever should. Great things both in nature and grace, come from small and contemptible beginnings.[9]

There is not much to choose between Boyle and Flavell as mediators, although each has individual stylistic features. That Swift chooses not to imitate individual stylistic features suggests that the specifics of style are not his consuming interest. A bright undergraduate with a modestly good ear could come much closer to Boyle than Swift does; unless we judge Swift a thoroughly incompetent personator, we must assume that his interests here lie beyond parody that is individual and personal.

But the objects of laughter in Swift's *Meditation* suggest a cogent and coherent satiric target that would explain Swift's parodic aims and at the same time answer the recurrent charges that it was at least uncharitable, if not downright impious, to attack a man of Boyle's righteousness in the first place. Four things call undue attention to themselves in Swift's version of meditation. First is the strained analogy set up between the broomstick and a human being, based on an inversion of the traditional topos comparing man to a tree. Second is the subtly self-congratulatory, egocentric, even solipsistic, manner in which the analogy is asserted:

> When I beheld this, I sighed, and said within myself Surely Mortal Man is a Broomstick. . . .

Third is the fact that the broomstick is a chance object for meditation. It is simply something at hand—"this broomstick in that neglected corner"—and seems to the speaker as good as any other as a possible object of meditation, rather like Donne's flea or Marvell's dewdrop, which also take their cue from the homiletic tradition of concrete exempla: "Mark but this flea . . ." and "This single stick . . . ." The fourth feature is what gives Swift's Meditation away as a parody rather than a failed serious effort. The object in question is not a natural object but a man-made one, and this distortion of a meditationist's procedure calls quick attention to the fact that the meditator was stretching the rules, as observed by the likes of Boyle and serious imitators like Flavell, for they had usually concentrated on human activities and observation of objects or patterns in the natural world. Boyle, for example, had meditated "Upon the Sight of some variously-coloured clouds," "Upon the sight of a fair milk-maid singing to her cow," and "Upon one's talking to an echo," and Flavell upon such inspired subjects as "Upon the Sudden Withering of a Rose" or "Upon the Pulling up of a Leek."

But Boyle and Flavell were stretching the rules too; they seriously distort the earlier meditative tradition. The tradition of Christian meditation had regularly devoted itself to biblical events, especially highlights in the life of Christ, or to set contemplations that produced a proper state of serene devotion in the meditator.[10] Meditations were not random, nor did they concentrate on trivial objects or observations. The distortion of the new meditators was conscious as well as contrived. Boyle's explanatory preface and a long and tedious introduction to his meditations claim the invention of a new kind of exercise, which Boyle calls "Meleteticks":

> There is scarce any thing, that may not prove the subject of an occasional meditation; . . . natural propensity . . . unperceivably ingages us to pry into the several attributes and relations of the things we consider, to obtain the greater plenty of particulars, for the making up of the more full and compleat parallel betwixt the things

whose resemblances we would set forth. By which means a man often comes to discover a multitude of particulars, even in obvious things, which . . . common beholders take no notice of.[11]

Boyle's meletetics is a distinctively "modern"—that is, eighteenth-century modern—version of meditation; its use of material meditative objects, its adaptation to the individual experiences of common men, its emphasis on the power of any individual to interpret adequately, its quiet allegiance to the methods and assumptions of empirical science, its assertion that great truths can be revealed through sense experience: these methods and attitudes and the assumptions that sponsor them seem more crucial to Swift's righteous ire than any particulars of style. Boyle's panegyric on modern writing and his ubiquitous progressivist assumptions might well have irritated or angered Swift, and certainly his confidence in human discovery and interpretative ability seem, when put beside Swift's beliefs, easy and radically optimistic. Here is a taste of Boyle's explanation of why he feels free to depart from classical decorum in language: rules-makers disagree with each other, he says, and

> I see no great reason to confine my self to the magisterial dictates of either ancient or scholastick, writers. For, living in this age, and in this part of the world, where we are not like to have those for readers that died before we were born, I see not why one may not judge of decorum by the examples and practices of those authors of our own times and countries. . . .[12]

Boyle's meletetics, widely influential and imitated, especially among dissenters, carry the every-man-his-own-priest idea to an extreme, and, like many other modern epistemologies and writings attacked by Swift, stressed the validity of individual experience as a means to eternal truth. Boyle and his followers democratized revelation to an incredible degree, turning the Book of Nature into a kind of cosmic book of associations with as many meanings as there are perceivers or even moods. That attitude was not likely to win Swift's approval. Swift does not mention Boyle in his letters (or at least in those that have survived) or elsewhere in his published works, except for a late marginal manuscript note in his copy of Burnet's *History of his own Time* in which he calls him a "a very silly writer."[13] However great a scientist, Boyle was a mannered writer, pedestrian theologian, and sometimes flatulent reasoner, and he had other characteristics likely to infuriate someone of Swift's sensibilities.

He had, for example, made much of his religious conversion at the age of fourteen, and he had repeatedly refused to take holy orders on the grounds that he had not had an inner call. Thus, although a faithful Anglican, Boyle in his personal life as well as in his writing acts more like Swift's dissenting contemporaries than like Swift the High Churchman, and Boyle's lifelong attempts to harmonize religion with empirical science, his fondness for scientific jargon, his scarcely disguised self-praise in *The Christian Virtuoso*, and his founding of the Boyle lectures on physico-theological subjects (Bentley was the first lecturer) all represent commitments that Swift regarded as at best misguided, at worst downright perverse.

We need not wonder, then, why Swift would feel free to attack "so great and pious a man as Mr. Boyle" (it is Sheridan's phrase) or whether his Broomstick hoax had any force of philosophical belief behind it.[14] In fact, the thrust of Swift's hoax aims far more broadly than at the single figure of Boyle. Rather than stylistic parody in the usual sense, *A Meditation upon a Broomstick* is generic or class parody—that is, parody of a kind of writing and the assumptions it is based on, and crucial to its working power is the recognition of the philosophical assumptions that underlie it rather than simple identification of the writer. In *A Tale of a Tub* Swift hints at his characteristic procedure:

> Some of those Passages in this Discourse, which appear most liable to Objection are what they call Parodies, where the Author personates the Style and Manner of other Writers, whom he has a mind to expose. I shall produce one Instance, it is in the 51st page. Dryden, L'Estrange, and some others I shall not name, are here levelled at, who having spent their Lives in Faction, and Apostacies, and all manner of Vice, pretended to be Sufferers for Loyalty and Religion. So Dryden tells us in one of his Prefaces of his Merits and Suffering, thanks God that he possesses his Soul in Patience: In other Places he talks at the same Rate, and L'Estrange often uses the like Style, and I believe the Reader may find more Persons to give that Passage an Application.[15]

Personating more than one writer at a time is at least as difficult as imitating the individual traits of a single writer, and this kind of class parody—personating writers who share a disagreeable trait of some sort—is rampant in Swift. This is one reason why parody in Swift is so hard to pin down and why so many critics, in despair of being precise, have turned to denial of parody instead. I agree with Edward W. Rosenheim's definition of satire as an attack upon "discernible historic particulars,"[16] but that definition is easy to pervert in studying Swift, for the particular may be a group of writers or a class of thinkers or a category of believers just as easily as an individual. To insist that Swift aims at a single writer in his personations is not only to deprive his prose of much of the larger force that he demonstrably exerts but also to make him more of a lampoonist than thinker. Artist and marksman that he was, Swift could hit several antagonists and their foibles with a single shot, and we need not blame him for our own "either/or" instances, which, if I am right about Swift's *Broomstick,* Swift refused to honor even when it would have been easiest. Swift can, of course, be very particular when he wants to be, and there are times when he singles out a particular knave or fool instead of providing a family portrait. What is surprising is how seldom this occurs as a matter of style, for even in many particularized passages the focus is still on generic or class parody; when, for example, Swift inserts in *Gulliver's Travels* almost verbatim passages in seaman's jargon from Sturmy's *Mariner's Magazine* or when his scientific language is taken directly from the *Transactions* of the Royal Society, his parodic object is the broad and mindless use of these jargons, not Sturmy or the *Transactions* as such.

What I am saying does not mean, of course, that Swift does not invite us to find individuals within the family portraits he concentrates on, and, just as in *Meditation upon a Broomstick* he allows us to think of Boyle while attacking what Boyle stands for, so in many other passages he invites us to think of particular authors that exemplify the qualities embodied in his generic parody. The *Tale of a Tub* passage that I have alluded to, for example, names Dryden and L'Estrange for us and then suggests that we ourselves can find additional examples: "I believe the Reader may find more Persons to give that Passage an Application." Sometimes he gives names that exemplify, and sometimes he provides other clues. We have, I think, hardly begun to find the authors that, in his words, "he has a mind to expose," because we have looked too exclusively for stylistic parody and paid too little attention to other telltale details that can help to identify targets that are not to be identified stylistically.

2

Gulliver's Travels has generally resisted efforts to consider it parodic, and some Swift critics lurch toward apoplexy when the

very idea of parody is broached within reaching distance of
Gulliver's Travels.[17] And yet Swift's consciousness of contemporary writing is nearly as apparent there as in *A Tale of a Tub,* and
if passages that specifically echo another writer—such as the
plagiarized passage from Sturmy's *Mariner's Magazine*—are rare,
a large awareness of contemporary writing habits and the prevailing tastes of readers is visible at nearly every turn. Swift's
awareness of contemporary travel writers—William Dampier, for
example—has been often remarked, and much of the fun in the
book's first appearance had to do with its solemn title page:
Travels into Several Remote Nations of the World, it advertised,
promising something quite other than what is delivered. Swift, in
one of his letters, has something of a lark in imagining literal-
minded readers who are gulled by such an expectation: he
speaks of an Irish bishop who, after reading *Gulliver's Travels,*
concluded that it was "full of improbable lies, and for his part, he
hardly believed a word of it."[18]

But quite beyond its evocation of travel literature, *Gulliver's
Travels* engages a whole tradition of fiction that was then in the
process of developing, and Swift saw that this new kind of
writing was beginning to codify a "modern," significantly new
way of perceiving the world. Contemporary narratives of personal experience—scandalous memoirs and chronicles of personal and public political intrigue, as well as books that charted
personal travel to far-off places or new experiences—were in-
creasingly sought by a public that wanted material, intellectual,
and psychological satisfaction in the conquest of space and the
accrual of experience. Because of its new popularity, this subjective writing, whether genuine or fictional, seems to offer a personal yet universal key to reality and, like Boyle's *Meditations,*
can only deliver on its promise by exaggerated and distorted
emblematicism and by verbal sleight-of-hand. The assumptions,
values, and forms that seem to be implicitly attacked in *Gulliver's
Travels* would be easy enough to defend on their own terms, and
in fact in our time most of us find it easier to understand them
than we do Swift's objections; but the *Travels* offers us persuasive
evidence that Swift perceived the brave new literary world of the
1720s much as Pope did, with the significant difference that
Swift merges its personalities and consciousnesses into composite figures who anonymously participate in the creation of a
single work that expressed their values and outlook, rather than
being named and even individuated by their antagonist.[19] Even
in their monotonous sameness, though, some identifiable charac-

teristics emerge, and in the choral voice one can pick out a few distinctive, personalized tones that remind us of a voice insistent on being subjective, authoritative, and modern.

Because Swift's parody works through an accretion and absorption of particulars, it is difficult to illustrate his method without a detailed consideration of the text and its contexts, but here I will be only suggestive through brief attention to one episode and its surrounding circumstances. The suggestive place I want to examine may at first seem a bit unlikely—Lemuel Gulliver's pockets as he empties them for his interrogation in Lilliput. Here is an inventory of what turns up concealed on Gulliver's person:

a handkerchief
a snuffbox
a diary
a comb
a razor
a set of eating utensils
a watch
a set of pistols
a pouch of gunpowder and another pouch of bullets
silver and copper money and several pieces of gold
a pair of spectacles
a pocket perspective
and "several other little Conveniences."

To appreciate the full effect of this pocketful, we have to remember that Gulliver is supposed to have swum ashore—in dangerous stormy waves—with his pockets jammed like that, and he is also wearing a full set of clothes, a hat, and a large sword.

Because this information is not all presented at once, one might read the Travels several times and not notice Gulliver's rich and varied cargo. Gulliver, being Gulliver, does not tell us that his swimming was impeded by his load, nor does he tell us why he hung onto the material things that connect him to his past when, buffeted by waves that threaten to scuttle him, it would have seemed sensible to discharge himself of some of his burdens. The things are, to be sure, useful to Swift in initiating Gulliver's dialogue with the Lilliputians, but they are not necessary, as subsequent voyages show. Swift pretty clearly is having some fun at Gulliver's expense in making him such a dull-witted freighter, and his point seems crucially connected, on the one hand, to a contemporary joke, and, on the other, to Swift's perceptions about first-person narrative and the mind-numbing absurdities it sometimes offered to readers of contemporary narrative.

The joke was seven years old in 1726. It had involved a slip of Defoe's pen in *Robinson Crusoe*—a slip that, when corrected, still exposed a lapse in memory or lack of factual knowledge. When Defoe has Crusoe swim to the shipwreck at one point, he allows him to strip off his clothes to make the journey easier, but a little later we see Crusoe on shipboard stuffing his pockets with biscuits. Defoe later explains that Crusoe had left on his seaman's britches, but as a contemporary, Charles Gildon, pointed out, Defoe didn't thus improve his marks as a purveyor of information about seamen, for seaman's britches usually do not have pockets, and even when they do, the pockets are tiny ones, much too small for biscuits: Defoe's explanation had only pinpointed and elaborated his ignorance. For Gildon, Defoe here makes Crusoe perform unlikely, even absurd actions, and his attack is on the false realism in Defoe, just as in *Gulliver's Travels* the thrust is to demonstrate what the realism and pseudo-factuality of contemporary travel accounts and fictional narratives come to at last.[20] Gildon's joke on Defoe was, by the way, well enough known and remembered in 1725—six years after *Crusoe* and a year before *Gulliver*—that the *London Journal* can speak of the pocket episode as "a most notorious *Blunder*," which had given "Abundances of Pleasure [to] many of his Readers."[21]

Gulliver's pockets, then, work something like this: they remind us of Defoe's mistake and how authors who try to pass off genuine memoirs often are tripped by simple facts. The pockets also remind us of larger points quite beyond the comical allusion— that first-person narrators, in their haste to make a point and glorify themselves, are hopelessly inaccurate, obtuse, and pretentious; that long lists and particular details do not necessarily add up to some larger truth, and that attempts to read the world and its purpose through the recording of sense impressions and the imparting of symbolic qualities to things and events (as done in *Robinson Crusoe* and in the emblematic tradition represented by meletetic meditators like Robert Boyle) is finally an arrogant, self-serving, even solipsistic way of regarding the world. *Robinson Crusoe* comes up for examination in *Gulliver's Travels* quite often in various ways: in the opening paragraph in which the particulars of Defoe's life (his career as a hosier, his imprisonment as a debtor, his prudent marriage to a woman with a large dowry) are alluded to; in the preparatory events that preface each voyage proper; in the vague motivation for Gulliver's decisions to go repeatedly to sea because of "rambling Thoughts" and an unaccountable sense of destiny; in the habitual phrases that fall from Gulliver's lips and link him repeatedly but not constantly to the consciousness of Crusoe; in the ending in which Swift provides a sharp contrast to Crusoe's homecoming.[22] Defoe, exploring what man can do to achieve salvation and deliverance within a providential pattern, has Crusoe readjust to the company of human beings and society generally with relative ease, giving no hint that lack of conversation, human companionship, sexual relationship, and exile from the familiar for more than a quarter century offer any obtrusive problems in readjustment, and Crusoe returns to find himself remembered, beloved, and provided for by partners and well-wishers who have preserved and improved his property and investments so that he is now a rich plantation owner, soon to be a happy new husband and father. Alexander Selkirk, often said to be the prototype of Crusoe and in any case an island castaway who lived in isolation only a fraction of Crusoe's tenure, found postvoyage life far otherwise, returning to his home a silent misanthrope who avoided all company, living altogether by himself, some say in a cave he himself dug as an emblem of his psychological space. Swift's portrait of Gulliver neighing quietly to himself in his stable, unable to stand the company of his wife and children, his nose stopped with lavender, tobacco, and rue so that he cannot smell human smells, stands in sharp relief to Crusoe's homecoming and tacitly reminds us realistically of historical figures like Selkirk and of civilization and its discontents.

The example of the allusive pockets suggests that *Gulliver's Travels* is, among many other impressive things, an accreting generic or class parody not only of travel narratives per se but also of a larger developing class of first-person fictional narratives that make extraordinary claims for the importance of the contemporary, the knowableness through personal experience of large cosmic patterns, the significance of the individual, and the imperialistic possibilities of the human mind—a class parody, in short, of what we now see as the novel and the assumptions that enable it.

3

Indulge me in a preposterous claim. *A Tale of a Tub* is also, among other things, a parody of the emerging novel. But how can there be a parody of something that does not yet exist? you may well ask, and I admit that I do not want to be taken altogether literally. Still, I am serious about the slight dislocative shock that such an unlikely assertion may provide, and I want to make three quick points about it: one historical, one having to do with Swift's powers of cultural analysis, and one relating back to things I have implied about Swift's tendency to collapse and merge parodic targets, accreting a style and structure that is identifiable as generic or class parody.

First the historical point. Attempts to describe the beginnings of the novel as we know it almost invariably land on a cultural moment and a specific work so that the publication of a particular novel becomes the crucial event; in this view a specific "father" of the novel is usually identified, and a moment of birth can thus be found for the genre, be it 1719, or 1740, or 1749, or whatever—the choice depending ultimately on how one defines the novel and on what sorts of fiction one excludes from the definition. This preoccupation with "firsts" is understandable, given the way an opposite school of literary historians is prone to push origins back, as it were, *ab ovo*, and ultimately end up with Heliodorus or Homer or Ham as the first modern novelist. And the attraction of biological and organic metaphors is certainly appealing to a humanist tradition that wishes to think of literature as an art form to be privileged above mere material existence. I would, however, hate to have to defend a notion of genre that included in it the necessity of firsts, for it seems quite clear that most genres grow out of the shifting and rearranging of conventions, usually in response to some major cultural change, often involving a technological breakthrough that influences the possibilities of existing art without leading immediately to a full-grown, totally defined form that exemplifies and exhausts possibility. I would certainly agree that the modern English novel as we know it comes to exist sometime around the beginning of the eighteenth century, and I would argue that the exploding amount of narrative fiction then, together with distinctive and definable changes in the nature of extended narrative, mean that we can specify the emergence of a genre even if we cannot pin it down to a particular Friday afternoon. But the context of ferment is somewhat broader, even if it does not stretch back to classical times. And I think we need to consider more fully the fiction written in England in the later years of the seventeenth century, which, if not actually describable as novelistic, points clearly to what is going to happen when the talents of particular writers become more focused on the emerging cultural and technological possibilities. Here, for example, is the kind of self-conscious narrative writing one finds in an extraordinary work of 1691, John Dunton's *A Voyage Round the World, or The Life and Travels of Don Kainophilus:*

> Should I tell you, as the *virtuosi* do, that I was shaped at first like a Todpole, and that I remember very well, when my Tail *Rambled off,* and a pair of little Legs sprung out in the Room on't: Nay, shou'd I protest I pulled out my Note-book, and slapdashed it down the very minute after it happen'd,—let me see,—so many Days, Hours, and Seconds after Conception, yet this Infidel World wou'd hardly believe me. . . .[23]

Dunton has been suggested as a "source" for *A Tale of a Tub,* and many passages from his work—in the *Voyage* and elsewhere—could easily be cited to bloster a claim that Dunton is one of the hacks Swift has in mind as a parodic model for the tubbean author.[24] Dunton's life and works could in fact stand for much of what is under attack, in religion as well as in learning in *A Tale of a Tub,* for Dunton's publishing ventures, religious attitudes and experiences, and his rather volatile personal life make for racy reading that is in many ways symptomatic of the contemporary culture Swift is describing. We are likely to hear more in coming years of Dunton's place in the history of the novel, a place that is far more important than has been recognized.[25] But my point here is that Dunton is one of several writers one might cite—another is Francis Kirkman—to show that novelistic tendencies were already highly developed by 1694 when Swift began work on the *Tale,* even if no full-blown novel of artistic consequence yet existed.

Clearly, Swift saw the handwriting on the wall, a handwriting leading to a new world of print. *A Tale of a Tub* emphasizes the now, the subjective, the rambling recording of the present moment of an individual consciousness, digressiveness from the basic narrative movement, uncertainty of direction, and the portentousness of every word within a framework of fragmentation, lost passages, metaphors run wild, and syntactic madness; what Swift does with these emphases is to provide almost a catalogue of devices appropriate to the attitudes and values inherent in a new conception of writing and artistry then taking shape. Ultimately, it is too much to say that Swift's performance in *A Tale of a Tub* amounts to a parody of the novel, but his parodic representation of modern writing suggests how the wind was blowing, and he isolates a number of features that go on to find their proper home in the new narrative form then in the process of emerging. Swift isolates a number of features that became crucial in the new fiction: narrative interests merging with discursive ones only to be interrupted by the vagaries of individual consciousness; a preoccupation with subjectivity for its own sake; a concentration upon an individual of negligible social importance and an elevation of that individual's claims to significance; an almost boundless faith in the potential of particulars to lead to grand patterns of divine or natural order, empiricism vastly extended. In isolating such features, Swift provides an acute cultural analysis of forces deeply at work in English culture, and if he does not exactly prophesy some of the central features in the writing of Defoe, Richardson, and Sterne, he shows himself already aware of the inevitability that the culture's structure will find its appropriate form at the same time that he distills the implications of what is emerging as modernity by giving it a parodic form even before it has fully defined its own paradigm.

Swift's style in *A Tale of a Tub*, although it bears features of the style of Dunton and Dryden, Roger L'Estrange and Aphra Behn, Wotton, and Bentley and of perhaps scores of other contemporaries, is finally not that of any one hack but instead that of Everyhack. A knowledge of the particulars of writings relevant to the context of the *Tale* can only enhance our appreciation of what Swift does there, not because we are likely to find any one writer or work toward which Swift directs all of his satiric anger but because he collapses them into a chorus made up of individual voices barely distinguishable from one another and, in any case, contributory to what the Augustans soon heard as a universal hum. From hymn to hum, that is the way the Augustans perceived the breakdown of ritual and tradition and the separation from orality, as traditional values and ideas of order slipped into those of novelty. If the novel goes on to provide a different and less gloomy perspective, the vision of Swift is still a perceptive and prophetic one in its articulation of the emerging world's directions and cultural forms.

Like *A Tale of A Tub*, *Gulliver's Travels* is a vast many things generically, and the novel is only one of the forms that enables Swift's satiric art. Travel books, philosophical voyages, scientific translations, beast fables, children's fantasies, and a host of other formal and informal "kinds" play their part in Swift's act of imagination, and some of them, like the emerging novel, play a prominent role for readers in their ability to receive and perceive the text. Unlike *Don Quixote, Gulliver's Travels* does not contain both type and antitype, both paradigm and parody. But its negative representation of what was and what was to be involves Swift's shrewd (if ultimately doomed) vision of where western thought and western art would go in his own time, and in its response to the directions and assumptions of first-person, fictional narrative, *Gulliver's Travels* is a kind of testimony to a new tradition about to be invented, a form almost formed, a genre nearly generated, as well as a credo, call to arms, a solvent against solipsism. In a way it transcends its form, its credo, and its values, but it realizes those things too, against a new tradition rigorously engaged if only partly understood.

Notes

1. In *The Prose Works of Jonathan Swift*, ed. Herbert Davis et al. (Oxford: Basil Blackwell, 1939–68), 9:41. Henceforth referred to as *Prose Works*.

2. George P. Mayhew, "Jonathan Swift's Hoax of 1722 upon Ebenezor Elliston," *Bulletin of the John Rylands University Library of Manchester* 44 (1962): 366.

3. "The last Farewell of Ebenezor Ellison to this Transitory World," reprinted as an appendix in *Prose Works*, 9:366.

4. Most such "confessions" are very much alike, and the conventional wisdom is that someone, often the prison ordinary but sometimes a bookseller's hack, ghostwrote wholesale for the condemned prisoners. Collections of these last words were very popular early in the century; see, for example, *The Wonders of Free Grace: or, a compleat history of all the remarkable penitents that have been executed at Tyburn, and elsewhere* . . . (London, 1690). Elliston's last words are unusually rambling and oral, and it may be that we have here an attempt to transcribe something like what he actually said of himself.

5. See Herbert Davis's Introduction to vol. 1 of *Prose Works*, pp. xxxiii–xxxiv.

6. *Prose Works*, 1:239–240.

7. "Reflection 1," in *Occasional Reflections upon Several Subjects* (1665), reprinted in *Works* (London: 1772), 2: 359–60.

8. In the *Miscellanies in Prose and Verse*, (London: Benjamin Tooke, 1711), p. 231, Swift said his meditation was "According to the Style and Manner of the Honourable Robert Boyl's Meditations."

9. *Husbandry Spiritualized: or, The Heavenly Use of Earthly Things* (London: Robert Boulter, 1669), pp. 254–55.

10. The best description of the meditative tradition is still that of Louis Martz, *The Poetry of Meditation* (New Haven: Yale University Press, 1954).

11. "A Discourse Touching Occasional Meditations," in *Occasional Reflections*, reprinted in 1772 *Works*, 2:343.

12. "An Introductory Preface," in *Occasional Reflections*, reprinted in 1772 *Works*, 2:329.

13. See *Prose Works*, 5:271.

14. See Thomas Sheridan, *Life of Swift* (London, 1784), p. 42.

15. "Apology," in *A Tale of a Tub*, ed. A. C. Guthkelch and D. Nichol Smith, 2d ed. (Oxford: Clarendon Press, 1958), p. 7.

16. See *Swift and the Satirist's Art* (Chicago: University of Chicago Press, 1963), p. 31.

17. A happy exception is C. J. Rawson. See *Gulliver and the Gentle Reader* (London: Routledge and Kegan Paul, 1973).

18. Swift to Pope, 27 November 1726, in *Correspondence*, ed. Harold Williams (Oxford: Clarendon Press, 1963) 3:189.

19. Carole Fabricant, *Swift's Landscape* (Baltimore: Johns Hopkins University Press, 1982), esp. pp. 3–4, usefully reminds us that Swift's and Pope's positions need often to be distinguished from one another, but on this issue they seem to have seen eye to eye. For a good discussion of Swift's distrust of overreading natural phenomena, see Martin Price, *Swift's Rhetorical Art* (New Haven: Yale University Press, 1953), pp. 89–90.

20. Gildon's attack, published as *The life and strange surprising adventures of Mr. D—DeF—, of London Hosier . . . With remarks serious and comical upon the life of Crusoe*, had two editions in 1719 and another in 1724.

21. *London Journal*, 4 September 1725, p. 1.

22. John Robert Moore long ago pointed out that the opening paragraph of *Gulliver's Travels* reviewed satirically the life and career of DeFoe ("A DeFoe Allusion in *Gulliver's Travels*," *Notes and Queries* 178 (1940): 79–80. The whole issue of Defoe's relationship to Swift needs to be studied afresh, John Ross's study of the subject now being sadly outdated.

23. *A Voyage Round the World*, 3 vols. (London, 1691), 1:30.

24. See J. M. Stedmond, "Another Possible Analogue for Swift's *Tale of a Tub*," *Modern Language Notes* 72 (1957): 13–18. Stedmond, among others, has also studied Sterne's debt to Dunton, but the whole subject needs much more detailed analysis.

25. I have discussed some aspects of Dunton's importance in "The Insistent I," *Novel* 13 (1979): 19–37. See also Stephen Parks, *John Dunton and the English Book Trade* (New York: Garland, 1976) and Robert Adams Day, "Richard Bentley and John Dunton: Brothers under the Skin," *Studies in Eighteenth-Century Culture*, ed. O M Brack, Jr. (Madison: University of Wisconsin Press, 1986) 16:125–38.

Like Me, Like Me Not:
Gulliver's Travels as Children's Book

M. Sarah Smedman

Gulliver's Travels, like *Pilgrim's Progress* and *Robinson Crusoe*, has for more than two and a half centuries been a book read for pleasure by children. How a religious allegory or adventure novel underlaid with social, economic, and philosophic implications can appeal to children is a question rarely asked. On the other hand, how and why a bitter satire aimed at eighteenth-century political, religious, and cultural targets has attracted child readers is a question that has continually puzzled scholars. Most recently, John Traugott, in his fine essay "The Yahoo in the Doll's House" discusses play and game as the dominant figure of *Gulliver's Travels*. However, he reads the book primarily as one about childhood rather than as one for children, reasoning that children's make-believe, "a naive version of irony," is, like Swift's sophisticated irony, an "echo," an imitation of form emptied of meaning.[1] Traugott interprets *Gulliver* from the perspective of an adult, looking back *nostalgically* (emphasis mine, but a word he uses often) at recollected joys of childhood games such as romping with adults on the floor (like Gulliver in chains) and sailing boats in the bathtub (like Gulliver towing the Blefuscudian navy to Lilliput). But children themselves do not know nostalgia. For children at play, play has intense meaning; it is the adult's retrospective vision that descerns "a signifier without signification." Traugott focuses on the transference from child's play to Swift's rhetoric of irony as the key to understanding *Gulliver's Travels*. It is, on the contrary, *Gulliver's Travels* as children's literature, the appeal of the book to the child reader, that interests me.

1

Consideration of children's literature as a genre is problematic, for, like literature in general, that for children comprises many genres, each of which is defined by the elements of the literary work itself, not in terms of its audience. Although many have grappled with the question of what constitutes children's literature, none have been able to confine it within the popular conception that there is a kind of writing suitable only for children: a literature limited to child characters, restricted in subject matter, range of emotion, nature and quality of language. Good writers for children have never subscribed to such limitations. Jill Paton Walsh regrets "our habit of making false dichotomies," pointing out that "the distinction between children and adults can be a false crux; and that children though less well able to articulate their responses than adults, probably react similarly to aesthetic stimuli." She stresses the necessity of being honest about all dimensions of human existence "so that the child may know the nature of the game he is playing and may take a direction and make purposeful moves."[2] Natalie Babbitt asks, "Where do we get the idea that a children's book is gentle and sweet?" Children's writers, she adds, "Have a particularly tenacious view of life as an experiment in possiblity without compromise."[3]

Readers, writers, and critics agree that the best children's literature has characteristics that may or may not be found in adult literature, qualities that enrich rather than impoverish the works: a good and comparatively simple story; a strong moral theme (to be sharply distinguished from didacticism); honesty; a sense of wonder; an appreciation for the world; and a hopeful resolution, not to be confused with wish-fulfillment and happily-ever-after. Discussions of the nature of children's literature point, finally, to the inference that while no inherent qualities distinguish it exclusively from adult literature, the closure of a good children's book intimates something positive, "something which turns a story ultimately toward hope rather than resignation."[4]

Measured by the preceding criteria for children's literature, *Gulliver's Travels* fits well.[5] The book has many qualities to delight child readers, qualities deriving from the child always alive in the Swift whose favorite maxim was *vive la bagatelle*, and from the comic Swift, who for many adult readers gets buried under the bitterness of the misanthropic Gulliver, whose realistically hopeful creator dramatizes the dangers of staring too fixedly at human folly. Swift's dramatic vision seems one with his moral vision, an idealistic though not optimistic vision that admits of the coexistence, sometimes precarious, of irony and hope. Whatever else *Gulliver* is, it is an adventure story told with precision and logic in straightforward, unadorned prose, neither inflated nor magniloquent; Swift's logic delights children, whose own thought processes are so direct. Set in fantasyland, always the province of children, the story evokes wonder, is inventive and rich in detail and infused with the writer's passionate concern for his subject.

Swift's narrative perspective is in some ways that of a child. Like a child, Swift was possessed of an intensity born of the ability to see things clearly, "as if for the first time, in their original radiance and darkness."[6] Like a child, Swift wished to bring what he saw up close for examination. Not only did he discover Lilliput and the other countries of his imagination, he mapped them, described them, limned their inhabitants and their culture. Young readers, still sorting out the relationship between story and truth, are quite capable of perceiving the authenticity of Swift's vision, exaggerated as it may become in the telling. As George Orwell so graphically reminds us:

> A child, when it is past the infantile stage but still looking at the world with fresh eyes, is moved by horror almost as often as wonder—horror of snot and spittle, of the dog's excrement on the pavement, the dying toad full of maggots, the sweaty smell of grown-ups, the hideousness of old men, with their bald heads and bulbous noses. In his endless harping on disease, dirt, and deformity, Swift is not actually inventing anything, he is merely leaving something out.[7]

Samuel Holt Monk was wont to say that Swift's only insanity was his terrible, unbearable sanity, a state comprehensible perhaps only to those with unclouded, childlike vision.

An inherent problem with criticism of children's books is that adults must presume to speak for children. Because adults write, edit, publish, purchase, and review books for children, their opinions tend to override those of children themselves. What children do or do not like to read is not equivalent to what adults believe is or is not appropriate for them. Although histories and anthologies of children's literature invariably cite *Gulliver's Travels* as a classic and hundreds of editions have been published for juveniles, from the date of the book's publication adults have disagreed over its fitness as a companion for youth.[8] Diverse points of view reflect adults' various preconceived notions of childhood and the proper education of children. John Gay, responding to the fun in the *Travels*, tacitly approved it for children in his letter to Swift dated 17 November 1726, just two days after the anonymous publication of the book: "From the highest to the lowest it is universally read," Gay wrote, "from the Cabinet-council to the Nursery." He added that although lady-critics might construe it as an "insult on Providence, by depreciating the works of the Creator," the book "hath pass'd Lords and Commons *nemine contradicente;* and the whole town, men, women, and children are quite full of it."[9] By 1728, however, Jonathan Smedley, Dean of Clogher and a Whig, impervious to irony and disgusted by Swift's satires on religion and government, published *Gulliveriana,* in which he venomously attacks *Gulliver's Travels* as an "Abominable Piece," a "Book made up of Folly and Extravagance." Unable to perceive the reverence beneath the impious veneer of Swift's book, Smedley painstakingly emphasizes its pernicious effects upon impressionable young minds and judges it "Wicked, for a Man whose Vocation it is to preach the Holy Gospel, to spend so much precious Time purely to tempt Youth to misspend it."[10] Similarly, in the midnineteenth century, when it was the presupposition that all literature for children should be solemnly didactic, Thackeray, who admired the "fable" of *Gulliver,* misconstrued its moral as "horrible, shameful, unmanly, and blasphemous," and accused Swift of lacking "softness," of entering "the nursery with the tread and gayety of an ogre"; Thackeray believed no one but Swift could have found it possible to write *A Modest Proposal* because most people melt at the thought of childhood, fondle and caress it.[11] A century after Thackeray, George Orwell's assessment of Swift's masterpiece sounds more like John Gay's. *Gulliver's Travels,* Orwell declared, ought to be included among six books to be preserved when all others were destroyed. "I read it first when I was eight," he says, "and I have certainly not read it less than half a dozen times since. Its fascination seems inexhaustible."[12]

The controversy over whether or not *Gulliver's Travels* is suitable for children would seem to derive from two misconceptions: (1) an imprecise and often erroneous conception of children's literature; and (2) paradoxically, a single-minded focus on the complexities and bitterness of the book. The tenet, evinced in the statements of Smedley and Thackeray, that children's literature is simplistic moral pap, limited in subject matter to sweetness and light, limited in mode to romance or comedy, continues to be prevalent. Children themselves, of course, have never restricted their reading to the vacuous, which accounts for their adoption of *Gulliver's Travels.*

2

When *Gulliver's Travels* was published, the cultural ethos was conducive to its wide reception. Jonathan Smedley notwithstanding, children and their elders who were part of the society that Gulliver took by storm in November of 1726 would have understood children's ability to see the truth and the fun in the book. The popular audience for books in the early eighteenth century was still largely a single audience, as that for television is today. Not until midcentury did Thomas Boreman, followed by John Newbery, begin to publish specifically for children. Children were familiar with the same stories as their parents, heroes often familiar to them through both the oral and written traditions. Three of these stories widely known through popular chapbooks were particularly relevant to the immediate acceptance of Gulliver by children: *The History of Tom Thumbe, The History of Jack and the Giants,* and *The World Turned Upside Down.* These stories of pygmies amidst giants and of a topsy-turvy world—both situations universally appealing to children—had prepared young people for Swift's situations and inversions. Of the three stories, none is so relevant in its particulars to *Gulliver's Travels* as is that of *Tom Thumbe.*[13]

In his preface to the 1621 prose version of *The History of Tom Thumbe,* Richard Johnson addresses at some length various constituents of the single audience for whom he had chosen to write Tom's story:

> This is the Subject that my Pen means to make you merry with, and the only Story that (at noone dayes) may in time become the awaker of Sleepy Youth, prone to sluggishnesse: The ancient Tales of Tom Thumbe in the olde time, have been the only revivers of drouzy age at midnight; old and young have with his Tales chim'd Mattens till the Cocks crow in the Morning. . . .[14]

Although Johnson explicitly names Gargantua's story as one he eschewed in favor of Tom Thumbe's, Michael Patrick Hearn states in his preface to the Garland reprint that Johnson not only depended heavily on Rabelais's giant Gargantua, but "borrowed liberally" from the host of legends about Tom.[15] Hearn enumerates many similarities between the stories of Tom and Gulliver: Gulliver in Brobdingnag, like Tom, can be picked up by the middle between forefinger and thumb; just as Tom falls into his mother's pudding, Gulliver tumbles into a bowl of cream; both are attacked by animals, birds, and insects larger than themselves; from his perspective each finds the persons of court ladies physically offensive; King Arthur gives Tom a gold ring, which he wears as a girdle, whereas the Brobdingnagian queen gives Gulliver one he wears as a collar. A "huge blacke Raven" carries off Tom while he is attempting "to scarre away crowes . . . with a cudgell made of a Barley straw"; Gulliver is snatched by "some Eagle [who] had got the Ring of my Box in his Beak."[16] Hearn attributes both Tom's boast that he "can drowne a whole Towne with [his] pisse" and Gulliver's extinguishing the fire in the queen's palace with his urine to Gargantua's drowning of 260,418 people by the same means.[17] Hearn, however, takes no notice of the similarity between Swift's Yahoos, who climb trees to shower Gulliver with their excrement, and the giant in *Tom Thumbe*, who, to relieve the indigestion caused by Tom's "rumbling and tumbling in his guts . . . hyed he up to the toppe of his Castle wall, where he disgorged his stomacke, and cast out his burthen, at least three miles into the Sea."[18]

My point here is not to trace possible sources of *Gulliver's Travels* but to offer evidence that the book found a ready audience prepared by popular chapbooks. Citing also crude, scatalogical verses unabashedly published for children—the kind of rhymes that Francelia Butler has demonstrated are still part of skip-rope culture of children around the world—Hearn states what by today is a truism among students both of the eighteenth century and of children's literature:

> Adults of this period apparently thought nothing of giving their young unexpurgated editions of such popular literature as *Gulliver's Travels* . . . with its many references to bodily functions.[19]

Once having the book in hand, what do children find that has kept them coming back to *Gulliver's Travels* for more than 250 years? The strongest attraction, say most historians of children's literature, is the adventure in the book. Ahead of that I would put Swift's relationship to his material exhibited in the playfulness pervading the *Travels*, untainted by sentimentality or nostalgia. Sentimentality, never playful, cannot peacefully coexist with irony and is corrosive of common sense. Perhaps precisely because nostalgia, that entirely adult emotion, never intrudes into *Gulliver's Travels*, children of any century find easy access into the book, identifying with Gulliver as a person who sees things as they do. Since John Newbery's *Lilliputian Magazine* (1752) and such publications as John Harris's twelve-volume miniature *Cabinet of Lilliput: Instructive Stories . . .* (1802), children, because of their relative size, have been associated with the Lilliputians. In reality, children, often more sensible than adults, revel in Gulliver's benevolent power in Lilliput and share the troubles his size brings upon him in Brobdingnag.

The first two voyages, particularly, are imbued with Swift's childlike spirit, which evokes in young readers a sense of kinship. Not only the subjects Swift treats in many episodes but also his point of view, reasoning, and tone attest to his keen recollection of what it means to be a child. Consequently, he is able both to capture the essence of childhood and to speak its language. Most representative of the child still alive in the mature Swift is the understanding, lacking in many subsequent adapters of his work, that learning language, with its attendant frustrations and delight in sheer sound, is childhood's greatest task and triumph. Children appreciate the many incidents dramatizing failure to understand or be understood because of linguistic ignorance, learning the language, and consequent ability to communicate. In Lilliput children understand and enjoy the logic, as well as the naughtiness, of doing what comes naturally to extinguish the palace fire and are as baffled as Gulliver by his ostracism for having accomplished the feat. Statements like Gulliver's about the Lilliputian king—"He was then past his Prime, being twenty-eight Years and three Quarters old" (p. 30)—capture children's exactness about their own ages, the childish inability to recognize that "grown-up" does not mean "old," and the conception that everyone existing before their frames of reference belongs to the past, all of which is equally ancient history. For children, who quarrel and quickly make up, the causes of war might not seem so petty had Swift not taken such great care to trivialize them; they will wonder at the longevity of the discord. With their innate sense of justice, they will stand with Gulliver in his refusal to enslave a courageous people, just as, in their craving to be the center of attention, they will share his pleasure in the attendance of the Blefuscudian ambassadors. With Gulliver they will learn the pain of ingratitude. The voyage to Brobdingnag combines a clear reflection of what it means to be a child among big people and the child's desire to be seriously listened to by adults. Swift captures children's ambivalent attraction to and fear of other inhabitants of their world—rats, dogs, wasps, and bigger chilren who bully them. To timid children, all aliens are ogres. Children seeking independence sympathize with Gulliver's wish to deal with the frog who climbs aboard his boat by himself; his success will give them courage. Frequently the object of unwanted attention and inane remarks from strangers, young readers will squirm with Gulliver displayed as a freak in a circus. Especially, they will empathize with his having been able to live "happy enough in that Country if my Littleness had not exposed me to several ridiculous and troublesome Accidents" (p. 116), as well as with the effort it costs him to read and to play the piano. They will also laugh at Gulliver in these predicaments and thereby learn to laugh at themselves.

From the publication of *Gulliver's Travels*, the voyage to Laputa has been considered the weakest part of the book. Arbuthnot and Gay wrote Swift, respectively, that it was the "least brilliant" and the "least entertaining," although Gay added that "this hath its defenders too."[20] Among the defenders will be those children fascinated by a flying island and its flappers, by the detailed directions on how to drive it, by the opportunity to summon dead heroes, and by the picture of what it might be like to live forever. Children are curious about, fascinated with, and fearful of death from a very early age; the misery of the Struldbruggs' existence should quell any desire to live forever, though the full impact of that vivid narrative may remain half-submerged until the child is old enough to believe in his or her own mortality. It is impossible to believe that Natalie Babbitt's novel for young readers, *Tuck Everlasting*, does not at least in part derive from her desire to counterbalance the Struldbruggs with the Tucks, destined to live forever a pleasant life without aging. Babbitt's point, however, like Swift's, is that being cut off from the natural wheel of life-death is an undesirable fate.

Young people, too inexperienced to be cynical, are more likely to read Gulliver's fourth voyage as comedy than malevolent cynicism. Amused by the topsy-turvydom of a world where horses behave like passionless but perfect humans and humans behave like Yahoos, the average child, having persevered to the end, cannot miss the blatant ironies of the final chapter:

Thus, gentle Reader, I have given thee a faithful History of my Travels . . . wherein I have not been so studious of Ornament as of Truth. I could perhaps like others have astonished thee with strange improbable Tales; but I rather chose to relate plain Matter of Fact in the simplest Manner and Style; because my principle Design was to inform, and not to amuse thee. (p. 291)

Through the irony, the average child will also glimpse the truth. Swift wrote "to vex the world," yes, but the ingenuousness of his hero, his childlike delight in games, verbal and physical, the clarity of his view of life and his exaggerated expression of it— these not only amuse but were designed to do so.

3

Since 1726, there have been innumerable editions of *Gulliver's Travels* for children in English—including abridgments, expurgations, retellings, textbook editions, shorthand editions, some which can only be called prostitutions. Each abridgment or retelling reflects an adult's conception of childhood and of what is or is not suitable material for children, both in content and in difficulty of language. To see what changes have occurred in the real *Gulliver's Travels* and in attitudes toward childhood through the years, I examined fifty-five versions published between 1727 and 1985 in the United States and Great Britain in a survey that does not pretend to be comprehensive but does intend to be representative. The survey includes editions that have been published specifically for children or have been recommended for them by specialists in children's literature: editions that include only part 1 or part 2, parts 1 and 2, parts 1 through 3, as well as those which include all four parts. I examined all eighteenth-century abridgments to which I had access—including the first (1727)—and tried to locate at least one edition meeting my specifications from each decade of the nineteenth and twentieth centuries.[21] The books surveyed range in format from cheap chapbooks, like Redpath's Books of the Campfire and the tiny paperback from Ross's Juvenile Library series, to artistically designed, expensively bound copies, such as the Excelsior Edition of Standard Juvenile Fiction and the Oxford Illustrated Classics edition included in *British Book Design 1956*. Of the fifty-five editions studied, twelve include only the first voyage; one, only the second voyage; eighteen, both the first and second; one, the first three; and twenty-three include all four voyages, two of the latter (1947, 1963) combining the third and fourth in one. These figures provide some basis for questioning the statement appearing in most histories of children's literature that children's editions contain only the first two voyages. It is more difficult to contest the assumption that children read only the first two voyages, but an educated conjecture is that those youngsters to whom the four voyages have been available, having read the first two, would not stop there.

Other general discoveries prove interesting. Of the fifty-five editions in the sample, forty-three retain the first person in which *Gulliver's Travels* was originally written, many of these retellings as well as abridgments; twelve are retold in the third person. No editor comments on his or her reason for the change, so one can only infer that it may have been to approximate more closely the style of the fairy tale, an inference that seems valid in light of the fact that most of the third-person versions are for young children. Similarly, thirty-eight editions retain the word *Travels* in the title, while twelve use *Adventures* and four, *Voyages*—that is, *The Adventures of Gulliver in* . . . , or *Gulliver's Voyages to.* . . . Most editors decided that Swift's prefatory letters were too topical or subtle for young people, for few children's editions contain either of them, though the letter from Richard Sympson appears occasionally. Many of those not in cheap paper bindings contain biographical sketches of Swift, most of them to some degree antipathetic to Swift as a person. They tend to emphasize his eccentric temperament, to attribute to him a vision of despair, and to credit him as a brilliant stylist. The abridgments rarely alter Swift's diction or syntax except to modernize terms—for example, substituting *Australia* for *Van Diemen's land* and *pumpkin* for *pompion*. Even many of the versions that change the narrative to third person retain much of Swift's language. Retellings for younger children, such as Edith Robarts's and John Lang's, simplify as they delete.

To chart all the variations in the fifty-five editions is not possible here. However, it is possible to point to several incidents that may serve as touchstones in a brief survey of the process of editing for children: namely, Gulliver's observation upon the nurse's breast as she suckles the baby (p. 91); Gulliver's frolics with the maids-of-honor (pp. 112–13); his harmless sport of jumping cow dung (p. 124); the Lagadan experimenter's attempt to return human ordure back into food and Gulliver's fit of colic (pp. 179 and 181); descriptions of male and female Yahoos (pp. 223–24); and the attack of the female Yahoo upon Gulliver (pp. 266–67). These touchstone passages tend to be ribald and scatological but are not exclusively so.

What has happened to the story of Gulliver's putting out the palace fire, in the context of comparable incidents in Lilliput, illustrates something of the nature of emendations in children's versions of *Gulliver's Travels*. From the fifty-four editions that

include the voyage to Lilliput, eighteen retain Gulliver's vindication of the reputation of Flimnap's wife, but only five retain any
mention of his natural need for elimination, though all describe
in some detail what Gulliver eats and drinks. Thirty-four editions
excise the extinguishing of the fire in the queen's palace, the first
of which in my sample did not occur until 1829; the second, in
1840; the third, in 1886. Not until the late 1880s did that deletion
occur almost as a matter of course. Fifteen editions retain the
story of the fire just as Swift told it. One merely reports, "most
unfortunately, at this time, that Gulliver had offended the Queen
by a well-meant, but badly-managed effort to do her a service,
and thus he lost also her friendship."[22] Four editions retain the
incident, portraying Gulliver as victimized hero, but alter the
manner in which he puts out the fire. The first, the Excelsior
Edition of Standard Juvenile Fiction, published in the 1870s,
supplies an adjoining palace with a "reservoir of water kept for
the especial use of the empress." For any other person to use the
water was a capital crime. "But, necessity, [Gulliver] thought,

> had no law; so reaching over I lifted the tank, which might contain
> about four gallons of water, and applied it so well to the proper places
> that in three minutes the fire was wholly extinguished and the rest of
> that noble pile, which had cost so many ages in erecting, preserved
> from destruction.[23]

Gulliver in Lilliput, retold by Edith Robarts, provides Gulliver an
additional occasion for heroism and finds a use for his retrieved
hat, which he wears to the fire although he forgets his coat:

> It seemed a very dreadful thing that this beautiful palace should be
> burnt to the ground, and just as I was fearing this might happen, an
> idea suddenly occurred to me. This was to use my hat for a bucket,
> and by filling it at the lake in the palace garden, I emptied the lake
> and soon put out the fire! But to my horror I also nearly drowned the
> Queen and her royal children. The water quite filled the rooms in
> which the royal family were, and I had the greatest difficulty to pick
> them out at the windows. They were quite insensible, but soon after
> became conscious again, and were unhurt.[24]

Like the anonymous adapter of the Excelsior Edition, W. B. Scott
works an altered expedient into the framework of Swift's prose:

> In consequence of the great difficulty of providing me with washing
> accommodation inside the temple, a brewer's vat had been assigned

to me. This, for the convenience of obtaining a sufficient supply of water, was placed by the side of a well, near the entrance to the city, and, therefore, at no great distance from the palace. Coming home late the previous night I had washed myself before retiring to rest; and by great good fortune, as I thought, the suds had not been thrown away. I lost no time in carrying the vat to the palace, and as it contained nearly an English gallon of water, I was able to use it with such good effect that in three minutes the fire was wholly extinguished. . . .[25]

Not nearly so convoluted is the Usborne/Hayes Picture Classics *Gulliver's Travels,* which simply states: "Gulliver helped out and within minutes he had put out the fire. The palace was saved and he went back home to bed."[26]

Each interesting in its own way, every edition of *Gulliver's Travels* for young readers seems worthy of comment; some, however, have one or another feature that ought not go unremarked. For example, 1) a prefatory statement of motivation for abridgment of the original, which usually reveals a particular attitude toward children and their literature; 2) the very nature of the edition or its significance in the history of children's publications; 3) inventive interpolations or substitutions; or 4) simply a uniqueness which eludes classification.

The first abridged edition, pirated in 1727 by Stone and King, was apparently published with no thought of children as a special audience. Its stated purpose is to "lessen the Expence" of the original, thus making the best-seller available to a greater number of readers. The publisher promised that the abridgment would be "faithful," would answer "the intention of the Author," and would not deprive "the Original of those Ornaments which recommend it to the Judicious." "It is true," the introduction acknowledges, "that some Passages in the Original, which the Generality of Mankind have thought immodest and indecent, are entirely omitted."[27] For the most part, however, the touchstone passages remain intact. What is "contracted into a very narrow Compass" are the lengthy descriptions of the lands, their customs and laws, and the philosophical disquisitions between Gulliver and various rulers.

The first abridgment of *Gulliver's Travels* published in America was for children, that by Young and M'Culloch in Philadelphia in 1787: *The Adventures of Captain Gulliver in a Voyage to the Islands of Lilliput and Brobdingnag.* According to A. S. W. Rosenbach, this first juvenile edition goes back to a John Newbery original.[28] A retelling in the third person, its various printings by different publishers keeps much of Swift's language, including:

> Mr. Gulliver could not help wondering at the intrepidity of those diminutive mortals who [ventured to mount and] walk upon his body, while one of his hands was at liberty, without trembling at the sight of so prodigious a creature as he must appear to them.[29]

The vocabulary was apparently quite within the range of nearly seven-year-old Thomas Dow, who, according to an inscription in a 1794 copy, was presented with the book on 4 December 1811. A second inscription reads: "Thomas Dow was born February the 2 Day A.D. 1805."

In a Smedleyan vein, though milder, Edwin O. Chapman in the introduction to his "New Edition, Edited for Young Readers" (1888) damns Swift with the faint praise that he was "an able writer and a great scholar" but never "a good man nor a happy man." Chapman grants that though there is much in *Gulliver's Travels* that is "of no interest to" or "unsuitable for" children, the "romantic adventures of Gulliver will always have for young readers the attractions of a fairy tale." Chapman concludes:

> This editor has faithfully preserved these attractive features and as mercilessly cut out the objectionable portions. His only excuse for taking such liberties with the author's text is that the work may with propriety be placed, where it has so long been improperly classed, among books for children.[30]

Chapman's is properly an edition, preserving Swift's prose but deleting or sanitizing all touchstone incidents.

In his "Introductory Sketch" to the 1896 Riverside Literature Series edition of *The Voyages to Lilliput and Brobdingnag,* Horace Scudder, of landmark significance in the history of children's magazines, addresses children as intelligent and literate but betrays his prejudice against Swift, occasionally propounding factual inaccuracies. The "Sketch" begins:

> It is curious fortune for a book to be written as a political satire and to come finally to be read by the young for their entertainment, with no thought at all of the satire except as it is pointed out by students of literature.[31]

Unlike Defoe's mind, Scudder suggests, Swift's was perverted: he had "an imperious intellect," which tyrannized over his sense of "natural play, and life, instead of being humanized by it, was rendered more cruel and passionate." Scudder does pay tribute to Swift's genuine love of "language used skillfully and exactly," not only in word but by retention of the original prose in his edition. He justifies his categorical judgment—"the greatest interest centred on Lilliput, for it appealed to people much as fairy tales appeal to children"—by reference to the eighteenth century as a time when "people had little abundance of imagination, and not much faith in supernatural life." Comparing himself with "all editors who have prepared these *Travels* for popular reading," Scudder, too, omits "such passages as show an unseemly coarseness." He equates "popular reading" with reading for children.

William Dean Howells's introduction to the 1913 Harper publication illustrated by Louis Rhead is interesting because he says that before he read the book when he was "ten or twelve years old," he knew from his father that *Gulliver's Travels* was one of the great books among different literatures. Howells recognizes the personal and cultural satire but also "the far more subtle and sanative irony which plays through these most delightful studies of human Nature"; but he does not

> expect the boys, or even the girls, who more than grown people, will delight in the witchery of one of the most amusing fables ever invented, to feel the play of undercurrent in it.[32]

On the contrary, the entire design of the Macmillan Classics 1919 *Gulliver's Travels* edited by Padraic Colum assumes that children are aesthetically sensitive and intelligent readers. Beautiful as an object, the book has powerfully fine and funny illustrations by Willy Pogany. In the 1962 reissue, Clifton Fadiman, in his pointed afterword, tells young readers that "this particular edition is a kind of compliment to you":

> Your editor, Padraic Colum, is a man who knows something about youth. He is confident that you are capable of reading all of Swift's masterpiece in a form very little different from the original version.[33]

Colum indeed compliments young readers: his introduction contains an excellent, objective biographical sketch of Swift, which places the author in human perspective and literary context, and also an analysis of *Gulliver's Travels* focusing on Swift's "one idea firmly held." Colum clearly explains satire and its function in the book, Swift's love of language and its impact on the

Travels, and the place of affection and wonder in readers' responses to the stories. Differing markedly from Howells, Colum addresses children as capable of understanding many of the layers of meaning and literary techniques in Swift's book and possesses the Swiftian skill of conveying penetrating insights in terse and lucid prose. While many commentators liken *Gulliver's Travels* to fairy tales and Andrew Lang includes a simplified retelling in his famous collection of folktales from many cultures, the 1889 *Blue Fairy Book,* it is the differences which interest Colum:

> *Gulliver's Travels* is a fairy tale inverted. In the fairy tale the little beings have beauty and graciousness, the giants are dull-witted, and the beasts are helpful, and humanity is shown as triumphant. In *Gulliver* the little beings are hurtful, the giants have more insight than men, the beasts rule, and humanity is shown, not as triumphant, but as degraded and enslaved.[34]

In 1962, after twenty years of successful publishing, Golden Press released *Gulliver's Travels* as one of its Illustrated Classics. This retelling by Sarel Eimerl deletes all references to political discussions, to scatalogical and sexual incidents, and to humans as diminutive, contemptible animals, and it greatly abbreviates parts 3 and 4. Sentence patterns tend to be simple and syntactically repetitive. The pictures by Maraja in brilliant primary colors are profuse, many of them decorative as well as illustrative. Because of Golden Press's philosophy of publishing well-written stories by reputable authors and illustrators in durable but cheap format, the Golden Books edition undoubtedly reached a wider audience than more authentic but expensively bound books.

Textbook editions of the *Travels* include an abridgment of Lilliput and Brobdingnag published by Ginn in 1886, and also an adaptation "retold" by Frank L. Beals, assistant superintendent of the Chicago schools, and published by Sanborn in 1946. Beals thought *Gulliver's Travels* "interesting and fascinating" but "too difficult" to be read by children in the middle grades. Humbler in tone than Chapman, having fewer expectations of children than Colum, Beals notes that the "present rewriting is not an effort to improve upon *A Voyage to Lilliput,* but to simplify it and make it available to the young people of today."[35] Too pedestrian to excite wonder, each of the fourteen short chapters is followed by questions calling for recall, interpretation, or opinion, plus vocabulary words. Brief definitions accompany a "word list" at the end of the text. Several passages are explicitly didactic, appropriate perhaps to a textbook, never to a good story, and certainly not worthy of Swift's subtlety. What the original Gulliver thinks about the Lilliputian emperor's desire to enslave the Blefuscudians and his own refusal to cooperate, Beals spells out in wooden, moralizing dialogue.

Perhaps taking its cue from Laputa's school of languages where the professors' "first Project was to shorten Discourse by cutting Polysyllables into one" (p. 185), in 1895 A. L. Burt published the *Travels* in "Words of One Syllable" by Mrs. J. C. Gorham. Interesting if only because it evinces the challenge posed by a clever game, the book has a liveliness of style derived from varied sentence patterns and apt diction. Gorham cheats only a little when she divides the months of the year into hyphenated words. Another attempt of a similar kind, the Dolches' *Gulliver's Stories for Pleasure Reading* (1960) is one of their series of classics rewritten in language limited to their famous basic list of the first thousand words for children's reading. Unlike Gorham's, the Dolches' adaptation is a travesty, stifling rather that stimulating the imagination.

The Macmillan edition illustrated by Charles E. Brock (1894, 1923) displays an eagerness to uphold the integrity of the legal profession and its practioners. Into Gulliver's account of lawyers and the adjudication of the case of his cow, the anonymous adapter reinserts a lengthy passage from the original 1726 edition which Swift had deleted in 1735:

> The numerousness of those that dedicated themselves to this Profession were such that the fair and justifiable Advantage and Income of the Profession was not sufficient for the decent and handsome Maintenance of the Multitudes who followed it. Hence it came to pass that it was found needful to supply that by Artifice and Cunning which could not be procured by just and honest methods. . . . [Dishonest] practioners were by Men of discernment called Pettifoggers . . . and it was my ill Hap as well as the Misfortune of my suffering Acquaintance to be engaged only with this Species of the Profession.[36]

The ensuing account of the practice of following legal precedent is extended to emphasize that not all lawyers are crooked. Nowhere else does this editor, whoever he was, attempt to justify a class of people, a custom, or a law that Swift villifies. This passage with a few changes in diction and capitalization appears again in the editions of W. B. Scott (1911) and Rand McNally's Windemere Series (1912).

Patrick Bellew is one among several editors and retellers of Gulliver's adventures who injudiciously delete the language Swift fabricates for the inhabitants of his fantasy lands, particularly the Lilliputians. However, Bellew's edition (1945) is unique in that it creates his own nonsense language in which the Lilliputian king and Gulliver converse:

> *Schmoz garumph kabob!* said the little man.
> *Wazzat?* said Gulliver.
> *Kiwee galurki chimpoo!* replied the midget.
> Neither understood the other, but from Gulliver making chewing motions and swallowing, the little man finally appeared to understand, although at first he thought Gulliver wanted to eat him.

Later, when the king's horse shies before the Man-Mountain, the following conversation takes place: "*Nok urak goydoo!* [the king] cried." Not understanding, Gulliver "tried the only other language he knew."

> *Parlez-vous Français?*
> *Novak prum bagoz yewohee-hee*, was all he got in exchange.
> *Je ne vous comprends pas*, he replied.
>   As this seemed likely to go on forever, Gulliver tried sign language, which seemed more successful, and soon he began to gather what the King wanted.[37]

Once Gulliver can speak a bit of Lilliputian, Bellew translates an occasional phrase into English. When Gulliver visits Mildendo, the inhabitants shout, "*Helugi galumph!* meaning *Hail and Welcome!*" Gulliver replies, "*Yugosi pizzu*, that is *The same to you.*" Bellew also changes Flimnap's name to Floogumph, probably because the combination of the roundly hollow and thudding sounds better match his own "little language" than the thinner, lighter Flimnap. Purists may castigate Bellew as a corruptor, but he captures something of Swift's spirit of fun and love of language.

An unusual, jolly *Gulliver in Lilliput* is a British pop-up version illustrated by Vojtech Kubasta and printed by Artia in Prague. The cover is a puppet theater with royalty in the audience and a little girl holding her doll by one hand at stage edge. Gulliver appears in the proscenium arch, hand to his hat. When the book is opened, Gulliver, inside the front cover, doffs his hat and bows:

Hello, children!
Allow me to introduce myself. My name is Lemuel Gulliver and I am
a ship's surgeon. . . .[38]

Through the slim volume, Gulliver speaks cozily to the children,
the anonymous narrator attributing to him details that not only
increase merriment but, like Swift's, poke fun at contemporary
culture. A few samples convey the flavor. During the noisy astonishment of the Lilliputians when Gulliver stands to his full
height, Gulliver confesses that it was "a wonderful feeling—
something like being born a second time"; then he records:

> local police tried in vain to keep order. The official news agency
> published a report that ten people were trampled to death by the
> crowd, but two hours later it denied this.

More specifically directed to children are Gulliver's accounts of
boys' and girls' games:

> Children played hide-and-seek in my hair, finding it extremely good
> fun, for nowhere else did they have so many hiding places. Once a
> little girl got lost there and could not find a way out. She cried and
> cried until I helped her disentangle herself and set her down on the
> ground again.

On the day of the parade of the royal troops between Gulliver's
legs,

> . . . drummers drummed, the emperor's jester outdid himself in being
> funny, flags and banners fluttered from the towers, and the sun
> looked down in surprise at all this unusual activity. The boys, who in
> Lilliput just as elsewhere, painted all kinds of signs on the wall,
> waved their little flags, and one of them even climbed on the top of
> the Castle parapet, although this was strictly forbidden.

Despite the fact that at least from the time John Newbery published the *Lilliputian Magazine*, children have been associated
with Swift's little people, this Artia version of the story is the
only one in the sample in which children may identify with the
Lilliputians rather than with Gulliver.

The texts and formats of the four 1980s editions recapitulate
trends in the publication of *Gulliver's Travels* during its long
lifetime. Both the two retellings and the two reissues differ from
each other in nature and quality. The Usborne/Hayes Picture

Classics retelling of the voyage to Lilliput is a glossy, garish paperback, only a cut above the comic book in design and quality of illustration. The text is insipid. By contrast the 1983 version of the first two voyages illustrated by David Small has a verve of its own, enhanced by its brevity. Certainly the text pales by comparison with Swift's, but it has more regard for the sound and sense of words than most retellings. Unfortunately, nothing in the book corrects the title-page indication that Swift wrote the text as it appears; the storyteller remains anonymous. The oversize book has strong, expressionistic, heavily-lined illustrations. Sadly, because of its fine bookmanking, it will not have the mass market appeal of the Usborne/Hayes "Classic."

Schocken's 1984 one-volume, moderately priced issue of the *Travels* illustrated by Rex Whistler makes available to a wide audience an example of book illustration that had previously been limited to an edition of only two hundred copies (1930). The text is that of the 1735 edition. Nonetheless, the book is marketed for children, and Lawrence Whistler, the illustrator's brother, in his preface refers to the story as "inescapably, a spendid children's book," wisely commenting that the author "probably enjoyed arousing wonder in minds that as yet had no grasp of the satirical."[39] The artist's preliminary colored sketch of the frontispiece is on the book jacket, though the final illustrations are in pen and ink, for Whistler is "not in favour of colour, as destroying unity even while it added charm." The 1985 edition illustrated by Arthur Rackham is a version of a book printed in various formats since its appearance in 1900. A new edition, including additional colored illustrations, was published in 1909; another, in 1952. In contrast to the attractively designed volume of 1909 bound in gilt-engraved covers, the 1985 book is cheap, with all the colored plates lumped together in the middle of the book, a caricature of both Rackham as illustrator and of quality children's books.

A complete history of the editions of *Gulliver's Travels* for children might well prove to be a paradigm of the history of children's books, for even my sample includes a wide variety of publications passed off as children's literature: (1) pop-up books for toddlers, complete editions for adolescents, and editions aimed at every age in between; (2) texts of *Gulliver's Travels* in syntax and vocabulary ranging from paraphrases in short, simple sentences composed of words from the Dolches' basic list, to editions retaining Swift's prose unaltered; (3) texts reflecting the belief that stories for children must be cute, sentimental, and didactic; (4) sanitized texts reflecting the belief that children must be sheltered not only from what is political, violent, and vulgar but also from anything that has to do with natural bodily functions; and (5) unexpurgated texts reflecting the belief that though young people may be inexperienced, they are intellectually and emotionally capable of coping with several levels of meaning in stories. Of course, neither writers, critics, nor young readers would consider every edition of equal merit. Like other books marketed for children, some editions of Gulliver's Travels have literary significance; others are pulp.

Children's expectations for a good story are basic and stringent: it should have a single trajectory along which the story develops; it should have clearly delineated characters and settings; it should have adventure beyond the actual; and it must be true, "real."[40] Good literature for children should simultaneously enlarge and enrich their imaginations and extend their insights into the patterns and meaning of life. Gulliver's Travels satisfies those expectations as well today as it did in 1726—or in 1927, when William Lyons Phelps wrote in The Yale Review: "'Gulliver's Travels' is the most terrible satire ever aimed at humanity; and it has diverted hundreds of thousands of children."[41] Perhaps Padraic Colum, in that fine introduction to his edition of the book, has best expressed the reason why Gulliver's story has so strong a hold upon children's—and adults'—imaginations. In contrast to modern writers, Colum says, Swift and his contemporaries referred to few ideas but illustrated them prodigiously. Swift's book has "abundance in power," for

> It is an illustration of one idea firmly held: Swift looks from above, down upon men, he looks from below up at them and then he looks at them from behind. He breaks into no complexity of idea. But he puts so much power into his statement that we know as much about the Lilliputians and the Brobdingnagians and the Houyhnhnms as if we had read our twelve volumes on each by the Gibbon of their respective empires.[42]

Undoubtedly this power is one reason Clifton Fadiman places Gulliver's Travels among the ten books he predicts will still be read by children in five hundred years.[43]

Swift's forceful representation of strange exterior worlds and the relationships that exist within them enables readers—children and adults—to understand their interior landscapes. Consequently, even today's children who adventure with Gulliver learn through the Lilliputians, Brobdingnagians, Houyhnhnms, and others much about human nature. Though they neither know nor care about topical or personal allusions, they will understand that people and their institutions can be corrupt; but they will realize, too, that they need not be so. Correctives are at hand, one of which children may imbibe (if their editions leave them the third and fourth voyages, as many do) is that we should not too proudly aspire to perfection and happiness through reason and technology. That way lies madness, as Gulliver portrays but never learns.

More important, young readers learn from Gulliver because they are intrigued and amused by his exploits. According to the study by Carleton Washburne and Mabel Vogel, eighty-nine percent of the boys and seventy-five percent of the girls who reported reading the book for pleasure ranked it in interest value somewhere between "a good book; I like it," and "one of the best books I ever read."[44] Surely a major cause of the continued viability of *Gulliver's Travels* is that children have always enjoyed it. Perhaps Fadiman is not far wrong when he claims, "Whether by accident or design . . . the gods tend to grant immortality to those books which, in addition to being great, are loved by children."[45]

Notes

1. "The Yahoo in the Doll's House: *Gulliver's Travels* the Children's Classic," in *English Satire and the Satiric Tradition*, ed. Claude Rawson (Oxford: Basil Blackwell, 1984), pp. 127–50.

2. Jill Paton Walsh, "The Writers in the Writer," *Signal* 40 (1983): 3; "The Lords of Time," in *The Openhearted Audience*, ed. Virginia Haviland (Washington, D. C.: Library of Congress, 1980), p. 198.

3. "Happy Endings? Of Course, and Also Joy," in *Children's Literature: Views and Reviews*, ed. Virginia Haviland (Glenview, Ill.: Scott, Foresman, 1973), p. 157.

4. Babbitt, "Happy Endings?", p. 158.

5. For this essay, children will be considered as those persons who have manifested some sense of story but who have not yet entered high school, that is, between approximately three and fourteen years of age. This delimitation allows for inclusion of editions of *Gulliver's Travels* for the preschool child as well as for those in early adolescence.

6. Edwin Muir, "A Child's World Is a Poet's," in *Children's Literature: Views and Reviews*, p. 269.

7. "Politics *vs.* Literature: An Examination of *Gulliver's Travels*" (1950), rpt. in *Shooting an Elephant and Other Stories* (London: Secker, 1957), p. 82.

8. At least two studies of twentieth-century children's reading allow youngsters to record the popularity of *Gulliver's Travels:* George W. Norwell, *What Boys and Girls Like to Read* (New York: Silver Burdett, 1958); and Carleton Washburne and Mabel Vogel, *What Children Like to Read: Winnetka Graded Book List* (New York: Rand, 1926).

9. *The Correspondence of Jonathan Swift,* ed. Harold Williams (Oxford: Clarendon Press, 1963), 3: 182–83.

10. *Gulliveriana,* facsimile rpt. as *Swiftiana 8* (New York: Garland Publishing, 1974), pp. 329 and 330.

11. "Swift," in *The English Humorists* (New York: Crowell, 1840), pp. 20 and 18.

12. "Politics vs. Literature," p. 78.

13. Repetitive and violent, *Jack and the Giants* (the first extant printing is 1711) delighted the boyhoods of Fielding and Boswell, among others, and inured children to blood and gore; actual public executions, however, more probably inspired Swift's account of the malefactor's death than Jack's many murders of multiheaded giants. Only a sample of the text of *The World Turned Upside Down, or the Folly of Man* is included in John Ashton's *Chap-Books of the Eighteenth Century* (London: Chatto, 1882); "Luckily," says Ashton, "the illustrations explain themselves" (p. 267). At least three of these may have direct bearing on Gulliver's fourth voyage: in one, two horses duel while astride the backs of men; in another, a horse grooms his master; in a third, an ass drives a miller weighed down under a heavy sack.

14. Richard Johnson, *The History of Tom Thumbe,* ed. Curt F. Bühler (Evanston, Ill.: Northwestern University Press, 1965), p. 2.

15. In *The History of Tom Thumbe* (New York: Garland Publishing, 1977), pp. ix–xi. Hearn calls Johnson "an undistinguished author of much popular literature" (p. viii).

16. Johnson, *Tom Thumbe,* p. 13; *Gulliver's Travels,* in *The Prose Works of Jonathan Swift,* ed. Herbert Davis et al. (Oxford: Basil Blackwell, 1939–68), 11:140–41. Subsequent references to Swift's original will be to this edition and will be given within the text. These bird scenes have always been attractive to illustrators: in his *Chap-Books of the Eighteenth Century,* Ashton includes a woodcut of a huge bird carrying in his beak a tiny, sticklike Tom Thumbe; illustrators of *Gulliver's Travels* almost invariably include a representation of an eagle carrying Gulliver's box in his beak.

17. Johnson, *Tom Thumbe,* p. 15. See Hearn, *Tom Thumbe,* p. xviii.

18. Johnson, *Tom Thumbe,* pp. 17–18.

19. Hearn, *Tom Thumbe,* p. xvii.

20. Swift, *Correspondence,* 3: 179 and 183.

21. Although my sample leans toward twentieth-century editions, it includes none published during the 1930s or 1970s; by contrast, the 1940s and 1960s were boon years for *Gulliver's Travels.* To date I have seen four 1980s editions.

22. *Gulliver's Travels in Lilliput and Brobdingnag,* Told to Children by John Lang (London: T. C. and E. C. Jack, 1908), p. 43.

23. *Travels of Lemuel Gulliver into Several Remote Regions of the World* (New York: American News Co., n.d.), pp. 63–64.

24. *Gulliver in Lilliput,* Retold by Edith Robarts (London: Ward, Lock, n.d.), pp. 60–61.

25. *Gulliver's Travels,* Adapted for the Young by W. B. Scott (London: Ernest Nister, 1911), pp. 63–64.

26. *Gulliver's Travels in Lilliput*, Retold by Angela Wilkes (London: Usborne/ Hayes, 1982), p. 25.

27. *Travels into Several Remote Nations of the World* (London: Stone and King, 1727), p. As–3.

28. Rosenbach, collector and author of *Early American Children's Books*, bases his conclusions on d'Alte Welch's "Bibliography of American Children's Books Printed Prior to 1821," *Proceedings of the American Antiquarian Society* 77 (1968): 378. The first American edition is the same as that published in London by P. Osborne et al. in 1785.

29. *The Adventures of Captain Gulliver* (Philadelphia: Young and M'Culloch, 1787), p. 15. The passage in the 1794 edition is identical, but the edition appearing in the 1820s includes the bracketed phrase.

30. *Gulliver's Travels into Several Remote Regions of the World*, Edited for Young Readers by Edwin O. Chapman (New York: Worthington, 1888), pp. 8–9.

31. *Gulliver's Travels: The Voyages to Lilliput and Brobdingnag* (Boston: Houghton Mifflin, 1896), [p. 5]. Subsequent quotations appear on pp. 10, 13, and 18.

32. *Gulliver's Travels into Several Remote Nations of the World* (New York: Harper, 1913), p. xv.

33. *Gulliver's Travels*, Retold by Padraic Colum (1919; New York: Macmillan, 1962), p. 259.

34. Colum, *Gulliver's Travels*, n. p. Fadiman concludes rightly: "Mr. Colum's introduction . . . tells you a great deal about Swift and explains how it came about that he could, apparently with approval, record the verdict of the King of the Brobdingnagians upon the species you and I belong to" (p. 260).

35. *The Story of Lemuel Gulliver in Lilliput Land*, Adapted and Retold by Frank L. Beals (Chicago: Benjamin H. Sanborn, 1946), [p. i]. The copy I used of the 1886 Ginn edition especially interested me, for it had been used by one William R. Jutte of Desk 14 in some school at some time. The skimpy introduction only mentions satire, but William's teacher must have stressed that dimension; inside the cover, opposite the flyleaf where he has written his name, he has noted:

	Personal
	on one man
	Political
Satire {	on parties
	General
	on customs
	Religious

At the end of part 1, chapter 5, a boyish hand has written, "8 examples of general satire for Monday"; in the margins of chapter 6, ten passages are marked off and "G S" written beside each.

36. *Travels into Several Remote Nations of the World* (1894; New York: Macmillan, 1923), pp. 284–85. A sophisticated edition, this is recommended for children by Emelyn E. Gardner and Eloise Ramsey, *A Handbook of Children's Literature: Methods and Materials* (Chicago: Scott, Foresman, 1927).

37. *Gulliver's Travels*, Adapted and Illustrated by Patrick Bellew (New York: Hyperion Press, 1945), pp. 8 and 11–12.

38. *Gulliver in Lilliput* (Prague: Artia, n.d.), p. 2. Subsequent quotations

appear on unnumbered pages 7, 11, and 13. Not listed in the usual bibliographies, this book was probably published between 1940 and 1963, when Dr. Irving Kerlan was collecting contemporary children's books; in the Kerlan Collection of the University of Minnesota's Children's Literature Research Collections, the volume bears a descriptive note in Dr. Kerlan's hand.

39. *Gulliver's Travels* (New York: Schocken, 1984), p. 7. The subsequent quotation appears on p. 9.

40. The metaphor of a trajectory belongs to Jill Paton Walsh, "The Lords of Time," pp. 184–89: "There is such a thing as the plot of the order in which the writer unfolds his story: a kind of metaplot. Let us imagine this . . . as a trajectory, a flight path which must take the best, the most emotionally loaded route through the subject to the projected end. Whatever lies right on the trajectory is essential to a children's story. Anything else—a subplot, irrelevant description or philosophizing—makes a story too complicated for children."

41. "A Note on Gulliver," *The Yale Review* (October 1927): 93.

42. Colum, *Gulliver's Travels*, p. xv.

43. "Books for Children," in *Party of One* (Cleveland: World Publishing, 1955), pp. 382–85.

44. *What Children Like to Read*, p. 117.

45. "Books for Children," p. 385.

Gulliver's Travels
Selected Editions for Children

Travels into Several Remote Nations of the World. London: Stone and King, 1727.

The Adventures of Captain Gulliver. Adorned with Cuts. Philadelphia: Young and M'Culloch, 1787.

The Adventures of Captain Gulliver in a Voyate to the Islands of Lilliput and Brobdingnag. Adorned with Cuts. Philadelphia: W. Young, 1794.

The Adventures of Captain Gulliver. Boston: S. Hall, 1794.

The Surprizing Adventures of Captain Gulliver in a Voyage to the Kingdom of Lilliput. Illus. Philadelphia: B. C. Busby, 1808.

Adventures of Captain Gulliver in a Voyage to Lilliput. Ross's Juvenile Library. Edinburgh: G. Ross, n.d. (1814?).

Adventures of Captian Gulliver in a Voyage to Lilliput. Ross's Juvenile Library. Glasgow: J. Lumsden & Son, 1814.

Adventures of Captain Gulliver in a Voyage to Lilliput. Ross's Juvenile Library. Glasgow: J. Lumsden & Son, 1815.

The Adventures of Captain Gulliver in a Voyage to the Islands of Lilliput and Brobdingnag. Adorned with Cuts. London: J. Harris (Successor to E. Newbery), n.d. (1820s).

Gulliver's Travels into Several Remote Nations of the World. In *Jones's Cabinet Edition of Classic Tales*, Comprising in One Volume the most esteemed Works of Imagination by Various Authors. University Edition. London: Jones & Co., 1827.

Gulliver's Travels into Several Remote Nations of the World. London: R. Brown, 1829.

Gulliver's Voyage to Lilliput. In *Tales for Children.* Paris: Baudry's European Library, 1840. Pp. 41–70.

Gulliver's Travels into the Kingdom of Lilliput. Embellished with Neat Engravings on Wood. New York: J. Slater, n.d. (1850s).

Voyage to Lilliput. Books for the Campfire. Boston: James Redpath; N.Y.: American News Company, 1864.

Gulliver's Voyage to the Giants. Otley, Eng.: W. Walker & Sons, n.d. (1870s).

Travels of Lemuel Gulliver into Several Remote Regions of the World. The Excelsior Edition of Standard Juvenile Fiction. New York: American News Co., n.d. (1870s).

Gulliver's Travels into Several Remote Nations of the World. Illus. J. G. Thomson. Beeton's Boys' Own Library. London: Ward, Lock & Co., n.d. (1880s).

Gulliver's Travels: I. A Voyage to Lilliput. 2. A Voyage to Brobdingnag. Ed. for Schools, with Notes and a Sketch of the Author's Life. Boston, New York, Chicago, London: Ginn, 1886.

Gulliver's Travels into Several Remote Regions of the World. A New Edition, Edited for Young Readers by Edwin Chapman. Illus. New York: Worthington, 1888.

Lang, Andrew, ed. "A Voyage to Lilliput." *The Blue Fairy Book.* Illus. H. J. Ford and G. P. Jacomb Hood. London and New York: Longmans, Green, 1889.

Travels into Several Remote Nations of the World. Illus. Charles E. Brock. Preface by Henry Craik. New York: Macmillan, 1894. (Emelyn Garner and Eloise Ramsey in *A Handbook of Children's Literature: Methods and Materials* attribute the editorship of this edition to Joseph Jacobs.)

Gulliver's Travels into Several Remote Regions of the World. In Words of One Syllable. By J. C. G. [Mrs. J. C. Gorham]. New York: A. L. Burt, 1895. (First published New York: Cassell, 1888 in Cassell's Series of One Syllable Books.)

Gulliver's Travels into Some Remote Regions of the World. Illus. Altemus Young People's Library. Philadelphia: Henry Altemus, 1896.

Gulliver's Travels: The Voyages to Lilliput and Brobdingnag. Intro. Horace Scudder. The Riverside Literature Series. Boston: Houghton Mifflin, 1896.

Gulliver's Travels. Arranged for Young Readers. Illus. Philadelphia: Henry Altemus, 1899.

Gulliver's Travels into Several Remote Regions of the World. Illus. T. Morten. New York: McLoughlin, n.d. (1890s). (First published London: Cassell, Petter, and Galpin, 1865, with explanatory notes attributed to John Francis Waller.)

Gulliver in Lilliput. Retold by Edith Robarts. Illus. in Colour. Stories for Children. London: Ward, Lock, n.d. (after 1900).

Gulliver's Travels into Some Remote Regions of the World. Illus. Young People's Cloth Library. Chicago: W. B. Conkey, n.d. (after 1900).

Gulliver's Travels into Several Remote Regions of the World. Illus. Gordon Brown and Others. Caldwell's Juvenile Classics with Colored Illustrations. New York: H. M. Caldwell, n.d. (after 1900).

Gulliver's Travels into Several Remote Nations of the World. Illus. Arthur Rackham. Temple Classics for Young People. London: Dent, 1901.

Gulliver's Travels in Lilliput and Brobdingnag. Told to the Children by John Lang. Illus. F. M. B. Blaikie. London: T. C. and E. C. Jack; New York: Dutton, 1908.

Gulliver's Travels into Several Remote Nations of the World. Illus. Arthur Rackham (in color, with new illustrations). London: Dent; New York: Dutton, 1909.

Gulliver's Travels. Adapted for the Young by W. B. Scott. Illus. A. E. Jackson. London: Ernest Nister; New York: Dutton, 1911.

Gulliver's Travels. Illus. Milo Winter. Windemere Series. New York: Rand McNally, 1912.

Gulliver's Travels into Several Remote Nations of the World. Intro. W. D. Howells. Illus. Louis Rhead. New York: Harper, 1913.

Gulliver's Travels. Ed. Padraic Colum. Illus. Willy Pogany. London: George G. Harrap, 1919.

Gulliver's Travels into Lilliput and Brobdingnag. Illus. Jean de Bosschère. New York: Dodd, Mead; London: William Heinemann, n.d. (1920?).

Gulliver's Travels Among the Lilliputians and the Giants. Appropriately Illus. Favorite Fairy Tale Series, no. 135. Chicago: M. A. Donohue, n.d.

Travels into Several Remote Nations of the World. Illus. Charles E. Brock. Preface by Henry Craik. New York: Macmillan, 1923.

Gulliver in Lilliput. Illus. Vojtech Kubasta. Prague: Artia, n.d.

Gulliver's Travels. Adapted and Illustrated by Patrick Bellew. New York: Hyperion Press, 1945.

The Story of Lemuel Gulliver in Lilliput Land. Adapted and Retold by Frank L. Beals. Illus. E. E. King. Chicago: Benjamin H. Sanborn, 1946.

Gulliver's Travels. Revised & Slightly Abridged for Readers of Our Time. Illus. Aldren Watson. Illustrated Junior Library. New York: Grosset & Dunlap, 1947.

Gulliver's Travels. Ed. for Young Readers. Illus. Leonard Weisgard. Junior Deluxe Edition. Garden City, N.Y.: Doubleday, 1954.

Gulliver's Travels. Illus. Robin Jacques. Oxford: Oxford University Press, 1955.

Gulliver's Travels into Several Remote Nations of the World. Illus. Arthur Rackham. London: Dent; New York: Dutton, 1959. (This edition was first published in 1952.)

Gulliver's Stories for Pleasure Reading. Retold by Edward W. Dolch, Marguerite P. Dolch, and Beulah F. Jackson. Illus. Billy M. Jackson. Champaign, Il.: Garrard, 1960.

Gulliver's Travels. Ed. Elaine Moss. Illus. Hans Baltzer. New York: Duell, Sloan and Pearce, 1961.

Gulliver's Travels. Adapted by Sarel Eimerl. Illus. Maraja. Golden Illustrated Classics. New York: Golden Press, 1962.

Gulliver's Travels. Retold by Padraic Colum. Illus. Willy Pogany. Afterword by Clifton Fadiman. New York, London: Macmillan, 1962.

Gulliver's Travels. Revised and Slightly Abridged. Illus. Jo Polseno. Companion Library. New York: Grosset & Dunlap, 1963.

Gulliver's Travels in Lilliput. Retold by Angela Wilkes. Illus. Peter Dennis. Usborne/Hayes Picture Classics. London: Usborne; Tulsa: Hayes, 1982.

Gulliver's Travels. Illus. David Small. New York: William Morrow, 1983.

Gulliver's Travels. Illus. Rex Whistler. New York: Schocken, 1984.

Gulliver's Travels. Illus. Arthur Rackham. New York: Crown-Avenel, 1985. ("Previously published in a slightly different form under the title *Gulliver's Travels into Several Remote Nations of the World.*")

Gulliver's Travels and the Genre of the Illustrated Book

John F. Sena

Although we tend to think of the illustrated book as a nineteenth-century phenomenon, immortalized by Dickens and Thackeray, virtually all the major works of prose fiction published during the eighteenth century were illustrated. Of these no work was more frequently or more exhaustively illustrated in that period and throughout the nineteenth and twentieth centuries than *Gulliver's Travels*.[1] This should not be surprising when one considers the nature of Swift's artistry. *Gulliver's Travels* is a highly visual work: we are constantly being encouraged to picture in our mind's eye the appearance of people, buildings, and objects. Each part abounds with specific measurements and precise numbers: we know, for instance, that four yards to the right of the prostrate Gulliver a stage was erected eighteen inches from the ground, capable of holding four Lilliputians; that his body is equal to 1728 of theirs; that a Brobdingnagian breast is sixteen feet in circumference. Swift often describes the physical pose struck by a character, the expression on his face, as well as Gulliver's numerous gestures and those of the people he encounters. He is also careful to delineate in all four voyages the precise physical settings for Gulliver's adventures; we know literally where our hero stands. In addition to making a conscious effort to create verbal pictures, Swift's prose style contributes to the visual atmosphere of the work. His language is, for the most part, nonmetaphoric; sentences are filled with concrete nouns, adjectives appear in clusters to achieve a precise description, parenthetical statements and apositives are employed for further clarity and definition. In short, *Gulliver's Travels* lends itself to pictorial illustration.

While most readers respond with a sense of aesthetic pleasure at seeing an illustration, pictures have a more significant function than merely providing decorative ornamentation to a narrative. They are an inseparable part of the work they illustrate.[2] On the simplest level, illustrations reinforce the mimetic quality of a text; they help readers visualize a character or a scene. In a more complex manner, they have a profound effect on the reader's understanding of the printed word, for they continually interpret the text for us, providing a particular reading of an event or scene, conveying a specific point of view. In doing so, illustrations constitute a form of nonverbal criticism, a visual gloss that molds and shapes the way we view the written text. As we shift our attention back and forth between the written word and the visual image, we become aware of another voice in the work, of the presence of another storyteller, of an additional creator who shares the page with the author. At times this creator may even take precedence over the author in providing the reader with, in the words of J. Hillis Miller, more compelling "affirmations of the presence and appearance of the characters."[3] Most readers, I suspect, remember an illustration of Gulliver tied to the ground by the Lilliputians—and carry with them the details of that picture—more vividly than they recall Swift's description of the episode. An illustrated text, then, is qualitatively different from a text without illustrations; illustrations are an integral part of the work they accompany and are as much an element in establishing the meaning of a text and shaping the reader's response to the text as the language they illuminate and interpret. An illustrated text exists as a hybrid form, as a genre that combines simultaneously the verbal and the visual, the word and the graphic image, the primary text and a "reading" of that text.

While illustrations influence the meaning of the written text, their presence also affects in a number of ways the manner in which a reader approaches, perceives, and responds to the text. Illustrations, for instance, tend by their very nature to be concrete and specific. Thus, while a text may be abstract or metaphoric or even vague, illustrations continually move the reader toward the particular, the tangible, the solid, the definite. This is largely the result of the obvious appeal of illustrations to our sense of sight. Since they provide us with a visual depiction of a narrative, illustrations tend to stress the concrete and physical while largely neglecting the theoretical and abstruse. They also tend to emphasize for the reader the static elements in a text. A written text may facilely describe movement: it may transport us over great distances, conduct us over large stretches of time, or portray characters in action. Illustrations are for the most part poorly suited for conveying spatial or temporal or kinetic movement, and thus action in a text is frequently ignored by the graphic artist. Further, illustrations tend to convey meaning in a literal fashion, while words function symbolically. When we wish to picture the events described in a text in our mind's eye, we must translate verbal symbols into mental images; such a process is unnecessary with illustrations, for the artist provides us with the visual image. Thus illustrations tend to work more directly and immediately on the intellect and emotions of the reader than the written text. For instance, a picture of Gulliver tied to the ground by the Lilliputians conveys the idea of his capture and of their relative sizes more directly and immediately—and probably more forcefully—than the prose description of that event. With an illustrated text, the medium, as we have heard so often in recent times, is the message. An illustrated text is also capable of being understood by a broader, less sophisticated, and less literate audience than a written text.[4] In the example cited above, even a person incapable of understanding the complexities of Swift's language would be able to comprehend the Lilliputians' initial attitude toward Gulliver as well as his submissiveness. Thus, the mere presence of illustrations may attract readers to a work that they might otherwise have regarded as too arcane or difficult.

While illustrations work in conjunction with the text to convey meaning, their inherent beauty, the fact that they are aesthetically pleasing, often places them in competition with the text for the reader's attention. When such artwork is especially well done or is particularly unusual, as with many of J. J. Grandville's illustrations, for example, it draws some of our attention away from the beauty and complexity of the writer's prose and forces us to focus on the artistry of the illustrator. Or it may cause us momentarily to contemplate the illustrator's statement and not the author's. Ultimately, our attention, as I suggested above, is captured exclusively by neither but shifts back and forth between the two until we form in our mind an aesthetic and intellectual union of the verbal and visual. This process of reading—or viewing—an illustrated text, it would seem to me, accurately reflects the nature of this hybrid genre, for in an illustrated book the verbal and the visual, although separate and thus demanding individual attention, work synergistically to form a whole that is different from and greater than either taken independently. The act of reading an illustrated text, then, places more demands on the reader than is required by a text without illustrations, for the reader and not the author or the illustrator is responsible for the final creative act. We must interpret not only verbal symbols but graphic designs and fuse the two into a single, coherent whole.

Not all illustrations, of course, succeed in interpreting or commenting on a narrative. Many never go beyond a mere supplemental form of visualization. The lithographs of Edward Bawden recently published by the Folio Society of London, for instance, may be colorful and attractive, but they simply depict scenes from the narrative without demonstrating any attitude toward it. Illustrations like these are of little interest in a discussion of the qualitative impact of illustrations on a text and on the reader. Yet even after eliminating those which are primarily literal renderings of the text, one finds that there are still many more significant and provocative illustrated editions of *Gulliver's Travels* than can conveniently be discussed in a single essay. While undoubtedly the work of other illustrators could be substituted, the illustrated editions I have selected to examine are, I believe, illuminative of the manner in which graphic images affect our understanding and interpretation of a literary text.

Many writers have worked closely with their illustrators. Dickens, for instance, frequently offered lengthy and detailed instructions to H. K. Brown, better known as Phiz, for initial drawings for his novels as well as suggestions for their revision.[5] Thackeray himself drew initial letters, headpieces, tailpieces, and full-page illustrations that reflected the thematic motifs in his novels; in this case his fiction and his illustrations form a unified artistic whole, even though he worked in two media.[6] Neither situation occurred with Swift. Although he was willing, even desirous, to have *Gulliver's Travels* illustrated, he did not collaborate with any illustrator. In fact, a number of his opinions communicated to Benjamin Motte concerning possible illustrations have been largely ignored, even rejected, by graphic artists for the past 250 years. He thought, for instance, that part 2 did not lend itself to illustration as well as part 1 because Gulliver would have to be too "diminutive a figure" to be seen. Historically, part 2 has been illustrated as often as part 1; in fact, illustrators have not only failed to have the difficulty Swift predicted in maintaining the proper proportions, I do not think that any book of *Gulliver's Travels* has been more imaginatively illustrated. Several of the scenes from part 1 that Swift thought should be illustrated—"The Ladyes in their Coaches driving about his table. His rising up out of his Carriage when he is fastned to his House . . . His Hat drawn by 8 Horses"[7]—have rarely been illustrated. Although Swift remarked to Motte that he did not know how the projectors could be drawn, they have been by far the most frequently illustrated group of characters from part 3. He thought, on the other hand, that part 4 would "furnish many" scenes for illustration; in reality, it has been the least illustrated book of Gulliver's Travels and the one that appears to have given illustrators the greatest difficulty. It is ironic that a writer whose work lends itself so well to illustration seems to have been unable to evaluate more perceptively the problems and potential of his narrative for illustration.

Within a year of its publication, illustrated editions of Gulliver's Travels appeared in England, Holland, and France; the illustrations from these editions were reproduced in subsequent editions throughout the century. Illustrated editions also appeared in Germany and Spain. The illustrations in all of these early editions are few in number and generally undistinguished in conception and execution.[8] Of the three illustrated editions that appeared in 1727, for instance, each contains only one picture per book, and that illustration is generally a literal visualization of the text. There is also a remarkable similarity in the selection of scenes to illustrate: all three depict Gulliver in part 1 with Lilliputians swarming over him and Gulliver about to board the Flying Island in part 3. Even the work of the best-known eighteenth-century illustrator of Gulliver's Travels, Thomas Stothard, fails to alter or mold significantly our understanding of or reaction to the text. Stothard, who subsequently produced outstanding illustrations for Clarissa Harlowe and The Seasons, designed four pictures in 1782—one for each book—for a popular edition of Gulliver's Travels that appeared in the widely read series, The Novelist's Magazine. He selected scenes that are inherently interesting and lend themselves to visual depiction; however, he succeeds in offering little more than an uninspired literal rendering of the text. His illustration, for instance, of Gulliver being pulled up to the Flying Island, by contrast with the fanciful depictions of that scene in nineteenth- and twentieth-century illustrations, is unimaginative and flat. The Flying Island appears merely as a large box floating in mid-air, with Gulliver being hoisted by a simple pulley and chain while sitting on a horizontal piece of wood. Gulliver's face, here as in Stothard's other illustrations of him, is totally without expression. Unfortunately, the illustration detracts from the text, for we are likely to have conceived of the island as a much more complex and elaborate place, filled with miraculous devices, and Gulliver as experiencing at this moment fear or awe or confusion or a combination of all three. Furthermore, Stothard's practice of placing an ornate border around each illustration has the effect of separating it from the text; it appears as a picture in a frame— suitable for hanging—rather than as an illustration to be integrated into our reading of the narrative.

Ironically, the most imaginative and artistically accomplished of the early illustrations of *Gulliver's Travels* was in part a literary hoax. In 1726, just two months after the publication of *Gulliver's Travels*, William Hogarth drew an illustration for the work titled: "The Punishment Inflicted on Lemuel Gulliver" (plate 1) and tried to create the illusion that the picture was commissioned by Swift or his publisher to serve as a frontispiece for the first edition.[9] He wrote at the bottom of the engraving: "The Punishment inflicted on Lemuel Gulliver by applying a Lilypucian fire Engine to his Posteriors for his Urinal Profanation of the Royal Pallace àt Mildendo which was intended as a Frontispiece to his first Volume but Omitted." Neither Swift nor his publisher, however, commissioned the work; in fact, Swift was at this time scarcely acquainted with the twenty-nine-year-old artist.

The illustration reflects Hogarth's political partisanship and the intensity of his vision. By reading the picture in a manner analogous to reading a page of text, beginning at the left and proceeding laterally to the right, our eyes are first drawn to Gulliver's buttocks, the single most dominant feature in the engraving. The exposure to the public of a private part of his anatomy suggests the exploitation and subjugation of Gulliver, who may be seen by the British political leaders as John Bull or the average Englishman. His submission to this indignity goes beyond the simple passivity that Swift describes in the early chapters of book 1; it implies a total acquiescence and subordination on Gulliver's part (i.e., the English) to the humiliating and demeaning treatment of the Hanoverian kings and the Walpolean ministry. After focusing on Gulliver's backside, our eyes are directed to the right along a plane established by the horizontally held enema. The wrinkled and grotesque faces of his captors stand in contrast to the smooth, almost childlike buttocks of Gulliver, which has the effect of increasing our sense of Gulliver's innocence and our sympathy for his condition. The urination on Gulliver's hat suggests a further assault on his dignity while also revealing the hypocrisy of the Lilliputians, for they are engaging

Plate 1

in an act analogous to the public urination for which Gulliver is being punished. To the far right, the emperor is seen directing the entire scene while sitting in a thimble. Overlooking the action below is a clergyman seated in a pulpit made of a chamber pot, implying that the church has become the willing handmaiden of the politicians in suppressing the English. Beyond these things, the rat gnawing on a child suggests the lack of care and attention by the child's parents and, by extension, the abandonment of the government's parental responsibilities for protecting its children. And the general state of decay of the building and arch in the background, like the disrepair of the buildings in *Gin Lane*, imply a city and a society that are declining and crumbling; the Hanoverians and the Whigs have failed to restore strength and virtue to the English nation.

Hogarth's engraving reminds us that illustrations do not necessarily have to depict an actual scene from the work they illustrate, for nowhere in part 1 does Swift describe or even suggest such a punishment for Gulliver. In fact, we are told in chapter 5 that the king pardons Gulliver for urinating on the palace and that only the queen harbors any resentment over the act. It is Hogarth and not Swift who conceived of this scene, and since Hogarth ironically suggests the illustration should be placed at the beginning of *Gulliver's Travels*, it is evident that he believed if it were placed there it would influence the reader's perception and interpretation of the work, that it would create expectations for the reader before he or she read the first word of Swift's text. Gulliver and the English, according to Hogarth, have been grossly exploited, basely abused, and subjected to unspeakable indignities by their leaders. In their childlike innocence and respect for authority, Gulliver and the English have failed to recognize their strength or their ability to rebel against Britain's petty tyrants. Hogarth has encouraged us, then, to approach the text of *Gulliver's Travels* with a specific partisan point of view, a preconceived notion of what we shall find and how we should interpret the events described.

A number of competently illustrated editions of *Gulliver's Travels* appeared in the first three decades of the nineteenth century. The illustrations of W. H. Brooks in 1808, T. Uwine in 1815, Henry and George Corbould in the 1820s, and McLean in 1823 stress the romantic and fanciful nature of Gulliver's journeys to exotic lands—the strange customs and unusual clothing he observed—rather than the satiric and moral dimensions of his travels.[10] Their illustrations are generally few in number and derivative. All this was to change in 1838 with the appearance of J. J. Grandville's illustrations for *Gulliver's Travels*. Jean Ignace Isidore Gerard (J. J.) Grandville, a French political cartoonist and book illustrator, produced the most important, influential, and artistically brilliant illustrations of *Gulliver's Travels* ever published. His four hundred illustrations have never been surpassed in their imaginative and graphic quality, their ability to intensify, transform, and interpret Swift's text, and their power to delight, excite, and move the reader. Not only have his illustrations been widely reproduced—a total of fourteen times, including a 1935 edition of *Gulliver's Travels* published in Moscow and more recently in a facsimile edition published in this country—Grandville's influence on other illustrators of the *Travels* is ubiquitous in the nineteenth and twentieth centuries. When his illustrations appeared in a two-volume edition of *Gulliver's Travels* in England in 1840, where it was an immediate popular and critical success, Thackeray proffered perhaps the finest compliment that could be given to Grandville: he referred to him as "the Swift of the pencil."[11]

While most illustrators up to this point were satisfied with illustrating fairly predictable episodes—Gulliver being captured by the Lilliputians, the dwarf shaking apples on him in part 2, the appearance of the Flying Island, Gulliver's initial encounter with a Houyhnhnm—Grandville goes beyond the predictable and commonplace to illustrate virtually all aspects of Swift's text. The articles, for instance, that Gulliver is required to swear to in Lilliput in order to gain his liberty are presented as a scroll with an elaborate border placed along both sides of the page, creating the illusion that one is actually reading an unfurled official document. The border contains iconography that highlights Lilliputian life: two shoes, one with a high, one a low, heel; three eggs in egg cups; a quiver filled with arrows laid next to a bow. In part 3 we see one of several attempts Grandville makes to narrate through a rapid succession of pictures: in the school of political projectors, for instance, he describes the process of deciphering secret messages concealed in seemingly innocuous words by providing us with twenty illustrations, each separated by a brief phrase, a strategy that allows us to observe the movement of the satire rather than restricting us to a single static image. He also begins each chapter in all four books with illuminated letters that are so delicately and imaginatively executed that they alone would have brought this edition of *Gulliver's Travels* widespread acclaim.

Grandville's function as a critic aiding us in comprehending the text may be seen in these illuminated letters. He begins chapter 2 of part 2, for instance, with a huge eye staring at Gulliver with the letter M in its pupil (plate 2).[12] This illustration alerts the reader to a recurring pattern of imagery in the chapter. The Brobdingnagians do not simply maintain eye contact with Gulliver, nor do they merely look at him; rather, as Grandville implies, they stare at Gulliver, scrutinize him visually, devour him with their eyes. Gulliver becomes in chapter 2, it will be recalled, the property of a farmer who examines him visually and invites others to stare at him as well. He is transformed into a curiosity, a being described by all who come to look at him in the same manner as one would characterize an animal one was attempting to classify: he has the shape of a human, imitates human actions, speaks a language of his own, walks erect on two legs, is tame and gentle, and obeys commands. When another farmer comes to inspect him, Gulliver behaves as a freak in a circus. He is placed on a table, walks on command, draws his hanger, pays homage, and tells the visitor he is welcome in the Brobdingnagian language. The farmer, who wishes to stare at him more closely, puts on his "spectacles." Gulliver is then brought to a town and forced to perform before the intent gaze of the public. After returning home, he is once again put on display for the inspection of the neighbors, only to be taken on a more elaborate

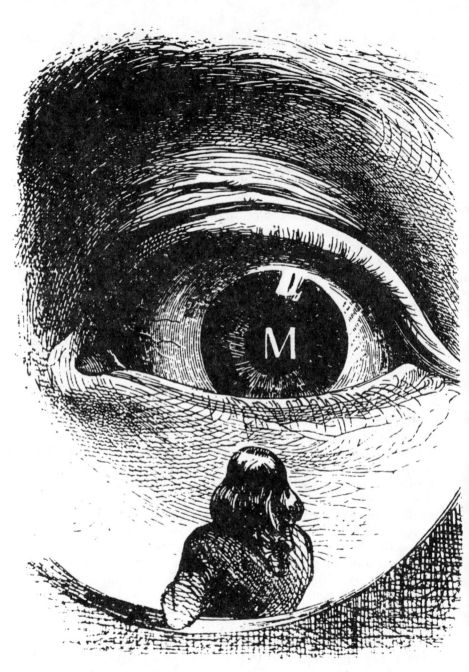

Plate 2

tour where he is stared at by the public ten times a day. By beginning this chapter with a huge eye looking at Gulliver, Grandville draws our attention to the act of staring, while inviting us to contemplate its significance. Staring, gawking, and looking intently are acts we generally direct toward a nonperson. One stares at an artifact, an animal in a zoo, a freak in a circus, but not at other humans. By staring at Gulliver, the Brobdingnagians are able to express their disbelief that human nature could be mimicked by such an insignificant and petty creature. It is a vivid rejoinder to Gulliver's inflated self-esteem, as well as an injunction for the benefit of the reader and Gulliver against pride in human nature and in human accomplishments. To the Brobdingnagians, Gulliver is not a representative of the highest form of sentient life but is something less than human: an artifact, animal, or a freak. In this illustration, then, Grandville has functioned as a critic by drawing our attention to a motif and encouraging us to reflect on its function in the narrative. Indeed, the Brobdingnagian stares not only at Gulliver but past Gulliver and into the reader's own eyes. Grandville has literally and figuratively illuminated the text for us.

The manner in which an illustration can interpret a text and shift the emphasis of an author may be seen in two successive illustrations Grandville provides of Gulliver's first glimpse of a Brobdingnagian. Swift does not expand on the physical appearance of the first Brobdingnagian seen by Gulliver and his shipmates. He simply describes him as a "huge Creature," and then proceeds to dwell not on his size but on the movement of the characters in the scene: the Brobdingnagian is "walking" and taking "prodigious strides" toward the sailors; they are rowing feverishly to escape him, and Gulliver, who simply wants to remove himself from the area, "ran as fast as I could" and "climbed up a steep hill."[13] In Grandville's illustration of this scene, the intense movement described by Swift, which is difficult for a graphic artist to convey, is minimized; instead the ominous and mysterious appearance of the Brobdingnagian and the sense of foreboding cast by him, which lend themselves to visual depiction, are stressed. Grandville places his illustration immediately below Swift's description of the Brobdingnagian as a "huge Creature," and by hiding his face with shadows he prevents us from conceiving of him as anything other than a creature, one whose genus and species are unknown. His pose, which recalls the Colossus of Rhodes standing guard, adds to our impression of his total physical dominance as well as to his mysteriousness.

Grandville holds us in suspense as to precisely what this creature looks like until we turn the page and are given a full-length view of a Brobdingnagian (plate 3). Since the picture of the Brobdingnagian takes up virtually an entire page, he, rather than the text, commands our attention; it is unlikely that one would read Swift's prose before examining the illustration. We are immediately struck by his prodigious size, which is emphasized by the amount of space given to the picture, and by the perspective from which Grandville has the reader view the Brobdingnagian. We are, like Gulliver, looking up at him. Thus the Brobdingnagian's head appears small in comparison to his legs, as it would to one standing on the ground. The perspective employed by Grandville resembles a low-angle shot in the cinema, a technique that, according to Louis Giannetti, makes the subject loom "threateningly over the spectator who is made to feel insecure and dominated. A person photographed from below inspires fear, awe, and respect."[14] Grandville's use of shading also emphasizes the imposing bulk of the Brobdingnagian: as our eyes move up his body, the shading becomes lighter, suggesting a greater distance from the observer. Although the Brobdingnagian is not moving but standing with both feet planted firmly on the ground (despite Swift's description of him as "moving" toward Gulliver), it is clear that he poses a direful threat to Gulliver, for at the compositional center of the picture is a large scythe, menacingly held in his right hand. Grandville directs our eyes to the scythe by framing it between several shafts of wheat, which are dark and prominent. He further intensifies the presence of the scythe by placing this picture immediately after Swift's description of the enormous size of the "Reaping-Hooks" held by the Brobdingnagians. By depicting the muscles in the Brobdingnagian's right arm as taut and his grip as firm, Grandville completes his transformation of the scythe from a farm implement into a destructive weapon. In another departure from Swift's text, which heightens the sense of imminent disaster to Gulliver, he places the farmer only several yards behind Gulliver, although Swift describes the reapers as being one hundred yards away.

Grandville's Gulliver is in this scene a much weaker and more pathetic figure than Swift's Gulliver. Through the prodigious size of the Brobdingnagian, his imperious expression, the centrality of the scythe in his hand, and the look of panic and fear on Gulliver's face, Grandville is able to convey the idea of Gulliver's

Plate 3

total vulnerability, his inability to protect himself, and his complete victimization from forces beyond his control. Even if the farmer does not wish to kill Gulliver, he can inadvertently destroy him. Since Gulliver is standing among stalks of wheat that are being harvested, he could unintentionally be sliced in half. Or he could simply be stepped on, for the Brobdingnagian, who is looking up and to the right, is seemingly oblivious to Gulliver's presence beneath him and to the left. Instant death may await Gulliver with the Brobdingnagian's next step. The futility of trying to escape from his plight is suggested by Gulliver's pose; his right leg is trapped between two stalks of wheat, and he appears to be stumbling forward. It is Grandville and not Swift, we should add, who first makes us aware of Gulliver's inability to escape, for Swift's description of the event is given on the following page: ". . . for the Stalks of the Corn were sometimes not above a Foot distant, so that I could hardly squeeze my Body betwixt them. . . . Here it was impossible for me to advance a step; for the Stalks were so interwoven that I could not creep through, and the Beards of the fallen Ears so strong and pointed, that they pierced through my Cloaths into my Flesh" (p. 70). Swift's description, while forceful, is anticlimactic, for we have already seen the extent and nature of Gulliver's predicament; here the text functions as a gloss on the illustration.

Swift writes that Gulliver reacted to this initial encounter with the Brobdingnagian with "Fear and Astonishment"; in Grandville's illustration we are left with the impression not of an astonished Gulliver but, as I have suggested, of a completely frightened, vulnerable, and intimidated Gulliver. In so depicting him, Grandville emphasizes and expands upon the theme in part 2 of man's physical fragility; the susceptibility of humans to injury, pain, and destruction; the precarious nature of human existence. Grandville's Gulliver, and by extension all mankind, is a creature whose life may be extinguished at any moment, either by chance or design, and one who is unable to escape his fate. Thus, this picture anticipates both the threats to Gulliver's existence, which will become an almost daily fact of life for him in Brobdingnag, as well as Swift's subsequent satire on pride of the body and on human nature itself. While later in part 2 Swift satirizes the concept of pride by allowing creatures below Gulliver on the great chain of being to attack him, Grandville intensifies the satire on man's vanity by placing Gulliver himself in a lowly position in the hierarchy of life. The Brobdingnagian's failure to see Gulliver even though he is immediately below him,

Gulliver's closeness to the ground, and the cover provided by low-growing vegetation, suggest a similarity in this illustration between Gulliver and members of the rodent family. While Swift will devote numerous subsequent pages to undermining Gulliver's pride, Grandville allows us to perceive in a single moment, through the economy of expression afforded by an illustration, the irony of a man dressed as an Englishman—hat in place, belt buckled, jerkin buttoned—desperately fleeing as a frightened animal.

Grandville's illustrations almost never simply reflect the text; as a creative artist he is constantly exploring the satiric possibilities that lie dormant in Swift's narrative, continually seeking to create his own statement by redefining, altering, or intensifying the text. An example of this may be found in his illustration of the dispute between the Big-Endians and the Little-Endians (plate 4). Swift satirizes the contentiousness between Catholics and Protestants by employing the literary technique of diminution: sublime religious doctrines are transformed into a common, material object—an egg—while theological debates over those doctrines are reduced to a trivial and meaningless argument over which end of the egg to break. Grandville takes Swift's reduction and diminishes it even further. In his rendering of the episode, the participants in the debate *become* eggs; that is, he combines the object of the debate and the protagonists in the controversy, both of which remain separate in Swift's narrative, by personifying the eggs and attributing to them openings at either their large or small end. In doing so, he is able to satirize not only religious controversy but also the degree of commitment of partisans in religious struggles: they literally become what they believe. Furthermore, while Swift's text makes religious zealots appear foolish by having them fight over inconsequential matters, Grandville's illustration makes them even more absurd by depicting them as warmongering eggs. The fight, of course, is portrayed in mock-heroic terms, carried out on a table top instead of a battlefield, using common, everyday eating utensils instead of implements of war. While one Big-Endian and one Little-Endian have fallen, it is doubtful that it is the result of combat. Given the fact that their weight is concentrated in their heads, it is more likely that they simply toppled over. Although Swift uses a highly imaginative metaphor in this passage, he keeps us rooted in historical reality by alluding in allegorical fashion to Henry VIII's break with the Roman Catholic Church, the death of Charles I, the forced abdication of James II, and the

Plate 4

Test Act. Grandville, however, creates in his illustration a bizarre
scene, devoid of historical grounding, populated by grotesquely
comic figures. His figures are literally egg-heads; in fact, their egg
heads are the same size as the rest of their body, while their torso
and legs are parts of an eggcup.

By personifying the eggs, Grandville has significantly altered
Swift's text; he has transformed an historical allegory into the
realm of fantasy. The essence of the fantastic, according to Eric
Rabkin, consists of a reversal of the fictional laws governing a
narrative: "Every work of art sets up its own ground rules. The
perspectives that the fantastic contradicts are perspectives legit-
imized by these internal ground rules."[15] Altering internal
ground rules is precisely what Grandville does to Swift's text in
this illustration. Although Lilliput is a miniature version of England, it is, we must remember, similar to England in all essential
characteristics: the Lilliputians, for instance, have a human anatomy, and the same physical laws that exist in England also
prevail in Lilliput. It would not be possible, then, in the fictional
context established by Swift, for inanimate objects to become

human. By personifying eggs and eggcups, Grandville has subverted Swift's "internal ground rules" and provided us with a fantastic episode. Although he has imaginatively transformed Swift's text, Grandville has not undermined its satiric thrust, for, as Rabkin reminds us, "satire is inherently fantastic" since both "reverse the perspectives of the world outside the narrative. . . ."[16] By introducing the fantastic, Grandville has, in effect, intensified the satire, for now the acts of religious zealots appear even further removed from the logic of our world and the rational behavior of humans. In fact, the acts of religious fanatics appear absurd even in the petty and trivial world of Lilliput.

When an illustrator, however, is as imaginative and talented in his medium as the author is in his, there is always the danger that an illustration will capture the attention of the reader to a greater extent than will the text. Such, I believe, is the case in Grandville's illustration of the operation described by the professor in the School of Political Projectors (plate 5). The professor, it will

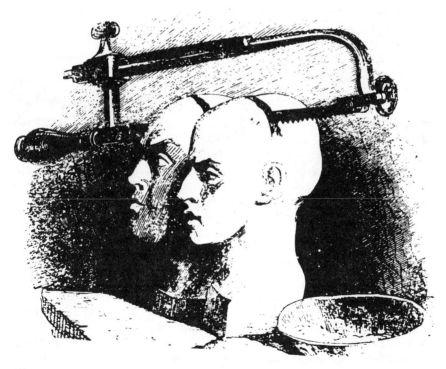

Plate 5

be recalled, describes a method of reducing political debate by dividing in half the brain of each disputant and exchanging them, "the two half Brains being left to debate the Matter between themselves within the Space of one Scull" (p. 189). Swift's satiric objective in this passage of restoring moderation to political disputes is all but lost in Grandville's illustration of two disembodied heads that have been sculptured out of marble. We are less likely upon glancing at this illustration to contemplate the foolishness of political zealots and their pointless, factional debates as we are to marvel at Grandville's creation of a macbre and surreal world where human-looking faces carved in an inanimate substance are operated upon as though they were humans; we are less likely to consider the need for moderation in our political disputes as we are to experience the intense discomfort and uneasiness caused by the presence of the hacksaw.[17]

Grandville's illustrations were followed by another extraordinary pictorial edition of *Gulliver's Travels* illustrated by Thomas Morten in 1865. Morten's illustrations, while indebted to Grandville, rival the pictures of the French master in both their comprehensive coverage of the *Travels* and their popularity: he designed almost four hundred plates, which were reprinted thirteen times in the nineteenth and early twentieth centuries in England and America. While each of Morten's illustrations reveal his attention to detail and skillful use of perspective, the strength of his artistry lies not merely in depicting individual scenes but in presenting a "progress piece," a series of illustrations that elucidate the development of a theme or a character and thus provide the reader with an interpretation of an entire book. In his illustrations for part 4, for instance, he presents us with his view of the "progress" of Gulliver: Morten's Gulliver begins as an arrogant and haughty Englishman who is transformed into a humble and disillusioned creature, one who perceives the folly and evil in himself and his countrymen.

In the first of Morten's fourteen plates for this book, Gulliver is depicted as a prideful colonizer who has landed in a strange country and is patronizingly greeting a Houyhnhnm. His self-esteem and self-importance may be seen not only in his pose and facial expression but in his clothing: he is impeccably adorned in a fashionable jacket with his sword hanging from his belt and his hat securely on his head. After becoming acquainted with the Houyhnhnms in the first three plates, his relationship to them undergoes a change, and Gulliver is seen in the next three illustrations as a curiosity, a strange animal that must be inspected and examined. Throughout these plates the superiority of the Houyhnhnms is emphasized. Their heads are held high, which conveys a sense of condescension toward Gulliver, while their eyes, which are disproportionately large, create the impression of intelligence, perceptiveness, and intensity. They are almost always drawn as taller than Gulliver, even when they are sitting, so that we see them as continuously looking down on him, literally as well as metaphorically. Gulliver's subordination to them may be seen in the fifth picture in Morten's series (plate 6), in which a group of Houyhnhnms gather to inspect him.[18] Morten's use of light and shadow in this plate is representative of his technique throughout his illustrations. The body of the large horse behind him and of the two colts to his right are heavily shaded. This dark background serves to direct our eyes to the one point of light in the center of the darkness: Gulliver's face. Morten further emphasizes Gulliver's face as the focal point of the picture by placing the horses around him in a semicircular fashion; the straight lines formed by the noses of three horses and their line of vision point directly to Gulliver's face. The expression on his face suggests a significant change in his attitude toward the Houyhnhnms. He now looks upon them not with condescension but with a mixture of awe, deference, and fright. Morten underscores this change by removing Gulliver's hat, which in the first picture helped to convey his self-confidence and dignity, and placing it on the ground. The stripping of Gulliver's pride, symbolized by the stripping of his clothing, continues in Morten's sixth picture, in which the Houyhnhnms have forced him to remove his pants.

At this point the focus of Morten's illustrations shifts from Houyhnhnmland to Europe so that the reader may reflect along with Gulliver on the brutality and corruption of the English. Morten's seventh picture depicts the wanton cruelty of an Englishman beating a horse to death, while the eighth picture in the series, a patent imitation of the second plate of Hogarth's *The Rake's Progress*, reflects the baleful effects of luxury and pride. Gulliver's total rejection of his past life and adoption of the virtues of the Houyhnhnms may be seen in the last two pictures from Houyhnhnmland. In picture nine he attempts to identify with the horses to the extent of imitating their gait. Unlike C. E. Brock's ironic depiction of this scene in his 1894 illustrated edition of the *Travels*, Morten does not explore its comic or satiric possibilities; rather, he presents us with a somber and serious Gulliver who has a pained expression on his face as he

Plate 6

tries with all the courage and strength he can muster to keep up with the Houyhnhnms' rapid pace. By the tenth picture, Gulliver's submission to the Houyhnhnms' way of life is complete: he kneels in front of the Houyhnhnm master and kisses his hoof. This illustration, which completes the evolution of Gulliver, stands in sharp contrast to the first plate, in which Gulliver had been pictured as a well-dressed Englishman patronizingly examining a Houyhnhnm. His hat has now been removed, his well-tailored jacket has been replaced by animal skins, and his sword is nowhere to be found. Morten's two final illustrations emphasize his "hard school" interpretation of part 4. In picture eleven, Pedro de Mendez's crew menacingly encircle Gulliver, guns and swords drawn and pointed at the hapless survivor. Their facial expressions suggest that they are ready to kill him. While Swift's text makes no mention of Pedro or his crew as posing a threat to Gulliver, here the first Europeans he meets confirm his belief in the cruel and predatory nature of mankind. This view is further emphasized in the final picture, in which English colonizers are shown pillaging a defenseless land, wantonly raping women and killing children.

Morten's selection of the episodes to illustrate and the content of his pictures reflect a specific critical interpretation of part 4, which he successfully conveys to the reader. By ignoring the irony in Swift's treatment of the Houyhnhnms and of Gulliver both in Houyhnhnmland and after his return to England—by ignoring, for instance, Gulliver's absurd and excessive behavior—Morten shapes his readers' response to Gulliver's experiences. We are encouraged to see the Houyhnhnms as ideal creatures who represent a standard for conduct that emerges in sharp contrast to the cruel and vicious behavior of western man, who is almost melodramatically presented in the final two pictures. We are invited to see Gulliver's submission to the Houyhnhnms not as an indication of his limited mentality, but as a logical reaction to their virtue; we are encouraged to see his misanthropy not as a foolish and excessive reaction to the weakness of man or as a failure to accept the imperfection inherent in human nature, but as a reasonable response to the evil in mankind. Morten's illustrations, then, provide us with a nonverbal interpretation of part 4 that is as clear, unequivocal, and persuasive as any act of verbal criticism.

While Morten's illustrations achieved a universal appeal, a number of illustrated editions in the late nineteenth century failed to transcend contemporary tastes. A. D. Lalauze designed a set of aquatints in 1875, for instance, in the pre-Raphaelite style, while V. A. Poirson reflected in an 1884 edition the interest of the period in orientalism. Arthur Rackham, however, returned to the satiric spirit and moral concerns of Swift's text in his 1899 illustrations. The success of his line drawings encouraged Rackham to revise some of his illustrations, to add new pictures, and to water color all but two for a highly acclaimed edition published in 1909. His twelve illustrations are graphically sophisticated and aesthetically pleasing: the pencil lines clearly show through the watercolor to define facial and physical features with precision, while the muted shades of red, green, yellow, and brown add a sense of realism and freshness to his depictions. The illustrations were so well executed, in fact, that the publisher conceived of this edition largely as a vehicle for Rackham's pictures: in a prefatory note he stated that he makes "no apology for a new edition since the fine drawings of MR. ARTHUR RACKHAM are a sufficient *raison d'etre*."

While most of Rackham's illustrations attempt to capture the serious elements of Swift's satire, especially of the plight of Gulliver in part 2, he is one of the few illustrators to reflect Swift's spirit of playfulness as well. In his illustration of a Laputan deep in thought, for instance, he depicts the eyes as not simply turned inward but as crossed, while the complex mathematical problem the Laputan contemplates is being solved by counting on his fingers. The poor man is so absorbed in abstract speculation that his next step will submerge him in a duck pond. In his illustration of the theory expounded at the school of languages in part 3 that we should use things and not words to communicate, Rackham provides us with a fanciful conception of what two individuals trying to talk in this manner would look like. They are pictured with lips tightly pursed, standing next to two huge sacks filled with the paraphernalia of any self-respecting peddlar: dolls, toy houses, bottles, clocks, forks, jars, and countless other items that may take the place of concrete nouns. These trivial and banal items are an apt reflection of the triviality and banality of the Laputans' thoughts: their ideas are nothing more than the junk collected and disgarded by hucksters.

One of Rackham's most colorful and imaginative creations is his illustration of the attack on Gulliver in part 2 by giant wasps (plate 7).[19] While most illustrators have provided a fairly literal visualization of this scene, Rackham has altered the thrust of Swift's satire, ultimately presenting us with a Gulliver who is more vulnerable and threatened than Swift's character. In Swift's

Plate 7

description of the attack by the wasps, it will be recalled, Gulliver emerges victorious; Gulliver tells us that when the wasps attacked him he took out his hanger and "dispatched" four of them and sent the rest flying away. He then removed the stingers from the fallen wasps to take back to the scientists at Gresham College (pp. 109–10). In Rackham's illustration not only is the satire on the Royal Society ignored, but Gulliver's bravura and success in the episode are undermined. Gulliver is depicted as a victim of the wasps, as a frail creature who is being mercilessly victimized by insects. The vertical pencil lines at the top half of the picture create a rapid swooping effect of wasps that are disproportionately large for the scale Swift established for Brobdingnag. While Gulliver may have been successful in warding off Brobdingnagian flies with his knife in the episode immediately before this one, he appears totally unable to protect himself from the wasps with his sword, for that weapon is held in a contorted manner with the back (rather than the inside) of his hand facing the reader. The billowing of his loose-fitting garment creates the impression of a bloated stomach that is being gnawed on by a wasp. This predatory aspect is emphasized by Rackham's placing the wasp on Gulliver's stomach at the structural center of the picture and having Gulliver's eyes direct our vision to his tormentor. Gulliver's body has also undergone a metamorphosis. In all but one other picture in this edition—that of Gulliver's being nearly crushed to death by apples—the narrator is depicted as a young man with a full face and smooth skin. Here he appears as an old, decrepit man. His face is drawn and wrinkled; his arms, wrists, and legs are emaciated; the subcutaneous fat in his hands has receded so that his hands and fingers appear shriveled. His aged and withered appearance, which has no basis in Swift's text, increases our sense of Gulliver's helplessness as well as our sympathy for him.

Rackham's selection of this particular episode to illustrate from chapter 3, as opposed to several other scenes that lend themselves equally well to graphic depiction, also affects our conception of Gulliver. Chapter 3 is filled with events that establish the physical inferiority of Gulliver in Brobdingnag: he is examined by three Brobdingnagian scholars; a dwarf drops him in cream; he is forced into the marrow of a bone; he is attacked by flies. Rackham could have illustrated any of these events, but by selecting the final episode of the chapter, the attack by the wasps, he has provided us with a sense of climax, a finale, to the crescendo of abuse experienced by Gulliver. While Swift ends this chapter in a more positive fashion with Gulliver warding off the wasps, Rackham has transformed the episode into the final and most dangerous assault on Gulliver's body and dignity in the chapter, leaving us with a firm and lasting impression of his— and, by extension, our—weakness and frailty and alienation. Man cannot protect himself physically, according to Rackham, even from those creatures below him on the great chain of being. The reader is forced, after examining this illustration, to seek solace in the fact that it is man's reason and not his body that has given him dominance over animal life. Rackham has prepared us for Swift's attack on the abuses of man's intellect in part 3.

Three years after Rackham's illustrations appeared, Louis Rhead produced one of the most notable illustrated editions of *Gulliver's Travels* published in the twentieth century. For the 1913 edition of the *Travels*, published by Harper Brothers and containing an introduction by William Dean Howells, Rhead provided sixty-one illustrations, thirty-three of which are full-page pictures, and illuminated letters at the beginning of each chapter. His illustrations of part 1 abound in detail; they are generally filled with Lilliputians, frequently between fifty and one hundred, who are so carefully and precisely drawn that we may observe objects in their hands as well as their physical gestures. His illustrations of part 2 are remarkable for his depictions of the animals which attack Gulliver: they are generally disproportionately large, even for the scale established by Swift, and resemble the drawings one would find in an early twentieth-century biology textbook. His illustration of the Struldbruggs in part 3 vividly captures the grotesquerie and tragedy of their plight through their facial ugliness and bodily deformities, while his portrayal of the experiments at the Grand Academy are among the most imaginatively conceived and precisely drawn in any illustrated edition. Throughout his work, Rhead employs contrasts between light and dark as well as shades of black, creating effects not unlike those of a mezzotint, to highlight characters.

While virtually all of his illustrations are worth discussion, Rhead's conception of the Yahoos is especially provocative and, as with any worthwhile illustration, affects the way we think of them. Illustrations of the Yahoos throughout the eighteenth, nineteenth, and twentieth centuries tend to share a number of characteristics. The Yahoos are virtually always depicted as bestial and violent creatures, wearing no clothes and covered with a great deal of hair; their facial features and physical posture make them appear to be either primitive or apish men. Rhead alters several of these traditional characteristics. For instance, he makes them appear much more human than most other illustrators. Their bodies, which are covered with less hair than one generally finds in illustrations of them, closely resemble a human body in both size and muscular formation. One of them, in fact, is shown running in an upright position, very much in the manner of a human. In so doing, Rhead underscores Gulliver's remarks that he "observed, in this abominable Animal, a perfect human Figure" (p. 214) and the Houyhnhnm master's declaration that Gulliver "agreed in every Feature of [his] Body with other Yahoos" (pp. 243–44). Their greatest dissimilarity to contemporary humans is in their facial characteristics: their pushed-in noses and low foreheads create the appearance of primitive men, although Rhead renders their ears as large appendages with high pointed tips, recalling the shape often found not in drawings of primitive man but in traditional illustrations of Satan.

By depicting the Yahoos as bearing a close resemblance to man's body, Rhead is able to suggest to the reader that the Yahoos should be seen as representing man "in the flesh." Since the body or "the flesh" was, as Roland M. Frye has reminded us, a traditional Christian symbol for man's natural depravity, we are encouraged to view the Yahoos as representing "those elements in his nature which man must distrust, and which, in Christian terms, he must seek to subdue."[20] Rhead's rendering of the Yahoos, then, calls the reader's attention to their moral significance and to Swift's use of traditional Christian rhetoric in his description of them.

Rhead also suggests the sinful nature of the Yahoos by placing a full-page illustration of several of them directly next to a page in part 4 in which a particular sin is described (plate 8): the sin of avarice.[21] On the page opposite this illustration, Gulliver describes the practice of the Yahoos, who "claw for whole days" in order to get "certain shining Stones" (p. 244). After obtaining these stones, which have no practical use, they carry them to their kennels, hide them from their cohorts, and protect them with their lives. Indeed, in the areas where the stones abound, the Houyhnhnm master has observed that the Yahoos have their "fiercest and most frequent Battles" (p. 245). When two Yahoos fight over a stone, a third, according to the master Houyhnhnm, will frequently take advantage of the situation and steal it. In Rhead's illustration we can see a Yahoo on the right running off

Plate 8

with a round stone in his hand, while two others, unmindful of this, fight to the death for possession of it. Gulliver, undoubtedly speaking for Swift, observes a similarity between the Yahoos' acquisitive nature and "the same Principle of Avarice which I had ascribed to Mankind," as well as between the violent confrontation of the Yahoos over possession of the stone and lawsuits in England; the only difference, Gulliver declares, is that the result of the Yahoos' struggle is "more equitable than many Degrees among us" (p. 245), for they lose only a stone, while plaintiffs and defendants in judicial proceedings in England are left totally impoverished.

This juxtaposition of illustration and text invites us to "read" both pages not in sequence but, in a sense, simultaneously by a process of shifting back and forth between the text and the illustration. It is, I believe, unlikely that a reader would finish the entire page of prose before looking at Rhead's illustration: it would be difficult, if not impossible, to restrain our curiosity or discipline our eyes not to gaze at it either before reading the text or periodically while reading it. Thus while Swift describes the Yahoos as exhibiting a trait commonly found among humans, Rhead's illustration allows us to see at the same time their physical resemblance to humans and their enactment of this human trait. The text and the picture become one unified expression, and through them we are left with a conception of the Yahoos as representing man both physically and morally. By creating naked, primitive creatures who resemble humans, Rhead has also entrapped us in the satiric mirror; he has forced us to look at ourselves as "bare-forked animals" without the trappings of civilization; he has made us see our rapacious, violent, and contentious nature, which we successfully cloak in civilized society under the euphemisms of financial pursuits and judicial proceedings.

While the illustrations of Rackham and Rhead were probably the most popular, influential, and accomplished drawings of the early twentieth century, there has not been a shortage of sophisticated and imaginative illustrations of *Gulliver's Travels* in the past fifty years. Rex Whistler, for instance, produced twelve large color pictures for an edition of the *Travels* published by the Cresset Press, which, unfortunately, has not been widely circulated.[22] While Whistler pays a great deal of attention to clothing and physical poses in his illustrations, it is in the frames for his pictures that his imagination and creativity may best be seen. The frames or borders are themselves elaborate pictures filled with iconography that comments on the action which is enclosed. One frame of an illustration for part 1, for instance, consists of mythological figures, columns, and various structures from classical architecture that are decayed and in disarray, suggesting the decline from the classical ideal in both Lilliput and Augustan England. A frame for an illustration of Gulliver's and Munodi's tour of Lagado consists of numerous scientists performing absurd experiments, buildings that are in disrepair, individuals totally absorbed in contemplation—in short, vignettes that effectively epitomize the entire satire on the Grand Academy. W. A. Diggins's illustrations, on the other hand, which are all done in shades of green, are exceptional in their use of perspective.[23] In his depiction of Gulliver pulling the Blefuscudian fleet, for instance, the viewer contemplates the scene from Gulliver's vantage point (we never see Gulliver in part 1). The entire bottom half of the picture consists almost exclusively of his massive arms and his hands, which are holding the strings fastened to the Blefuscudian ships; the prominence of his arms and wrists in the foreground of the picture forcefully conveys to the viewer a sense of Gulliver's physical might and superiority in Lilliput. While Whistler's and Diggins's illustrations have a significant effect on our perception and interpretation of the text, probably the most compelling and moving illustrations of *Gulliver's Travels* in the past fifty years have been done by Luis Quintanilla in the 1947 edition issued by Crown Publishers.[24] Many of his 184 drawings tend toward caricature, which heightens our response to even minor characters. His illustration of the maids of court in part 2 fondling Gulliver is dominated by voluptuous young women who are seminude; here, as in several other pictures that contain nude bodies, he captures the eroticism of Swift's text, a quality that has been generally ignored by Swift's illustrators. Following in the tradition of Blake, he engraved twenty-three of the printing plates himself. While not as compelling as Quintanilla's drawings, James Millar's illustrations for the Appletree Press edition, which celebrated the two-hundred-fiftieth anniversary of the publication of *Gulliver's Travels*, are undoubtedly the most unusual recent illustrations of Gulliver and the people he encounters.[25] Using a method of painting over linoleum in which thin lines are cut in the shapes and forms he wishes to reproduce, Millar created eighteen illustrations in which figures are defined by thin white lines over a black background. His pictures suggest his indebtedness to Henri Matisse.[26] His sitting and reclining figures are similar in pose and silhouettelike appearance to Matisse's *Nu couché* or *Nu rose*, while his frequent use of flowers floating in space are remarkably like Matisse's use of flowers in *Fleurs de neige*, *La Gerbe*, and scores of other paintings, as well as to his paper cut-outs, which appeared during the last twenty years of his life.

Finally, though the art work may not be as sophisticated or the text as reliable as the editions we have been examining, probably no illustrated edition of *Gulliver's Travels* has had a more profound influence on an entire generation of readers than the version published by Classics Illustrated, better known as Classic Comics. Classics Illustrated chose the voyage to Lilliput for one of its earliest issues (no. 16); published in 1946, this popular comic book probably provided many American readers with their first contact with Gulliver's adventures. The illustrations are detailed, imaginative, and colorful. The clothing of Gulliver and the Lilliputians ranges in style and period from the English Renaissance to the eighteenth century, while the illustrations of Gulliver capturing the Blefuscudian fleet, the naval battle between Lilliput and Blefuscu, and the Lilliputians preparing red-hot pokers to be used to blind Gulliver fill the reader with excitement, suspense, and a sense of adventure. Great liberties are taken, however, with the text. The story is told, for instance, not by Gulliver but by an omniscient narrator. At one point in the narrative Gulliver saves Mildendo from a devastating flood by diverting a rampaging river; he also defends the Blefuscudians by constructing giant slingshots (one of a child's favorite implements) and hurling stones at the Lilliputians. Gulliver is, in this rendering of Gulliver's Travels, a superhero of the 1940s. Even though the editor of Classics Illustrated, Albert Kantner, did not support the Comics Code Authority, which acted as a censor for material placed in comic books, the story is carefully bowdlerized for children.[27] The Lilliputians march between Gulliver's legs, but his pants are not torn and the troops do not look up. The episode in which Gulliver puts out a fire by urination is completely avoided; he is impeached instead for returning to the capital without giving sufficient notice.

There are, obviously, significant differences between a comic book version of a literary work and the type of illustrated editions we have been examining.[28] In the comic book, text and illustrations are more closely related than in the illustrated book, for prose and picture share the same frame. As we read the words, which are generally expressed through captions or balloons, we are simultaneously looking at the picture, so that the two blend in our consciousness into one organic whole. Furthermore, in the comics time is a function of space, for each frame represents a division of time. This allows the pictures in a strip to imitate the time-flow of a narrative more closely and realistically than the pictures in an illustrated edition; as our eyes move from one frame to another, we experience the movement in time of the narrative.[29] Comics are also especially well-suited to capture the kinetic and intellectual movement of a character; as we quickly view a succession of pictures we can see a character in action or undergoing change more distinctly than we can by looking at illustrations in a book separated by several pages of text. This tends to give to comics—at least to the Classics Illustrated version of Gulliver's Travels—the quality of a "progress piece": we see Gulliver's attitude change from boredom with his surroundings to intense involvement with the affairs of Lilliput and Blefuscu; we see the Lilliputians express first hostility to him, then admiration, then rejection, and finally friendship. It is interesting that Hogarth was one of the first artists to develop fully the use of captions and ballooning in a series of illustrations to be viewed sequentially.

While comics may integrate word and picture, the two are obviously not equal; the picture commands our attention to a much greater extent than the prose. The result is that comic-book versions of a literary work present a one-dimensional view. They stress the narrative element almost exclusively; they tell a story. They do not reflect the complexities of an author's language, his use of irony, imagistic patterns, shifts in point of view, or various subtleties of meaning. In the Classics Illustrated *Gulliver's Travels* we are not presented with verbal artistry but with an exciting story; on the other hand, we are reminded of a salient fact: *Gulliver's Travels* is, indeed, an exciting and engrossing series of adventures, filled with swift action and fascinating events. And it was probably this aspect of Swift's masterpiece that first attracted us to it and ultimately still accounts for much of its popularity.

It is evident, I believe, from the works we have examined that illustrated editions of *Gulliver's Travels* differ significantly from the text of Swift's satire without illustrations. The illustrations we have seen are constantly commenting on the text, clarifying a theme, shaping our response to a character, recasting a scene so that we can see it anew. One final, brief example of this may be seen in three well-known illustrations—by Lefebvre, C. E. Brock, and A. D. Lalauze—of the episode from part 2, chapter 5, in which Gulliver is brought to the chambers of the maids of honor.[30] In Lefebvre's illustration of this scene (plate 9), the women scrutinize Gulliver as one would examine an unusual artitact or a rare curiosity. The woman holding him and gazing at him through a magnifying glass has a studious aspect, while the facial expressions and gestures of her cohorts suggest a mixture of inquisitiveness, surprise, and wonder. Although in Swift's text Gulliver is described as an erotic toy, a source of sexual gratification for the young women, Lefebvre's depiction of the scene is decidedly nonsexual. The semiscientific examination, the manner in which Gulliver is being held, and his spread-eagle pose suggest that he exists for these women more as a specimen than as a human, more as an object of intellectual inquiry than as a sex object. The reader is inclined to recall the earlier examination of Gulliver by the king's scholars rather than to dwell on the suggestive description in Swift's text. C. E. Brock's illustration of the same scene (plate 10) also departs from Swift's text. Rather than depicting the women as nude or seminude, Brock presents them elaborately dressed in clothing that resembles a mixture of oriental and occidental designs. Gulliver's kissing of one woman's

Plate 9

Plate 10

finger, the gracious appearance of all three women, and their modest demeanor suggest that Brock wishes the reader to conceive of the relationship between Gulliver and the maids of honor to be one of mutual respect and courtliness; etiquette and civility have replaced the eroticism and exploitation present in Swift's text. Lalauze's illustration of this scene, on the other hand, emphasizes the sensuous appearance and erotic activities of the maids of court (plate 11). His picture is dominated by seminude women; Gulliver has disappeared from our sight, having been submerged within the bosom of one of the maids. While Lefebvre conceived of Gulliver as an object of scientific inquiry, Lalauze sees him as an object of sexual gratification; while Brock stressed Gulliver's courtly relationship to the women, Lalauze portrays him as little more than a convenient dildo. To a greater extent than either Lefebvre or Brock, Lalauze involves at least some readers in the illustration: males, I believe, are encouraged to share vicariously in Gulliver's experience.

In offering widely different interpretations of a text, illustrations may, then, function as a form of critical commentary. Unfortunately, we are so accustomed to thinking that critical explications can only be expressed in written language that we fail to recognize illustrations as critical statement: "Our education," James Steel Smith reminds us, "our language habits, our publishing and editorial and teaching patterns—all these operate as if critical thinking about the arts were inevitably verbal."[31] The commentary on the text provided by illustrations is no less serious or compelling or informative than a prose essay. At the same time, illustrations have a life of their own; they are acts of the imagination which have an autonomy apart from the text. Illustrations also make demands on the reader that do not arise during the reading of a nonillustrated text. In an illustrated text, for instance, we are continuously required to read two statements, the author's and the illustrator's. Yet the statements are being made in two different media. This demands that the reader constantly shift his or her critical orientation, from reading verbal symbols left to right to interpreting visual representations that exist on several planes. An illustrated text likewise demands that the reader be able to move rapidly from abstract to concrete, from kinetic to static, from metaphoric to literal. In addition, since a sequence of pictures, such as those by Morten, can be most profitably seen as forming a narrative rather than as isolated depictions of a scene, the reader must keep two narratives in mind simultaneously, one visual and one verbal; he or she must

Plate 11

remain cognizant of how each picture relates not simply to the text but to previous pictures as well.

Illustrated texts also raise a number of questions for the reader. The reader is, for instance, constantly being asked to integrate text and picture into one coherent statement. But what does one do if the text and the picture make radically different statements? Which should be granted primacy? Although illustrations are generally created at a point in time after the text is composed, to what degree is an author influenced in the composing process by his desire to have his text illustrated? To what degree does an author's wish to have the reader form mental pictures affect the chosen manner of expression? While we realize that illustrations influence our understanding of a text, to what extent do pictures elucidate and comment on other pictures within a text? To what degree does an illustrator assume the reader's familiarity, not simply with the text but with the works of other illustrators? If both the illustration and the written word compete for the reader's attention, what are the inherent advantages of each medium? These questions—and scores of others—that the reader must implicitly ask when confronting an illustrated text suggest the qualitative difference between it and its purely verbal counterpart. The difficulty in answering them suggests that the vigorous exploration in terms of both the theory of this hybrid genre and its application may be profitably continued in the future.

Notes

1. For a useful list of illustrated editions of *Gulliver's Travels*, see David Lenfest, "A Checklist of Illustrated Editions of *Gulliver's Travels*, 1727–1914," *Papers of the Bibliographical Society of America* 62 (1968): 85–123. A number of illustrations of the *Travels* may be conveniently found in Isaac Asimov's *The Annotated Gulliver's Travels* (New York: Clarkson Potter, 1980).

2. For informative discussions of the relationship between a literary text and its illustrations, see Merritt Y. Hughes, "Some Illustrators of Milton: The Expulsion from Paradise," *Journal of English and Germanic Philology* 60 (1961): 670–79; Kester Svendsen, "John Martin and the Expulsion Scene of *Paradise Lost*," *Studies in English Literature* 1 (1961): 63–73; James Steel Smith, "Visual Criticism: A New Medium for Critical Comment," *Criticism* 4 (1962): 241–55; Ralph Cohen, *The Art of Discrimination* (Berkeley: University of California Press, 1964); David Lenfest, "The Illustrations of *Gulliver's Travels*, 1727–1838, Considered as an Index of Interpretation," Ph.D. diss. University of Michigan, 1966; J. Hillis Miller, "Sketches by *Boz*, *Oliver Twist*, and Cruikshank's Illustrations," in *Charles Dickens and George Cruikshank* (Berkeley: University of California Press, 1971), pp. 1–69; Michael Hancher, "The Placement of Tenniel's *Alice* Illustrations," *Harvard Library Bulletin* 30 (1982): 237–52.

3. Miller, "*Sketches by Boz, Oliver Twist*, and Cruikshank's Illustrations," p. 43.

4. James Steel Smith, "Visual Criticism: A New Medium for Critical Comment," p. 250. Smith also discusses a number of the issues I have raised in this paragraph.

5. For an informative discussion of the working relationship between Brown and Dickens, see Michael Steig, *Dickens and Phiz* (Bloomington: Indiana University Press, 1978). Mark Twain, it should be noted, also carefully examined E. W. Kemble's illustrations for *The Adventures of Huckleberry Finn* and charged him to make specific alterations in many of them.

6. For an examination of Thackeray's illustrations, see J. R. H. Harvey, *Victorian Novelists and their Illustrators* (New York: New York University Press, 1971), pp. 76–102.

7. Swift to Benjamin Motte, 28 December 1727, *The Correspondence of Jonathan Swift*, ed. Harold Williams (Oxford: Oxford University Press, 1963), 3: 257. The inclusion of maps as well as illustrations of the Flying Island and the writing machine suggest that Swift was receptive from the very beginning to having his text illustrated.

8. The most artistically sophisticated illustrations of *Gulliver's Travels* in the eighteenth century were done by Lefebvre in a French edition published in 1797. This was a limited edition, however, and they do not appear to have had a significant influence on the British reading public. For an excellent discussion of Lefebvre's illustrations, see David Lenfest, "Lefebvre's Illustrations of *Gulliver's Travels*," *New York Public Library Bulletin* 76 (1972): 199–213.

9. The plate is reproduced from Ronald Paulson, *Hogarth: His Life, Art, and Times* (New Haven: Yale University Press, 1971). For Swift's view of Hogarth, see his poem "The Legion Club" (1736), lines 219–34.

10. For a discussion of the specific scenes these artists illustrated, see David Lenfest, "A Checklist of Illustrated Editions of *Gulliver's Travels*, 1727–1914."

11. Several of Grandville's illustrations are discussed by David Lenfest in "Grandville's Gulliver," *Satire Newsletter* 10 (1973): 12–24.

12. Grandville's illustrations may be conveniently found in *Gulliver's Travels* (Arlington, Virginia: Great Ocean Publishers, 1980).

13. *Gulliver's Travels*, in *The Prose Works of Jonathan Swift*, ed. Herbert Davis et al. (Oxford: Basil Blackwell, 1939–68), 11:69. All quotations from *Gulliver's Travels* are from this edition and will be cited parenthetically by page number.

14. Louis Giannetti, *Understanding Movies*, 3d ed. (Englewood Cliffs, N.J.: Prentice-Hall, 1982), p. 15.

15. Eric Rabkin, *The Fantastic in Literature* (Princeton: Princeton University Press, 1976), pp. 4–5.

16. Ibid., p. 146.

17. David Bland, *A History of Book Illustration* (London: Faber and Faber, 1958), refers to Grandville as "a precursor of the surrealists" (p. 94).

18. This plate is reproduced from *Gulliver's Travels* (London: Cassell, Petter, and Galpin, 1865).

19. This plate is reproduced from *Gulliver's Travels* (London: J. M. Dent; New York: E. P. Dutton, 1909).

20. Roland Frye, "Swift's Yahoos and the Christian Symbols for Sin," *Journal of the History of Ideas* 15 (1954): 208.

21. This plate is reproduced from *Gulliver's Travels* (New York: Harper and Brothers Publishers, 1913).

22. *Gulliver's Travels* (London: Cresset Press, 1930).

23. *Gulliver's Travels* (Mount Vernon, N.Y.: Peter Pauper Press, 1948).

24. *Gulliver's Travels* (New York: Crown Publishers, 1947).

25. *Gulliver's Travels* (Belfast: Appletree Press, 1976).

26. A number of Matisse's works, which may have influenced Millar's illustrations, can be found in Aragon, *Henri Matisse, roman* (Paris: Gallimard, 1971), and Jack Cowart, Jack Flam, Dominique Fourcade, and John H. Neff, *Henri Matisse Paper Cut-Outs* (St. Louis Art Museum and the Detroit Institute of Arts, 1977).

27. For a discussion of the Comics Code Authority, as well as a brief history of comic books in the United States, see Leslie Daniels, *Comix: A History of Comic Books in America* (New York: E. P. Dutton, 1971).

28. For an informative examination of "comic art," see the introduction by Maurice Horn to *Seventy-five Years of the Comics* (Boston: Boston Book and Art, 1971), pp. 7–16. I am indebted to his discussion.

29. Ibid., p. 12.

30. Lefebvre's illustrations were originally published in a limited edition as the *Voyages de Gulliver* (Paris: Didot l'Aîné, 1797); the illustration discussed here is reproduced from Lenfest, "Lefebvre's Illustrations of *Gulliver's Travels*." Brock's illustrations originally appeared in *Travels into Several Remote Nations of the World* (London and New York: Macmillan and Co., 1894); the illustration discussed here is reproduced from *Gulliver's Travels* (New York: Signet, 1960). Lalauze's illustrations originally appeared in *Gulliver's Travels* (Paris: Libraire Des Bibliophiles, 1875), and the illustration discussed here is reproduced from that edition.

31. James Steel Smith, "Visual Criticism: A New Medium for Critical Comment," p. 245.

Scientific Discourse:
Gulliver's Travels and The
Philosophical Transactions

Frederik N. Smith

The influence of *The Philosophical Transactions of the Royal Society* on *Gulliver's Travels* has been understood for close to fifty years, ever since Marjorie Nicolson and Nora M. Mohler published "The Scientific Background of Swift's *Voyage to Laputa*."[1] Nicolson and Mohler's thesis—that most of the zany experiments reported in part 3 are skewings of actual investigations from the pages of the *Transactions*—is so convincing as to have achieved the status of a *donné* in scholarship on Swift. Subsequent scholars have located in the *Transactions* additional sources for both *A Tale of a Tub* and *Gulliver's Travels* or have argued that the principles underlying the research sponsored by the Royal Society (especially the necessity of empirical observation described in the plainest of styles) were postulates Swift found it convenient to mock in his major satire. It seems safe to agree with R. C. Olson that Swift "was acquainted with it [*The Transactions*] over the course of the greater part of his lifetime" and with George R. Potter that the evidence "proves conclusively that Swift was a humorously critical and surprisingly careful reader of the *Transactions*."[2]

That Swift should have knowledge of this first scientific journal in the English-speaking world should not surprise us.[3] Britain's utter fascination with contemporary science at the end of the seventeenth and beginning of the eighteenth centuries meant that the *Transactions*—which contained the latest news on that science—were widely read, and not only by scientists (although just who and who was not a scientist at this time is itself problematic) but by well-read laymen generally.[4] In light of the size of this readership, I think that we can expand on Nicolson and Mohler's argument and that, moreover, we can consider Swift's

y to the *form* of the *Transactions*. The influence of the
ciety's linguistic and scientific program comes not sim-
way of the genre of the travelogue (although certainly the
gs of Dampier and others are important here), but more
ly by way of the scientific discourse of his day; the trav-
t. ue was only one example of this type of prose. Without
denying the connection between the Laputan experiments and
the actual experiments reported in the *Transactions*, we can take
advantage of an opportunity to look in some detail at how the
style of contemporary scientific writing spiked Swift's (sometimes satiric) imagination.

1

Scientific discourse had changed radically over the century
prior to the publication of *Gulliver's Travels*. Thus in 1634
Thomas Muffet in his *Insectorum Theatrum* (quoted here in the
1658 translation appended to Edward Topsell's *History of Four-
Footed Beasts*) could romanticize even the bite and excrement of
the common fly:

> When he bites, 'tis not out of rusticity or clownishness to get bloud
> only; but by way of love & humanity, and for that reason especially he
> seiseth upon the fairest: yea what a pretty thing it is to see a company
> of Flyes flying to and again playing and sporting with one another,
> and hanging upon a thred as it were dancers on the ropes? Moreover
> as the cleanly horse doth, she laies her ordure all in one place, so that
> upper wainscot and seiling of the rooms where they use are full of
> great spots which they make on that occasion, which is an argument
> that they are not altogether void of some kinde of memory also.[5]

This is the Elizabethan world picture. Thirty years later, however,
after the invention of the microscope and under the influence of
the Royal Society, Robert Hooke, in his *Micrographia; or, Some
Physiological Descriptions of Minute Bodies*, can describe the
magnified, labelled drawing of a blue fly as follows:

> Sixthly, at the under part of the face FF, were several of the former
> sort of bended Bristles; and below all, the mouth, out of the middle of
> which, grew the *proboscis* GHI, which, by means of several joints,
> whereof it seems to consist, the Fly was able to move to and fro, and
> thrust it in and out as it pleas'd. . . . This kind of Fly seems by the
> steams or taste of fermenting and putrifying meat (which it often

kisses, as 'twere, with its *proboscis* as it trips over it) to be stimulated or excited to eject its Eggs or Seed on it. . . .[6]

This is the new objectivity. Hooke aims for a prose that will not stand between the reader and the subject being described; he keeps his opinions to himself. Yet the sought-after neutrality cannot altogether maintain itself, as he lapses into metaphor ("as 'twere" betrays his self-consciousness) reminiscent of the style of the previous age.

Gulliver describes the flies that attack him in Brobdingnag in terms that reflect—but do not altogether approve of—the new objectivity:

> The Kingdom is much pestered with Flies in Summer; and these odious insects, each of them as big as a *Dunstable* Lark, hardly gave me any Rest while I sat at Dinner, with their continual Humming and Buzzing about mine Ears. They would sometimes alight upon my Victuals, and leave their loathsome Excrement or Spawn behind, which to me was very visible, although not to the Natives of that Country, whose large Opticks were not so acute as mine in viewing smaller Objects. Sometimes they would fix upon my Nose or Forehead, where they stung me to the Quick, smelling very offensively.[7]

Here man is not the center of the universe but the unwitting victim of his own invention of the microscope. If Hooke's scrupulous objectivity is a reaction against the unrealistic, anthropomorphized descriptions of Muffett and others, then the noisome flies in Brobdingnag serve to remind us that modern, intellectualized objectivity ignores the horrible reality of these insects. A fly does not bite out of love and humanity, nor is its excrement on the ceiling indicative of its memory; but then again, neither is its stinger a mere "*proboscis* GHI." The earlier science falsifies its object by imagining man himself in that object. Modern science falsifies its object by denying man, by limiting him to the role of observer only. Swift tacitly contradicts both tendencies and insists on the offensiveness of these insects and shows also how for Gulliver, not merely observing but living in Hooke's world, they pose a threat to human existence. There is an additional irony here: two pages earlier, Gulliver has reported that the Brobdingnagian king noted "how contemptible a Thing was human Grandeur, which could be mimicked by such diminutive Insects as I" (p. 107).

But before delving into the question of the general influence of the *Transactions* themselves, I want to look at one unmistakable

ise of the specific influence of the Royal Society's brand of
science on *Gulliver's Travels*. The example tells us something
about the necessary complexity of Swift's relationship to modern
science. In part 2 Glumdalclitch takes Gulliver into the city,
where beggars crowd to the side of the coach, providing him with
"the most horrible Spectacles that ever an *European* Eye beheld":

> The most hateful Sight of all was the Lice crawling on their Cloaths: I
> could see distinctly the Limbs of these Vermin with my naked Eye,
> much better than those of an *European* Louse through a Microscope;
> and their Snouts with which they rooted like Swine. They were the
> first I had ever beheld; and I should have been curious enough to
> dissect one of them, if I had proper Instruments (which I unluckily
> left behind me in the Ship) although indeed the Sight was so nau-
> seous, that it perfectly turned my Stomach. (p. 113)

Swift's reference to the observation of a louse through a microscope (Gulliver's naked eye in Brobdingnag is equivalent to a
microscope in Europe) is a clear allusion to Hooke's *Micrographia*, where Observation 54 is "Of a Louse" and where Hooke
appends a very large and repulsive drawing of a louse. The
original engraving folds out to reveal a louse a full sixteen inches
in length. Hooke's oversized illustration offered Swift the opportunity of quite literally seeing what Gulliver would see in Brobdingnag. Hooke's several references to the louse's "snout" may
also have supplied a hint for Swift's swine analogy.

By way of his references to the microscope and to Gulliver's
"curious" desire to dissect, Swift turns his narrator into a proper
observer for the Royal Society and then has him leave his instruments behind (a humorous allusion to Crusoe's similar forget-
fulness) and get nauseous at the mere sight of the magnified
louse. Gulliver in this passage is both a scientist and a layman
repulsed by a scientist. What Swift has done is to replace Hooke's
excitement at his discoveries—down to his admiration of the
"very lovely ruby colour" of his own blood pulsing through the
belly of the louse—with Gulliver's comical squeamishness.[8]
Nonetheless, behind the easy slap at Hooke and the new science
we can sense Swift's very real fascination with the microcosmic
world being revealed through this new invention. Or else why
would he have been attracted to Hooke's Brobdingnagian louse in
the first place? Or why write a whole book of *Gulliver's Travels* as
if he were looking through a microscope? Hans Aarsleff reminds
us that John Wilkins (one of the founders of the Royal Society)
"knew that wonder is the chief impulse to serious study and

experiment."⁹ Hooke shared this attitude, and in the preface to his *Micrographia* speaks of the "high *rapture* and *delight* of the mind" to be found in experimental philosophy.¹⁰ One is tempted to add that Jonathan Swift was keenly aware of a similar connection between wonder and satire.

It is of course a commonplace that the description of scientific writing as enunciated in Sprat's *History of the Royal Society* was a sort of touchstone for the latter seventeenth and early eighteenth centuries. The Lagadan philosophers who seek to replace words with things can in this context be viewed as humorous literalizations of Sprat's admonition "to return back to the primitive purity, and shortness, when men deliver'd so many *things*, almost in an equal number of *words*."¹¹ But the Royal Society's style—and Gulliver's—is not unlike that of scientists since the seventeenth century. "The purity of scientific language," Aldous Huxley reminds us, "is not the same as the purity of literary language."

> The aim of the scientist is to say only one thing at a time, and to say it unambiguously and with the greatest possible clarity. To achieve this, he simplifies and jargonizes. . . . When the literary artist undertakes to give a purer sense to the words of his tribe, he does so with the express purpose of creating a language capable of conveying, not the single meaning of some particular science, but the multiple significance of human experience, on its most private as well as on its more public levels.¹²

Contributing to the complexity of *Gulliver's Travels* is the fact that Swift's choice of genre—a literary work overlayed on a sort of travelogue the Royal Society might have sponsored—led him to employ the scientific and literary styles at the same time. Clear and simple and unambiguous, his book nevertheless bristles with the multiple significances of human experience.

2

In the final chapter of part 4, Gulliver admits that he has aimed at the objectivity of a scientific rhetoric:

> wherein I have not been so studious of Ornament as of Truth. I could perhaps like others have astonished thee with improbable Tales; but I rather chose to relate plain Matter of Fact in the simplest Manner and Style; because my principal Design was to inform, and not to amuse thee. (p. 291)

Swift means this ironically. If the overly proper "thee" (archaic by 1726) does not give it away, then the assertion that we *might* have had "improbable Tales" reveals the author's hand. In any case, this sort of overt claim to veracity was not uncommon in the prefaces to travelogues, as in the preface to Dampier's *Voyage to New Holland* (1699):

> It has been objected against me by some, that my Accounts and Descriptions of Things are dry and jejeune, not filled with variety of pleasant Matter, to divert and gratify the Curious Reader. How far this is true, I must leave the World to judge. But if I have been exactly and strictly careful to give only true Relations and Descriptions of things (as I am sure I have). . . .[13]

In 1814 Scott noted the similarity between Gulliver and Dampier, and in 1934 Willard Bonner explored the parallels between the stolid mariner and "cousin Gulliver" in exhausting detail.[14] But here again we need to keep in mind that travelogues are only one type of scientific writing.

Indeed Swift—a reader of *The Philosophical Transactions*—might in 1710 have come across the following afterword to Patrick Blair's "Osteographia Elephantina":

> I have rather chosen to address you in a plain and common Stile, than give the least suspicion of Disingenuity in a finer language; especially since it is History [i.e., scientific discourse] I have written, where Matter of Fact, and not Romance, where Eloquence, is the chief Design.[15]

Or he might in 1717 have read the following postscript to Thomas Bower's "Account of an extraordinary Tumour or Wen lately cut off the Cheek of a Person in Scotland":

> I have given a true and plain Account of this extraordinary Case from certain Information; I have contented my self to relate only Matters of Fact, without making any Observations or Reflections on it; for I leave it to the Philosophers and *Virtuosi* to make their own Reasonings and Refinements as seems best to themselves (no. 354, p. 717)

Or he might in 1722 have found the following note in Thomas Nettleton's "Letter Concerning the Inoculation of the Small Pox":

> I have given you a short and plain Account of what has occur'd to me concerning this Method of Inoculation; 'tis not any pains or care I have taken in writing this Letter, that can recommend it, for I have

been solicitious about nothing but Truth, my design being only to
give you a short History. . . . (no. 370, p. 46)

There are a number of common elements in these passages: an
apology for the plainness of the narrative; a desire (even in the
face of the "extraordinary") to stick to what are perceived as facts;
an avoidance of anything beyond the scientifically observable;
and a willingness (at least implicit) to let *others* offer hypotheses,
opinions, and judgments. I do not care to argue that any of the
above passages served as Swift's source. I want on the contrary to
suggest that what lies behind *Gulliver's Travels* is not a specific
source but the style and approach one can identify broadly with
the new science. Back of all these passages is the Baconian
notion of a science founded not on rhetoric but on a cautious,
neutralized observation of phenomena. The accoutrements of
this scientific prose are maps, diagrams, measurements, lists, the
accumulation of empirical evidence, and of course the plain
style advocated by the Royal Society. *Gulliver's Travels* has all of
these.

But the lengths to which Swift has gone in imitating the language of the new science has not been noticed. The style of
Swift's satire is not just plain but plain the way the scientific
discourse of his day was plain. For instance, Swift repeatedly
demonstrates his awareness of the odd jargon spawned by the
followers of Bacon, a limited lexicon of everyday terms (this is
apparent in the passages on factuality quoted above), which show
up over and over in the pages of *The Philosophical Transactions*:

strict	object	distinct
observation	exact	fact
curious	rarities	performance
particular	circumstance	description
acute	diligent	correct
veracity	perfect	history
agreement	virtuoso	matter
phenomenon	useful	information
discover	relation	ingenuous
explain	wonder	sign
truth	inquiry	manifest
plain	nice	operation
account	examine	report

Long before Swift was writing, each of these everyday words had
acquired a quite specialized meaning; and each appears (in some

form) in *Gulliver's Travels* more than once and on occasion carries the weight of Swift's purpose. Thus when the Brobdingnagian king calls in three scholars to identify his unusual visitor, Gulliver says, borrowing from the language of science:

> These Gentlemen, after they had a while *examined* my Shape with much *Nicety,* were of different Opinions concerning me. . . . They *observed* by my Teeth, which they viewed with great *Exactness,* that I was a carnivorous Animal. . . . One of them seemed to think that I might be an Embrio, or abortive Birth. But this Opinion was rejected by the other two, who *observed* my Limbs to be *perfect* and finished; and that I had lived several Years, as it was *manifested* from my Beard; the Stumps whereof they *plainly discovered* through a Magnifying Glass. (pp. 103–4, italics mine)

There is irony in the situation, for here Gulliver is not the Royal Society observer but the object of scientific observation. Indeed the reference to the scholars studying Gulliver's beard hairs under the magnifying glass is an explicit allusion to Antony van Leeuenhoek, who over many years had reported on similar such inquiries in the pages of the *Transactions.*[16] In the looking-glass world of Swift's satire, things have somehow gotten reversed. It is as if the louse were suddenly to look up at Hooke through his microscope. Or as if the dog in Lagado were to get up off the table and come at the scientist with a pair of ivory-tipped bellows. But beyond the situation, the supposedly neutralized vocabulary of science—in this literary context, very much reinvigorated—opens up for Swift some marvelously unobtrusive ironies, which we have now all but lost. It may be necessary to qualify Serge Soupel's blanket assertion: "Swift had written against the Royal Society, yet at no point in his long career did he focus his sarcasms on the *language* of the Society."[17] The plain style of *Gulliver's Travels* has been a major factor in maintaining its readability over two and a half centuries; but for its first readers that style played a significant role in conveying Swift's tone.

Swift likewise used for his own purposes another characteristic feature of contemporary scientific prose: the analogy. Although comparison employed for the sake of elaboration was *verboten* to the Royal Society reporter, comparison for the sake of better explaining the subject at hand seems to have been acceptable, or at least unavoidable. In order to explain to another *what he alone may have seen,* the scientist must be able to compare the familiar with the unfamiliar he has discovered at the other end of the microscope or the other end of the world. Thus a reviewer of Christian Huygens's *The Celestial World Discover'd* wrote in 1699: " 'Tis the most usual Method of discovering the insensible Parts of the World by their Similitude to the more Sensible, as in Anatomy we judge of the Parts of a Creature, by the Similitude we find they have to the Parts of some other before known" (no. 256, p. 340). Analogy in a scientific work serves much the same function as an illustration or a diagram; although these quick glances back at a reality the scientist presumes he shares with his reader are of no importance as far as the scientific phenomena themselves are concerned, they are absolutely critical to the communication of those phenomena.

Analogies dot *The Philosophical Transactions* from their very inception. The subject matter ranges from references to the parts of the human body, to everyday objects and natural phenomena, to items identifiable to fellow *virtuosi* only.

Human tooth: Six or seven hundred of these Pipes put together, I judg exceed not the thickness of one Hair of a Mans Beard. (no. 140 [1678]: 1002)

Rock formations: The tops of them looks very like the Pavements that are in some Gentlemens Halls, abating the irregularity of the sides, but these lie as close. (no. 212 [1694]: 172)

Native dress: They cover their Yard [penis] with a piece of Bark, or sometimes Silver, of the very shape and bigness of that paper case we use to put a dose of Pills in. (no. 262 [1700]: 540)

Spider's blood: Some particles of Blood, which according to all appearance were spherical, circulating in a liquid matter, as plainly as if you were to see so many small Pease rolling off a gentle Declevity. (no. 271 [1701]: 868)

Anatomy of a whale: The said Captain having inform'd me, that the Testicles of a Whale are as big as a Firkin of Butter that weighs about a hundred Weight (no. 334 [1712]: 439)

Still birth: He found within her a hard mass of the form and size of a large Ninepin-Bowl. (no. 367 [1721]: 127)

In every instance the correspondent is attempting to describe something which no man (at least no European gentleman) has seen before, and he has had to draw on his own experience, which he assumes is equivalent to his reader's. In this way he hopes quite literally to domesticate the foreign; it is like sending a dwarfish sheep or an oversized wasp stinger back to London for examination by the virtuosi and proper registration in the museum at Gresham College.

In part 4 Gulliver himself mentions the necessity of using "Similitudes" when communicating with someone who has not shared one's own experiences. Shortly after his arrival in Houyhnhnmland, his master asks him to tell his story. Gulliver hesitates:

> I assured him, how extreamly desirous I was that he should be satisfied in every Point; but I doubted much, whether it would be possible for me to explain my self on several Subjects whereof his Honour could have no Conception, because I saw nothing in his Country to which I could resemble them. That, however, I would do my best, and strive to express my self by Similitudes, humbly desiring his Assistance when I wanted proper Words; which he was pleased to promise me. (p. 243)

As it turns out, most of Gulliver's analogies occur *not* during his fourth voyage but during his first two:

> *Lilliputians at war:* I felt above an Hundred Arrows discharged on my left Hand, which pricked me like so many Needles; and besides, they shot another Flight into the Air, as we do Bombs in Europe. (p. 22)

> *Size of Lilliputian objects:* I have been much pleased with observing a Cook pulling a Lark, which was not so large as a common Fly; and a young Girl threading an invisible Needle with invisible Silk. (p. 57)

> *Brobdingnagian breast:* I cannot tell what to compare [it] with, so as to give the curious Reader an Idea of its Bulk, Shape, and Colour. It stood prominent six Foot, and could not be less than sixteen in Circumference. The Nipple was about half the Bigness of my Head. . . . (p. 91)

> *Dishes in Brobdingnag:* I had an entire set of Silver Dishes and Plates, and other Necessaries, which in Proportion to those of the Queen, were not much bigger than what I have seen in a *London* Toy-shop, for the Furniture of a Baby-house (p. 106)

Each of these analogies does indeed assist in locating the reader relative to Gulliver's experience. But in every case (with the possible exception of the second), Swift is also insinuating something *beyond* his narrator's analogy. Thus although *arrows* only "prick" a giant in Lilliput, we can imagine what *bombs* might do (the verb is effectively omitted) to an ordinary-sized human being in Europe. The other analogies work in like fashion. As with his clever manipulation of the scientific jargon of his day, Swift has here turned the analogy common to scientific discourse into a device of his satire. His fun at the expense of this style is evident in Gulliver's attempt to locate an informative analogy for the size of a Brobdingnagian nipple, and his settling on "about half the Bigness of my Head." His rhetorical options limited by the plainness of this prose, Swift has nonetheless come up with ways to make it resonate with literary meanings the contemporary scientists never intended.[18] His text becomes more than the safe conveyer of trustworthy observations; but it is a testimony to his art that while his Royal Society style frequently becomes *more* than itself, it never becomes something *other* than itself.

Behind matters of form, however, is the Society's advocacy of a certain methodology: the meticulous accumulation of physical evidence, the citation of only the most credible witnesses, and an extremely cautious approach to argument from "matters of fact" to hypotheses or opinions. In its third year of existence the following appeared in the minutes of the Society:

> A curious and diligent process of making experiments; wherein a most severe inquiry may be made into all particulars, both of the manner of making experiment, and the circumstances observable in any of the effects; and every of these trials to be repeated twice or thrice at least, and so recorded and ranged into several orders or degrees; in every of which places they may stand like so many witnesses, to give testimony of this truth, or against that error. And a most severe examination of these witnesses must be made, before a jury can warrantably give their verdict, or a judge pronounce sentence, for branding one proposition or hypothesis as erroneous and absurd, or for establishing another for a truth or axiom.[19]

The neutral jargon of the new science is present here. But so too is evidence of the Baconian approach to phenomena refined and adumbrated by the early members of the Royal Society, with a vengeance. It is easy to smile at the legalism of this prose; for the virtuosi, however, the analogy was very real and perhaps serves to explain the quasi-legal nature of much scientific writing in the late seventeenth and early eighteenth centuries. And the assumption behind this methodology is difficult to reject. "If a scientific work does not refer back to a means of confirmation," claims Roman Ingarden, "then it can still transmit certain results of

cognition; but it becomes much more difficult to verify the assertions made in the work, and the fundamental value of the work
becomes less."[20]

The principle underlying this modern science was the process
of induction—the accumulation of particulars that can be com-
bined by means of a hypothesis into a tentative order. "Knowledge was advanced," Paul G. Arakelian says,

> not only by observing phenomena (as even Browne had done) but by
> limiting conclusions to those observations. Thus, the origin of color
> or the meaning of color does not interest Newton who instead mea-
> sures, records, experiments, and then hypothesizes about color. New-
> ton's data controls his conclusions, and only after he makes a
> hypothesis can he generalize his theory to other phenomena. Unlike
> rhetoricians, who deal with self-evident truths, the new scientist
> works with demonstrable truths which force him to be conscious of
> progression: how one idea leads to another, not how one idea com-
> pares to another.[21]

This is the Baconian spirit that informs *The Philosophical Transactions*. Although reports of the Royal Society descend at times
to a naive Baconism similar to certain passages of *Gulliver's
Travels*, it is important to keep in mind that what motivates the
new science is quite simply an admirable desire to restrain the
all-too-human tendency toward partiality and mere subjective
speculation. It sounds funny now, but in 1662, on the death of
Lawrence Rooke, one of the Society's first Fellows, a eulogy was
read that praised him above all for his typical response when
asked his view of a hypothesis: "I have no opinion."[22]

This attitude determined in large measure the form of the
Transactions; and the emphasis on factuality had its implications for contributors as well as readers. In a 1683 preface, in a
passage that offers a belated justification for the *Transactions* and
the genre of the scientific journal (then almost twenty years old),
the publication is described as a "Register" of knowledge:

> Although the Writing of these *Transactions*, is not to be looked upon
> as the Business of the *Royal Society:* Yet, in regard they are a *Spec-
> imen* of many things which lie before them; Contain a great *Variety* of
> Useful Matter; Are a convenient *Register*, for the Bringing in, and
> Preserving many *Experiments*, which, not enough for a Book, would
> also be lost; and have proved a very good Ferment for the setting [of]
> Men of Uncommon Thoughts in all parts a work [i.e., *to* work]. (no.
> 143, p. 2)

In this respect the *Transactions* serve a purpose very near the Society's collection of curiosities in its Gresham College "repository." The facts—largely unorganized—are simply displayed, and the viewer or reader is intended to draw his or her own conclusions. "There is no doubt," claims Hans Sloane in a 1699 preface, "but the more discerning will make a great difference between what is related in them [the *Transactions*] as Matter of Fact, Experiment, or Observation, and what is *Hypothesis*" (no. 248, n.p.). It would seem that this is likewise the responsibility handed over to the reader of *Gulliver's Travels*, who during three very factual books must supply his or her own tentative hypotheses, and who in part 4 must avoid taking Gulliver's singular hypothesis as equivalent to universal truth.

3

The care with which the Royal Society approached the impartial recording of phenomena is everywhere apparent. Nonetheless, its correspondents were confronted always with a dilemma: on the one hand, people at this time (scientists and laymen alike) had developed an insatiable appetite for novelty, and on the other they wanted to be satisfied that what they were reading was unquestionably true. This was a rhetorical problem.[23] The following examples dramatize the difficulty of conveying information about far-fetched phenomena to a highly skeptical audience. Note in each case the emphasis on writing:

The so-called "Giant's Causeway": Prolixity in a Philosophical Description I'm sure you'l pardon; for I was very exact in getting it from a person that was *rei compos*, perhaps *peritus*; a Scholar (a master of Arts in *Cambridge*). . . . (no. 199 [1693]: 708)

Solid objects voided by urine: I here set you down as I had it from the Pen of the Physician concern'd, who is alive, and the Truth of it well known in and about the Town where it happened. (no. 323 [1709]: 421)

Huge teeth unearthed recently: I procured the Loan of them, so long as to examine them particularly, make some Remarks, and take the following correct Sketches, that express their Form truly, just as big as the Life. (no. 346 [1715]: 371)

Unusual lights in the sky: 'Tis hoped a good History of the *Fact*, deduced partly from our own Observations, and partly collected from

the uniform Relations of credible Persons, or from the Letters of
such. . . . No. 347 [1716]: 406)

Water spouting out of the ground: The account I took of it when I first
saw it, I put into Writing; and upon a second Inspection, finding it to
be pretty exact, I thought a Transcript of it, would not be ungrateful to
you. . . . (no. 363 [1719]: 1097)

The paranoic fear of being caught out. Of being accused by the
Royal Society of not having made every effort to assure the
accuracy of one's written observations.[24] The Society's correspondents use every conceivable means of establishing the credibility of what they are reporting: personal observation;
testimony of firsthand witnesses, trustworthy witnesses, and
multiple witnesses to the same phenomenon; maps, drawings,
and even written affidavits; the submission of physical evidence
or the promise to make such evidence available; reliance on
meticulous measurement; the use of scientific instruments such
as the microscope, telescope, or various sorts of navigational
equipment; and the step-by-step recounting of the very process of
acquiring the information being reported. The plain style—the
accepted medium of the new science—was only one aspect of
this nervous factuality.

But here lies a paradox. It is interesting to note that the overrid-
ing desire to record observations in such extreme and often
personal detail meant that most of the submissions to the Society
have an anecdotal quality; efforts to achieve a foolproof credibility serve to make parts of the *Transactions* read very often like
"stories," and thus the difference between one of them and a
work like Defoe's "True Relation of the Apparition of one Mrs.
Veal" (1705) is scarcely arguable. Jan V. Golinski has made a
similar point recently about Robert Boyle's *Sceptical Chymist*
(1666):

In contrast to the dominant forms of the tradition which he crit-
icised, Boyle's experimental essays were *narrative,* as opposed to
exhaustively methodical; *suggestive,* rather than conclusively de-
monstrative; and *subjective,* in the sense that they included personal
and circumstantial details which would not be thought relevant by
many subsequent scientific writers.[25]

Indeed such literary contamination of scientific writing is a
prominent feature of the majority of the accounts in *The Philosophical Transactions.* It would seem that while the Royal So-

ciety had some success in demystifying the language of science in the latter half of the seventeenth century, the emphasis on empirical evidence, immediacy, and personal testimony gave to scientific reporting a literary license it would not otherwise have possessed. The function of storytelling in the emerging science of this period brought it closer to fiction, at least fiction as practiced by Defoe and Swift, than the Royal Society would have liked to admit.

A good example of the narrative approach to scientific report-ing in this period is William Oliver's five-page "Relation of an Extraordinary Sleepy Person, at Tinsbury, near Bath," which appeared in the *Transactions* in 1705. Many of the conventions of realistic fiction-writing are to be found here: detailed descrip-tion of setting and events, a focus on the chronology of happen-ings, emphasis on one major character and the sketchier presentation of other characters, the creation of suspense for the reader, and the evolution of the first-person narrator. The account begins like a police report, although the insistence on scientific accuracy soon leads to a kind of meticulous handling of detail that we tend to associate with prose fiction:

> *May* the 13th, *Anno* 1694, one *Samuel Chilton,* of *Tinsbury* near *Bath,* a Labourer, about 25 years of age, of a robust habit of Body, not fat, but fleshy, and a dark brown Hair, happen'd, without any visible cause, or evident sign, to fall into a very profound Sleep, out of which no Art used by those that were near him, cou'd rouze him, till after a months time. (no. 304, p. 2177)

Chilton's mother, fearing her son would starve in "that sullen humour, as she thought it," every day put food beside him, which by the following day was gone, although no one ever saw him eat or drink. There is more than one mystery here.

Two years later, Chilton fell into a second sleep. "After some days they [his family] were prevail'd with to try what effect Medicines might have on him,"

> and accordingly one Mr *Gibs,* a very able Apothecary of *Bath,* went to him, Bled, Blister'd, Cupp'd and Scarrified him, and used all the external irritating Medicines he could think on, but all to no pur-pose. . . . (p. 2177)

Like Swift's woman flayed, this man is treated not as a person but as an object of scientific curiosity. Chilton's family, however, seems anxious to preserve him; they manage to pour some wine through a quill slid between his clenched teeth. This second time Chilton slept seventeen weeks, then woke, put on his clothes, walked around his room, and could not be persuaded he had slept so long, "till going out into the Fields he found every body busy in getting in their Harvest, and he remember'd very well, when he fell asleep they were sowing of Barley and Oats, which he then saw ripe and fit to be cut down" (p. 2178). The sensory detail is a matter of proof to Chilton himself, but note that it is introduced from his point of view, not Oliver's. Although the sleeping man was somewhat thinner when he woke from his sleep, "yet a worthy Gentleman his Neighbor" claimed that he seemed, if anything, spunkier than ever; his testimony is proffered as scientific evidence, but it functions well as a human, nicely literary, outside perspective.

A little over a year later, Chilton fell into his third, and longest, sleep. "Being then at the *Bath*, and hearing of it," interjects the first-person narrator, "I took Horse on the 23d, to inform myself of a matter of fact I thought so strange."

> When I came to the House, I was by the neighbors (for there was no body at home at that time besides this sick man,) brought to his Bedside, where I found him asleep, as I had been told before, with a Cup of Beer and a piece of Bread and Cheese upon a Stool by his Bed within his reach. (p. 2179)

Again, the quest for scientific accuracy has led to a detailed, highly visual image. Dr. Oliver is unable to awaken the sleeping man, but turns (like the apothecary before him) to torture in the name of science:

> I was resolv'd to see what effects *Spirit* of *Sal Armoniac* would have, which I had brought with me, to discover the Cheat, if it had been one; so I held my Viol under one Nostril a considerable time, which being drawn from Quick-lime, was a very piercing Spirit, and so strong I would not bear it under my own Nose a moment without making my Eyes water, but he felt it not at all. (p. 2179)

Can we be so sure he didn't feel it? Dr. Oliver next proceeds to pour half a bottle of "this fiery Spirit" into Chilton's one nostril, which makes his eyes water and his nose run; yet nothing wakes him. The good doctor then crams that same nostril with powder of white hellebore: "I can hardly think any Imposter cou'd ever be insensible of what I did" (p. 2180). "Having made these my Experiments I left him," he coolly observes, "being pretty well satisfied he was really asleep, and no sullen Counterfeit, as some people thought him." Others follow Dr. Oliver to Tinsbury in order "to satisfie their Curiosity in a Rarity of that Nature"; they find Chilton in the same condition, only his nose understandably inflamed and swollen, his one nostril blistered and scabby. At last Chilton's family is forced to protect him from the men of science: "His mother upon this for some time after wou'd suffer no body to come near him, for fear of more Experiments upon her Son" (p. 2180). But soon the tortures begin once more. An apothecary sneaks into Chilton's house and bleeds him. In moving the poor man to another house, his head is knocked against a stone as he is carried down the stairs. Dr. Oliver arrives again and this time stops the victim's nose and mouth, and "a Gentleman then with me ran a large Pin into his Arm to the very Bone, but he gave us no manner of tokens of being sensible of any thing we did to him" (p. 2181). And still, in all this time, Chilton has not been observed to eat or drink. " 'Tis farther observable," adds our faithful narrator, "he never foul'd his Bed, but did his necessary occasions always in the Pot." How is this possible? questions the curious reader. And how can Dr. Oliver be so sure? Finally, after sleeping almost six months, the patient begins to have intermittent spells of consciousness and awakens at long last, fortunately unable to remember a thing. "I have no reason to suspect this to be any Cheat," concludes Dr. Oliver (p. 2182). "I am as well satisfied as I am of the best grounded matter of fact," says Defoe at the end of Mrs. Veal's story, published in the same year.[26]

This scientific report has many of the same features as *Gulliver's Travels*. Written in a plain, readable prose, the story is told in the first person and insists throughout on demonstrating the truth, without feeling, of an occurrence that is really very hard to believe; here, as in Swift's book, we have an interesting confrontation between modern science and happenings that are beyond belief. Moreover, at least implicitly the authenticity of any kind of verbal statement is questioned. If Chilton is a counterfeit, could not Dr. Oliver be one? If Gulliver intentionally deceives his Houyhnhnm master, could not he deceive us as well? Both *Gulliver's Travels* and this account from *The Philosophical Transactions* raise questions about the relationship between fact and truth and also turn back on themselves, disturbingly posing a further question about the trustworthiness of the very text we are reading.[27]

Gulliver's Travels was written in the context of this laudable search for reliable truths that are always just beyond reach. What

is averred in one number of the *Transactions* is likely to be
challenged in the next, commented on by a second correspondent, or emended before the letter has been posted. Paradoxically, in attempting to be so cautiously inclusive and wary of
jumping to conclusions, the Royal Society scientists are forced to
encounter the impossibility of their own method. Scientific writing—especially that which reports the collection of data—is by
definition an ephemeral thing, an open-ended groping toward a
truth that is not entirely in hand at any given moment. *The
Philosophical Transactions* record knowledge-in-process. So
does Swift's book. At least until Gulliver seeks a premature
closure in part 4 by leaping to a hypothesis that has not been
justified by the evidence he possesses to date. Although humanly
understandable, Gulliver's impetuosity leads him to the rash
equation of "Houyhnhnm" with "Perfection"—based on the
Houyhnhnm's own etymology and only a few months' experience with these intelligent beasts. But Gulliver's neat conclusion
is not Swift's. It seems to me that in allowing his character to
contradict the scientific paradigm inherent in the rest of the
book, Swift must have wanted us to remain more open-minded,
or open-minded longer, than Gulliver. It has been said before:
Gulliver's Travels raises fundamental questions but scarcely answers them. Like the reader of the *Transactions*, the reader of
Swift's book is given pieces of a larger argument and then left
pretty much on his or her own. As contemporary scientists knew
very well, the problem of identifying and verifying a "fact" was
difficult enough. Arriving at an acceptable hypothesis based on
those facts was even more problematic.

4

Roman Ingarden remarks that all assertions in a scientific work
are judgments, whereas a literary work contains no genuine
judgments. The scientific work asserts something about an unquestioned reality outside the text; its sentences are in this respect practically transparent and should not draw attention to
themselves. The literary work is different, for it refers to its own
built-up "realities" within the text; its sentences quite rightly
draw attention to themselves as depicters of these "realities."
Thus in reading a scientific work, aesthetic issues should be
ignored and ambiguity neither sought nor tolerated. "Just as the
literary work of art is not read as a work of information, and in

particular not as a scientific work," says Ingarden, "so the scientific work must not be treated as a work of art."[28]

But herein lies one of the delightful complexities of *Gulliver's Travels*. For Gulliver it is a scientific work, and thus its language functions as a means of referring to several different (and supposedly real) worlds outside itself. For Swift, however, the book is a work of fiction that aims to create its own realities apart from the actual world, although some of its textual referents have more than a textual existence, like Europe or England, London Bridge or Gresham College. Swift's literary work does not prevent us from being cognizant of Gulliver's scientific work, but ultimately it subsumes it, fictionalizing even its science. Scientific fact and literary truth debate each other on practically every page of *Gulliver's Travels*: and the generic doubleness of Swift's book—mimetic fiction overlaid on scientific discourse—is effective in getting his reader to consider some important questions regarding the assumptions of both genres, one that was relatively new to England, one that was only now emerging.

Gulliver's striptease before his Houyhnhnm master is a good illustration of such generic doubleness. The observer in these travels always verges on becoming the observed, but this scene is especially comical and poignant:

> My Master observed the whole Performance with great Signs of Curiosity and Admiration. He took up all my Cloaths in his Pastern, one Piece after another, and examined them diligently; he then stroaked my Body very gently, and looked round me several Times; after which he said, it was plain I must be a perfect *Yahoo*; but that I differed very much from the rest of my Species, in the Whiteness, and Smoothness of my Skin, my want of Hair in several Parts of my Body, the Shape and Shortness of my Claws behind and before, and my Affectation of walking continually on my two hinder Feet. He desired to see no more; and gave me leave to put on my Cloaths again, for I was shuddering with Cold. (p. 237)

Underscoring the ironic reversal of roles in this paragraph is Swift's use of the same scientific terminology he has employed elsewhere when Gulliver was in charge: "observed," "Performance," "Signs," "Curiosity," "examined," "diligently," "plain," and "perfect" are all words drawn from the scientific lexicon of the day. There are in the present situation a few ironies in the use of this vocabulary: while "curiosity" and "diligence" may be good qualities in a natural historian, when one is the *victim* of the age's thoroughgoing scientific inquisitiveness, things are not so funny; and while to be able to say that something is "plain" (the facts being clear) is likewise a positive state of affairs and while we may understand the master's epiphany ("a perfect *Yahoo*," says he), we may find it difficult to sympathize—for any discovery about Gulliver is also a discovery about ourselves. Focusing as it does on Gulliver's external, physical self, this passage shows us the master—truly the "master" here—dealing with Gulliver not as a fellow creature of this world but as a representative of a "Species"; the scientist, that is, anxious in the face of something new, is set on resolving the ambiguities of this strange creature, and his approach is to locate an intellectual category into which he can put Gulliver. In this exercise, appearances are everything. Gulliver's feelings—and even, rather surprisingly, his mental capacity—have no role in the process of identification.

The neutrality of diction in the paragraph is shattered only three times: once (potentially) in the reference to the master's stroking of Gulliver's body "gently," a word used positively throughout *Gulliver's Travels* and suggesting a certain sensitivity on the Houyhnhnm's part;[29] again in the master's comment on Gulliver's "Affectation" in walking on his hinder legs, a rather nasty sarcasm directed at Gulliver (and us) but also indicating a humorous ignorance of comparative anatomy; and finally, in that marvelous concluding image, which suddenly makes us aware of Gulliver not as an object of scientific curiosity but as a creature with his own feelings and sense of dignity. A being, we might say, not altogether unlike the Houyhnhnm master himself. There is of course no clear indication that the master recognizes Gulliver's discomfort; indeed that final clause—"for I was shuddering with Cold"—would seem to have been left intentionally ambivalent, suggesting either that the master orders Gulliver to put on his clothes because *he saw* he was shuddering or that Gulliver *was ready* to put on his clothes because he was shuddering. In any case, however, this paragraph, dominated by the language and supposed objectivity of modern science, is deliberately and effectively tinkered with, made more complex, more problematical. That is, ambiguity—precisely what science eschews—undermines and finally explodes the untroubled surface of scientific discourse. Royal Society travelers are expected to keep their distance, and to them all novelty is grist for the learned reading public back home. But Swift's unwillingness to remain within the genre of the travel book shows his impatience with such an approach; the style of fiction enables him to question the often unfeeling, narrow-minded, condescending practice of Baconian science.

Here and elsewhere Swift's prose resonates with mimetic and ironic alternatives that offer a powerful generic foil to the meticulous monodimensionality of the Royal Society travelogue. We are forced to confront the assumptions behind the two modes. We come to realize that scientific discourse aims at uneditorialized description and replicable apprehension of experience; ambiguity and opinion are to be kept out. Mimetic fiction, on the other hand, working by way of imagery, focuses on the uniqueness of experience and welcomes rhetorical ambiguity as one way of being honest to the complexity of real-life situations. Whereas Defoe conflated the two genres, denying the differences between them, Swift only pretends to integrate them, wanting us instead to remain sensitive to the wide differences between their approaches to their subjects. Who is Gulliver? There is simply no way that the methodology of empirical science can come to terms with this question; viewed as a specimen, as an exhibit on a slide, as a representative of a species, he is too easily stereotyped into a walking, talking category, not a man. On the contrary, the image of the shuddering Gulliver—an image like one that might be found in a novel—compels us to deal with the immediate presence of a single, sensate individual. Welcoming ambiguity and seeking not closure but a fuller understanding, fiction embodies an altogether different conception of truth. It is no coincidence that things that are not explained give Gulliver the most difficulty and the most pleasure: things like the petty jealousy of the Lilliputian minister, the unspoken feelings of Glumdaclitch, the Sorrel Nag's understated affection for his "gentle Yahoo." Nor is it surprising that Swift's most important truths exist somewhere outside Gulliver's persistent observation; *Gulliver's Travels* testifies to Swift's fascination with science, but ultimately it lays bare the limitations of contemporary science and heralds the old truths to be uncovered by the new genre of mimetic fiction.

Notes

1. "The Scientific Background of Swift's *Voyage to Laputa*," *Annals of Science* 2 (July 1937): 299–334. Rpt. in Marjorie Nicholson, *Science and the Imagination* (Hamden, Conn.: Archon Books, 1976), pp. 110–54.

2. R. C. Olson, "Swift's Use of the *Philosophical Transactions* in Section 5 of *A Tale of a Tub*," *Studies in Philology* 49 (1952): 460; George R. Potter, "Swift

and Natural Science," *Philological Quarterly* 20 (April 1941): 104–5. See also C. M. Webster, "Swift and the Royal Society's *Philosophical Transactions*," *Notes and Queries* 161 (8 August 1931): 99–100; Marjorie Nicolson and Nora M. Mohler, "Swift's 'Flying Island' in the *Voyage to Laputa*," *Annals of Science* 2 (October 1937): 405–30; Leeds Barroll, "Gulliver and the Struldbruggs," *PMLA* 73 (March 1958): 43–50; and Leland D. Peterson, "On the Keen Appetite for Perpetuity of Life," *English Language Notes* 1 (1964): 265–67. Connections made between the style of *Gulliver's Travels* and the plain style advocated by the Royal Society are too numerous to mention.

3. Dorothy Stimson, *Scientists and Amateurs: A History of the Royal Society* (New York: Henry Schuman, 1948), pp. 65–66, points out that in 1665 the *Transactions* barely missed being the oldest scientific journal of all, the *Journal des Savans* appearing only three months earlier.

4. On the membership of the Society, which included politicians, clergymen, and scholars in addition to "men of science," see A. Rupert Hall's introduction to Thomas Birch, *The History of the Royal Society of London* (New York: Johnson Reprint Corporation, 1968), pp. xix–xxx.

5. *The Theater of Insects: or, Lesser Living Creatures*, vol. 3 of *The History of Four-Footed Beasts and Serpents and Insects* (New York: Da Capo Press, 1967), p. 931.

6. *Micrographia* (New York: Dover Publications, 1961), pp. 183 and 185. Hooke was one of the founders of the Royal Society, and his book was published under its sponsorship.

7. *Gulliver's Travels*, in *The Prose Works of Jonathan Swift*, ed. Herbert Davis et al. (Oxford: Basil Blackwell, 1939–68), 11:109; subsequent references will be to this edition and will be included within the text. A more dramatic example of Gulliver's encounter with Hooke's world is the scene in which he is attacked by wasps.

8. Hooke, *Micrographia*, p. 213. Stimson, *Scientists and Amateurs*, p. 77, reports that Robert South is said to have said that "They [the virtuosi] can admire nothing but fleas, lice and themselves." Cf. Pope's *Essay on Man*, 1.195–96: "Say what the use, were finer optics giv'n,/ T' inspect a mite, not comprehend the heav'n?"

9. *From Locke to Saussure: Essays on the Study of Language and Intellectual History* (Minneapolis: University of Minnesota Press, 1982), p. 249. For an enthusiastic expression of this sense of wonder and curiosity closer to Swift's time, see *The Spectator*, no. 519 (25 October 1712).

10. *Micrographia*, [p. 15].

11. Thomas Sprat, *History of the Royal Society*, ed. Jackson I. Cope and Harold W. Jones (St. Louis: Washington University Press, 1958), p. 113. For a recent argument against the prevailing view that the tenets of the Royal Society had a major impact on the prose style of this period, see Brian Vickers, "The Royal Society and English Prose Style: A Reassessment," in *Rhetoric and the Pursuit of Truth: Language Change in the Seventeenth and Eighteenth Centuries* (Los Angeles: William Andrews Clark Memorial Library, 1985), pp. 1–76.

12. *Literature and Science* (New York: Harper and Row, 1963), pp. 12–13.

13. *Voyage to New Holland*, in *Dampier's Voyages*, ed. John Masefield, (London: E. Grant Richards, 1906), 2:342.

14. Willard H. Bonner, *Captain William Dampier: Buccaneer-Author* (Stanford: Stanford University Press, 1934), pp. 156–81; Scott's observation can be located most easily in *Swift: The Critical Heritage*, ed. Kathleen Williams (New

York: Barnes and Noble, 1970), p. 293. See also Arthur Sherbo, "Swift and Travel Literature," *Modern Language Studies* 9 (1979): 114–27; and Jenny Mezciems, " 'Tis not to divert the Reader': Moral and Literary Determinants in some Early Travel Narratives,": *Prose Studies* 6 (1982): 2–19.

15. No. 327, pp. 152–53. Subsequent references to the *Transactions* will be included within the text.

16. In fact at Leeuenhoek's death in 1723, he bequeathed twenty-six micro-scopes to the British scientists who had been so supportive of his work, and these were sent to London with many slides still in place. An account appear-ing at the end of the year in the *Transactions* reports that Leeuenhoek's own register of these exhibits mentioned "A crooked Hair, to which adheres a Ring-Worm, with a Piece of Cuticle," and also "A small Hair from the Hand, by which it appears these Hairs are not round" (no. 380 [1723]: 448).

17. "Science and the Mid-Eighteenth-Century Novel: Literature and the Lan-guage of Science," in *Literature and Science and Medicine* (Los Angeles: William Andrews Clark Memorial Library, 1982), p. 32.

18. Compare the following. Leeuenhoek describes the appearance of a human hair (seen through the microscope) in domestic terms: "The broadest part of it had six Flesh Particles, and in the middle of the six there lay part of a seventh Flesh Particle, and so made the likeness of a Weaver's Shuttle" (no. 315 [1708], p. 120). Gulliver describes the loadstone used on the Flying Island in comparable terms: "But the greatest Curiosity, upon which the Fate of the Island depends, is a Loadstone of a prodigious Size, in shape resembling a Weaver's Shuttle" (p. 168).

19. Recorded in Thomas Birch, *The History of the Royal Society of London for Improving of Natural Knowledge* (Hildesheim: Georg Olms Ver-lagsbuchhandlung, 1968), 1:202.

20. "Remarks on the Cognition of the Scientific Work," in *The Cognition of the Literary Work of Art* (Evanston, Ill.: Northwestern University Press, 1973), p. 147.

21. "The Myth of a Restoration Style Shift," *The Eighteenth Century* 20 (1979): 243. For an interesting discussion of the Royal Society's (not wholly consistent) view of hypothesis, see M. B. Hall, "Science in the Early Royal Society," in *The Emergence of Science in Western Europe*, ed. Maurice Crosland (London: Macmillan Press, 1975), pp. 57–77.

22. Recorded in Birch, *The History of the Royal Society*, 1:98.

23. In *Probability and Certainty in Seventeenth-Century England* (Princeton: Princeton University Press, 1983), pp. 3–14, Barbara Shapiro has similarly argued that members of the early Royal Society, despite their attacks on rhet-oric, were engaged in a project that was fundamentally rhetorical.

24. In 1699 there appeared in the *Transactions* an essay attempting to calcu-late algebraically the various degrees of credibility in human testimony: the relative veracity of a single reporter, of successive reporters who agree, and of both oral and written testimonials (no. 257, pp. 359–65).

25. Golinski, "Robert Boyle: scepticism and authority in seventeenth-century chemical discourse," in *The Figural and the Literal: Problems of Language in the History of Science and Philosophy, 1630–1800* (Manchester, England: Man-chester University Press, 1987), p. 68.

26. *Robinson Crusoe and Other Writings*, ed. James Sutherland (Boston: Houghton Mifflin, 1968), p. 303.

27. See Golinski, who cites various contemporary suspicions of Boyle's ex-

perimental narratives. Note also the way scientists writing into the Society on occasion, Scriblerus-like, even admit their quests for certainty have been fouled up in the process of publication: "I did not intend to publish this Memorial, till I had bestowed some further Consideration upon it, had not some learned Men of my Profession, and my honoured Friends, perswaded me to it" (no. 337 [1713] p. 143); "I have farther to add, that the Observation was publish'd entirely without my Knowledge about a Year after it had been read at a meeting of the *Royal Society*" (no. 350 [1716], p. 541).

28. Ingarden, "Remarks on the Cognition of the Scientific Work," p. 163.

29. Or perhaps his concern about damaging a rare specimen? See "gently," pp. 21, 31, 36, 46, 47, 65, 85, 88, 89, 93, 103, 107, 117 (twice), 122, 132, 159, 160 (twice), 205, 225, 237, 282 (twice), and 285. Cf. "gentle," pp. 72, 96, 241, 285, and 291, and "gentleness," p. 38.

Gulliver and the Origins of Science Fiction

Paul K. Alkon

Samuel Delany reports an incident that for him has a happy ending but that for readers of this volume may seem more like a horror story. A historian gradually stopped reading anything but science fiction in his spare time. Finally he began to doubt that he could ever again read anything else. Worried, he picked up an old favorite, *Pride and Prejudice,* to see what might happen. To his relief, he enjoyed it more than ever. But he saw it in a different way: whereas before he appreciated Austen for her masterful portraits of human nature acting as it might in the real world, now, as he read he asked himself what kind of world must be postulated in order for the events of her story to have happened as she relates them. The answer, somewhat to his surprise as an expert in early nineteenth-century history, was that for the tale of Elizabeth and Darcy to unfold as it does in *Pride and Prejudice* one must assume a world quite different from that in which Jane Austen actually lived. Delany does not spell out the differences noted by his friend between Austen's real and fictive worlds but simply draws an encouraging moral: that any kind of imaginative literature can be recuperated by reading it as though it were science fiction. Delany even suggests the possibility that doing so "may be the only hope for literature."[1] You may shudder.

Whether or not Delany is right in claiming so much, however, science fiction certainly makes possible a new way of reading many older works. I am skeptical about the advantages of this for Jane Austen's novels. Other writers offer more obviously rewarding candidates, some of which can even be transformed *into* science fiction without violence to authorial intentions and thereby acquire a place in our account of its origins. Thus Mary Shelley's *Frankenstein* is now widely acknowledged as the first instance of the form, although in calling it science fiction, as

163

Mark Rose observes, "we are retroactively recomposing that text under the influence of a generic idea that did not come into being until well after it was written." This procedure is in fact common in writing the history of many forms. It depends on "conceiving genre as a social phenomenon, as a set of expectations rather than as something that resides within a text."[2] Genre, so defined, is constituted by reading conventions that allow or compel attention to focus on a particular set of textual features that (if present) will accordingly seem most prominent. A complicated text may offer several options that are not always mutually exclusive, and it may therefore play some role in the history of many genres as, for example, Gulliver's Travels certainly does in the development of prose satire, the novel, the imaginary voyage, utopias, and science fiction. On this view of form as a function of reading conventions, moreover, Gulliver's role in the history of any one genre will also change as that genre evolves. Science fiction, arguably now the twentieth century's most significant as well as its most characteristic form, has of late evolved very rapidly indeed while serving as a vehicle for writers as excellent (and as diverse) as H. G. Wells, Aldous Huxley, George Orwell, Stanislaw Lem, Doris Lessing, Anthony Burgess, Joanna Russ, and Ursula K. Le Guin.

As one consequence of this accelerated evolution, for reasons that I want to outline here, there are now two very different ways of seeing Swift's relationship to the origins of science fiction: Gulliver's Travels may be relegated to a place among this form's distant precursors or else proposed as science fiction's very archetype. Accordingly, we now have yet another choice among interpretations of Gulliver and are confronted by one more Swiftian controversy: this time between partisans of what might be called the old wave and new wave schools of science fiction.[3] Both are alive and well, and adherents of both are strongly attracted to the Travels. The old wave school of reading Gulliver's Travels as no more than a remarkable forerunner of science fiction has for its champion Isaac Asimov. The new wave school of reading Gulliver is implicit in Delany's approach to science fiction (he does not discuss Swift) and explicit in Darko Suvin's compelling argument for taking Gulliver's adventures as an enduring archetype that sets the pattern for all science fiction. At stake in the choice between these schools is an ideology of response to science as well as consequences for critical theory and literary history.

1

There has long been agreement that *Gulliver* is somewhere among the honorable ancestors. In his now-classic 1955 essay, "The Pride of Lemuel Gulliver," for example, Samuel Holt Monk simply asserted, as a self-evident proposition requiring no further explanation, that *Gulliver's Travels* "is at once science fiction and a witty parody of science fiction."[4] When Kingsley Amis devoted his 1958 Christian Gauss seminar at Princeton to science fiction, he claimed *Gulliver's Travels* as "an ancestor of science fiction" on two grounds: because of "pains taken by Swift to counterfeit verisimilitude in the details of his story . . . to dispel that air of arbitrariness, of having no further aim than to be striking, which is characteristic of most fantasy"; and because "*Gulliver's Travels* . . . presents . . . a series of satirical utopias . . . chronicled with a great power of inventing details that are to be consistent with some basic assumption."[5] For Amis as for many others, science fiction is the genre of speculative tales plausibly grounded in some coherent assumption about variations in science or society and serving as a vehicle for social criticism. In a history of such tales the *Travels* will figure more prominently than Bacon's *New Atlantis*, Kepler's *Somnium*, Godwin's *Man in the Moone*, Cyrano's *L'Autre Monde*, or even More's *Utopia*.[6]

In the first book devoted to science fiction by an American university press (1970), Robert M. Philmus analyzed Swift's account of Lagado and Laputa to show that "although *Gulliver's Travels* is not science fiction, strictly defined, in . . . episodes like these a technique of presenting science as fiction can be perceived which anticipates the science fiction of later writers." Philmus makes the key point that, unlike previous satire on science in Shadwell's *Virtuoso* and the like, "Swift imaginatively transfigures scientific theory and experiment by describing the literal state of affairs they suggest." It is precisely "this literalizing of the abstract, which tends to enlarge metaphor into myth," Philmus notes, which is "a feature in the evolution of science fiction in the nineteenth century most prominent in writers like Samuel Butler and H. G. Wells, whose careful reading of Swift is apparent."[7] Thus by 1970 we have an established genealogy tracing textual affinities between *Gulliver's Travels* and science fiction. The main points of resemblance are the presence of explicit satire, speculative or utopian subject matter, and such stylistic features as techniques for establishing verisimilitude in nonrealistic tales and techniques for literalizing scientific abstractions to convert metaphor into myth.

In 1973 Brian Aldiss departed slightly from endorsement of that genealogy by stressing a major difference between the *Travels* and science fiction while nevertheless paying generous tribute to Swift: "It is fortunate that this masterly work does not count as science fiction, being satirical and/or moral in intention rather than speculative, for if it did so count, then perfection would have been achieved straightaway, and the genre possibly concluded as soon as it had begun." Aldiss, from the vantage point of a skillful writer of science fiction, here fastens in passing on the same feature of his genre that now attracts so much of Delany's attention: the priority of sheer speculative invention over explicit satire or moralizing. Of the *Travels*, however, Aldiss rightly adds that "the book comes clawing its way out of any category into which critics try to place it."[8] This protean quality is yet another reason why the recent evolution of science fiction has been able to provide a new way of reading the *Travels* without, however, displacing more conventional accounts such as that provided as recently as 1980 by Isaac Asimov.

At the beginning of this decade Asimov published a handsome, lavishly illustrated quarto volume entitled *The Annotated Gulliver's Travels*.[9] For many purposes this is an excellent reading edition. The text is based on Faulkner's Dublin edition. The pictures are well chosen from a wide range of Swift's illustrators over the centuries. Asimov's commentary, as we might expect, is intelligent, interesting, informative, and laced with judicious criticism. But for Asimov, who forged his standards under the tutelage of John Campbell during the heyday of *Astounding Science Fiction* in the genre's "golden age" of the 1930s and 40s, *Gulliver's Travels* is only intermittently science fiction. Thus of the flying island of Laputa, Asimov remarks:

> Others had invented fanciful flying cities before this, but Jonathan Swift was the first to attempt an explanation of its workings in line with the findings of contemporary science. This section of the book is therefore true science fiction, perhaps the earliest example we have of it. To include earlier works as science fiction involves broadening the definition of the genre to include works not strictly based on a scientific background, and thus little more than adventure fantasy— like, for instance, the first two parts of *Gulliver's Travels*. (p. 144)

Asimov singles out Gulliver's "Philosophical Account" of the flying island at the start of book 3, chapter 3 in particular as "excellent science fiction in the modern sense" (p. 154). Asimov also praises Swift's episode of the Struldbruggs for dealing as well as any subsequent science fiction with the theme of immortality, and for being the first realistic attempt to do so (p. 197). In relationship to the discovery of Deimos and Phobos in 1877, Asimov discusses Swift's mention of "two lesser Stars, or Satellites, which revolve about Mars," discounting this as prediction but accepting it as a nice fictional use of Kepler's speculation that Mars must have two moons (p. 158). Asimov does not quite limit science fiction to what C. S. Lewis called engineering fiction— the kind of writing, now usually termed "hard" science fiction, that confines itself to application of known science or technology.[10] But Asimov's commentary on Gulliver does keep to a strict construction of the genre that gives its affinities with science priority over its qualities as fiction.

This is no doubt partly because of Asimov's lingering "old wave," pre-Hiroshima optimism about science as an agent of progress. For him, as for so many writers of the golden age, one of science fiction's primary goals as a didactic genre is to encourage support for science in order to bring about a better future. This view of the form, however hard to maintain now, retains a certain nobility and nostalgic appeal perhaps tinged with comedy or pathos—depending on one's politics, temperament, and sense of the future. Certainly on this view of science fiction's main social role there is as much political urgency to the question of how the genre is defined as there is for any Marxist critic.

To those who believe with Asimov in the importance of devising a fictional rhetoric that will persuade readers to endorse science as an agent of progress, literature that is only adventure fantasy—like the first two books of Gulliver as Asimov reads them—may be delightful but will nevertheless remain marginal to the truly important concerns of our day. At stake in defining science fiction narrowly or broadly is thus the question of whether we accept as the twentieth century's most pressing issue the relationship of science and society, or whether other matters, especially the organization of social relationships, are given equal or greater priority on our agenda for political action. Hence too Asimov's preference for using science fiction as a means of advocating, not attacking, science. The Grand Academy of Lagado provokes Asimov to several spirited defenses of theoretical science and to a blunt statement that he is "completely out of sympathy with Swift's satire on science" (p. 147).

Asimov, however, superb storyteller that he is, knows better than most the dangers of being absolutely restrictive about any kind of writing. He hedges somewhat in applying his criterion that science fiction must keep "in line with the findings of contemporary science." In practice the line may be overstepped a bit so long as it remains in sight: "Swift's Mechanism to keep Laputa aloft and in motion wouldn't really work, but I suppose that's no surprise to anyone. The explanation sounds scientific and impressive and that's all that counts" (p. 157). So too, of the ointment the Lilliputians give Gulliver to ease the sting of their arrows, Asimov comments: "It is part of the stock in trade of the science fiction writer to allow strange peoples convenient advances in science when it helps smooth the progress of the plot" (p. 13). Thus for Asimov the requirements of scientific accuracy may sometimes give way to the purely artistic demands of story, although not at the expense of maintaining at least an air of scientific verisimilitude if the work is to count as science fiction. Of the other requirements of this genre in relation to *Gulliver's Travels* Asimov says nothing. The rest of his commentary provides shrewd interpretation along with much information about historical and factual matters that may require explanation for most twentieth-century readers. Throughout these parts of his commentary, as in his explicit observations about *Gulliver* as science fiction, Asimov's eye is for the most part firmly fixed on the content of Swift's work in relationship to our world as it was in the eighteenth century and as in its physical dimension, according to current science, it still is.

2

The method of reading induced by science fiction, according to Delany, is distinctive by virtue of the degree to which it focuses attention upon disparities between our universe—of daily life or of ordinary discourse—and that evoked by a narrative: "In science fiction the world of the story is not a given, but rather a construct that changes from story to story. . . . With each sentence we have to ask what in the world of the tale would have to be different from our world for such a sentence to be uttered— and thus, as the sentences build up, we build up a world in specific dialogue, in a specific tension, with our present concept of the real."[11] Take the sentence from Robert A. Heinlein's *Beyond This Horizon* that has become for Delany and others a convenient example of the genre in action: "The door dilated." To read this properly we must understand that doors in our world do *not* dilate. We must also try to grasp the implications—visual, scientific, technological, and social—of a world where doors in fact open by dilation. We should think too about the significance of such differences between the imagined world and our own.

In isolation from its context that particular difference is of course trivial. How doors open seldom matters so long as they do. But the brief shock of nonrecognition created by Heinlein's verb is nevertheless characteristic of effects that may become important. Think of the golden chamber pots in More's *Utopia*. Think of the readjustment from perhaps comfortably imagining a mildly annoying insect to imagining—what?—that takes place when readers arrive at the last three clauses of a sentence that Delany might well have used as another nice example: "In a little time I felt something alive moving on my left Leg, which advancing gently forward over my Breast, came almost up to my Chin; when bending my eyes downwards as much as I could, I perceived it to be a human Creature not six Inches high, with a bow and Arrow in his Hands, and a Quiver at his Back."[12] By some one striking change from what we are accustomed to, or even by aggregation of small individually insignificant details that differ from those familiar to the reader, there may be created the impression of an utterly strange place, time, or action. Part of the game for readers of science fiction is to infer—often from minor and sometimes apparently contradictory details slipped in without further explanation—the principles, whether of physical law, technological practices, or social custom, that govern an imagined world.

Putting together a coherent picture of a different world, or at least trying to do so, from a narrative jigsaw puzzle of bizarre details is a great part, though only part, of the distinctive pleasure created by much well-written science fiction. It is also surely one of the reader's keenest pleasures in the context of such a sentence as this, which Delany might also have cited: "While He and I were thus employed, another Horse came up; who applying himself to the first in a very formal Manner, they gently struck each others Right Hoof before, neighing several times by Turns, and varying the Sound, which seemed to be almost articulate" (p. 225). Sometimes, to be sure, an author may provide explanations that make it easy enough to put together a coherent picture of the strange place, or even too easy, as in science fiction modeled on static utopias like More's that embed almost every detail, right down to the chamber pots, in a web of sociological analysis accounting for those details in a way that leaves very little work for the reader's imagination. In the best recent science fiction, however, there is most often a mystery to be solved. By omission or *postponement* of any explicit accounting for the unusual, readers are forced to keep asking what must be the governing rules, whether social or physical, that explain strange objects or behavior described in the text.

Answers may be disconcerting, as when encountering this sentence from Thomas M. Disch's *Angouleme*: "Papa, the executive, remarried, a man this time and somewhat more happily."[13] Such a sentence may call for a reconsideration of the reader's values hardly less radical than the reassesment called for by this sentence from a much stranger story in which the only human character among a frightening group of aliens is told by his host: "I cannot but conclude the Bulk of your Natives, to be the most pernicious Race of little odious Vermin that Nature ever suffered to crawl upon the Surface of the Earth" (p. 132). Or, to take another of Delany's favorite examples, the text may demand specialized scientific knowledge for appreciation of its departures from current realities, as in a phrase mentioning "the monopole magnet-mining operations in the outer asteroid belt of Delta Cygni." To understand what is going on here one must recall, to begin with, that all known magnets are dipolar and that our solar system has only one asteroid belt. While this may sound more like the right stuff of science fiction than allusions to a world in which Papa's second marriage is to a man, it is the presentation of difference, whether social or scientific, that for Delany distinguishes the genre.[14]

This science fictional procedure can also be described as the substitution of a novel lexical field for the currently accepted one with its network of conventional relationships between signifiers and signified.[15] Consider how Swift makes such terms as *rational animal, man, beast,* and *vermin* aquire new and disturbing meanings for readers of the fourth voyage. About the imaginary world with its unconventional web of meanings thus constructed to account for such narrative details as dilating doors, homosexual marriages, monopole magnet-mining—or virtuous talking horses devoid of emotion who live in a land plagued with bestial humanoids—there will arise questions concerning value and significance. There will be induced in readers both heightened awareness of physical or social arrangements in our world that we ordinarily take for granted and a questioning of those arrangements. The moral advantage of science fiction is that without necessarily—or at its best, ever—devolving into mere preachment, science fiction is inevitably didactic. It always teaches—sometimes more and sometimes less important lessons, to be sure, depending upon the writer's skill. But it always teaches because *simply in order to be understood* it forces interrogation of things as they are in the light of things as they might conceivably be, whether for better or worse. Readers must apprehend their own world more fully, and they are invited to question its arrangements.

By defining science fiction in terms of reading conventions, which it characteristically enforces, Delany sacrifices some precision of definition in terms of subject matter. But he also escapes several embarrassments. There is no need to quibble over the exact borderline between science fiction and such related forms as fantasy, allegory, imaginary voyage, or utopia. In particular cases, each may to greater or lesser extent attain the effects most typical of science fiction, just as each of these forms, including science fiction, may also serve the purposes of satire. Any individual work may to a significant degree exemplify several genres at once. Implied here, by noteworthy coincidence, is the same kind of heuristic model postulating genres as "permeable" to each other that Raymond Trousson found indispensable for accurately writing the literary history of utopia.[16] This flexible approach to generic classification applies especially well to those new wave science fiction authors of the 1960s and afterwards, including Delany very notably, who have made a point of combining techniques from hitherto entirely separate kinds of writing.

From this perspective even the extent to which a story depends upon imaginary or real scientific concepts—whether used speculatively for purposes of extrapolation and prediction, or satirically—recedes to the status of a relevant but secondary consideration. What matters is evocation of significant differences between imagined and actual worlds—differences that invite reconsideration of our reality. *Frankenstein* may thus be accepted as science fiction without questioning very closely the actual science postulated by Mary Shelley to account for the monster. So may such diverse recent classics as Walter E. Miller's *A Canticle for Liebowitz*, which so prominently features the fantasy-figure of the Wandering Jew; Phillip K. Dick's *The Man in*

the *High Castle*, whose alternate reality of a world in which
America lost World War II is never accounted for by any scientific
explanation; and Delany's own *Einstein Intersection*, with its
aliens who in the far future take over our now-deserted planet
only to find themselves condemned for mysterious reasons to
relive such human myths as the legend of Orpheus and Eurydice.

Equally acceptable as science fiction from this perspective is
Gulliver's Travels. To appreciate the implications of thus regarding the entire *Travels* as science fiction, however, it is necessary
to be more precise about the consequences for readers of what
Delany calls science fiction's ability to instigate, by its very mode
of narration, "a world in specific dialogue . . . with our present
concept of the real." Every form of fantasy, allegory, utopia, and
satire, after all, is in some kind of dialogue with our notions of
reality. To specify essential differences between these forms and
science fiction—with which they may coexist in the same
work—Darko Suvin has argued persuasively for taking science
fiction as the literature of cognitive estrangement. Suvin derives
his idea of estrangement from the Russian Formalist concept of
"ostranenie" elaborated in Bertolt Brecht's definition of what he
called the *Verfremdungseffekt*: any mode of representation
"which allows us to recognize its subject, but at the same time
makes it seem unfamiliar."[17] Cognition is involved whenever the
defamiliarized subject is then understood on a more rational
basis as a contingent phenomenon whose conditions, if known,
may be subject to control or even alteration rather than simply
unquestioning acceptance. Brecht's example is Galileo's ability to
look at the swinging chandelier—not taking it for granted but
looking at it with sufficient detachment to see its movement as
strange enough to require an explanation, which he then provided in stating the laws governing pendulum motion.
Awareness of these laws, in turn, allows a measure of control
over such motion and application of it to new purposes. With
this example in mind, Suvin concludes that science fiction is "*a
literary genre whose necessary and sufficient conditions are the
presence and interaction of estrangement and cognition, and
whose main formal device is an imaginative framework alternative to the author's empirical environment.*"[18]

By stressing cognition in the Brechtian sense as a necessary
corollary of narrative devices of estrangement in science fiction,
Suvin discriminates between it and such forms as myth, folk tale,
and fantasy that do not so insistently call into question our sense

of the world as it is and therefore do not direct toward present reality that fictional "cognitive critique" whose "kinship . . . with the philosophical fundaments of modern science is evident." On this view, moreover, science fiction is not limited "to scientific vulgarization or even technological prognostication."[19] For Suvin as for Delany, examples of the genre do not have to be about science. Nor must they even necessarily resort to scientific or quasi-scientific explanation of their action ("take her to warp speed, Mr. Spock") in order to count. Another advantage of Suvin's view, which is no less latitudinarian that Delany's but carried a few steps further, is that a hierarchy of generic properties is established. Allegory, fantasy, utopia, satire—and even moments of realistic narrative confined to representation of the world we know—may be identifiable features within a work of science fiction. But they will be subordinated to cognitive estrangement if the work is to count as science fiction. That is to say that such elements will contribute significantly to effects of cognitive estrangement while also, perhaps, serving a variety of more conventional purposes. Conversely, patches of science fiction may be identifiable within works taking as a whole some other form, such as satire.[20]

   In the established genealogy of science fiction's ancestors that I have outlined above and that culminates in Asimov's annotated edition, *Gulliver's Travels* takes its conventional place as a satire with only enough patches of science fiction—most notably in the third voyage—to rank among science fiction's notable precursors. Considered in the light of those reading conventions as well as effects of reading enforced so strongly by recent, especially new wave, science fiction, and analyzed so well by Delany and Suvin, among others, *Gulliver's Travels* becomes far more important. Thus after discussing it for several pages, Suvin eloquently states the case for its primacy:

> By this utopian outrage, in his imaginary voyages and marvelous islands, Swift created the great model for all subsequent SF. It is a wise interweaving of utopias taking on anti-utopian functions and anti-utopias as allies of utopianism; of satire using scientific language and technological extrapolation as a grotesque; of adventures in SF countries, artificial satellites and aliens, immortals and monsters, all signifying England and the gentle reader. All the later protagonists of SF, gradually piecing together their strange locales, are sons of Gulliver, and all their more or less cognitive adventures the continuation of his *Travels*.[21]

By presenting the *Travels* as a model for all subsequent science fiction, Suvin does not really argue that it had a greater causal role than has been acknowledged in previous accounts of how the genre came into existence. Rather, he suggests that we look to *Gulliver's Travels* as the prime example of what science fiction ought to do for its readers and of what in ideal cases it does do.

Patrick Parrinder is right to say that "Suvin's is not so much a descriptive theory of science fiction . . . as a highly normative one which asserts that SF has the presentation of a 'distancing' vision, leading to social criticism, as its essential (but usually unfulfilled) promise or purpose."[22] The same might be said of Delany; his account of how the genre focuses attention on differences between real and imagined worlds, or on differences between accepted and unconventional lexical fields, does not apply equally to all science fictions. It singles out the most valuable. Other definitions are possible, but not, I believe, if one wants to characterize the genre at its best. For this purpose I am happy to accept Suvin's proposal of *Gulliver's Travels* as the touchstone. If everyone did so, science fiction would doubtless be much improved. In that as in so many things, the eighteenth century is exemplary. More to the point of this volume, however, are the consequences for reading *Gulliver's Travels* itself.

3

What I have for convenience called the old wave view of science fiction is concerned primarily with how it holds a mirror up to present or possible future reality, whether social or scientific, and with each author's explicit rhetorical purposes for doing so. Genre is defined narrowly in terms of subject matter in relationship to scientific concepts. The boundary between science fiction and other genres is clear. From this perspective the voyages to Lilliput and Brobdingnag are adventure-fantasy, no matter how much they may be inspired by the microscope and telescope. Gulliver's third voyage is science fiction, but only while he is on the Flying Island, in Lagado, and among the Struldbruggs. The fourth voyage is a variety of utopia. *Gulliver's Travels* as a whole lacks generic unity but is no worse for that. Insofar as it is science fiction it is deplorable for the very cleverness of its attack on science, but no more deplorable than any other kind of antiscientific rhetoric. Swift gets credit for being the first English writer of true science fiction but is reprehensible for his hostility to science and his lack of faith in the idea of progress. Partly on account of taking these negative attitudes as a rhetorical stance, the third voyage, despite its virtues as pioneering science fiction, seems the weakest.[23] Swift remains the foremost English satirist, but *Gulliver's Travel* is relegated to the remote past of science fiction.

For new wave theorists of science fiction Swift is our contemporary. The *Travels* is our great model. The eighteenth century is in dialogic relationship to the twentieth century. All the heroes of science fiction are more or less striking analogues of Lemuel Gulliver. The genre is defined in terms of how it affects the reader's perception of reality, and any technique or subject matter that can bring about cognitive estrangement is legitimate. There are fluid, not rigid boundaries between other genres and science fiction. It may as properly be used to attack as to defend science. *Gulliver's Travels* becomes a unified work with all of its components—imaginary voyage, utopia, antiutopia, fantasy, and satire—subordinated as parts of a coherent whole, because amid their other purposes they all help sustain cognitive estrangement. Other effects may predominate locally. But the *Travels* moves through varying degrees of strangeness and corresponding arousal of cognitive estrangement to an appropriate climax (not simply to a conundrum for critics) in the fourth part. Gulliver's last voyage, rather than part 3, becomes the most powerful science fiction in the *Travels* because, of all the creatures Gulliver encounters, the Houyhnhynms are the most genuinely alien— the most shockingly different.

Neither in their shape, their mentality, nor their social forms do they recall humans, that is to say, our world—as do the Lilliputians, Brobdingnagians, and even the mad scientists of Laputa and Lagado. The Houyhnhynms are truly *other*. Their appearance, their well-ordered society, their honesty, and above all, of course, their very ability to love or hate as we do drives Gulliver mad—and too often drives critics the same direction by their endless dispute over Swift's intentions. When the *Travels* are seen in the light of recent science fiction, however, there is no need to enter that hopeless debate. Rather than asking the unanswerable question of whether Swift intended readers to accept the Houyhnhynms as Gulliver does for a model in all things, we may take the evident difficulty of doing so as a measure of Swift's success in making readers look at humanity from a radically estranged perspective; that perspective forces any thinking person to assess the springs of human behavior instead of just taking note of the myriad forms of human folly satirized en route to Gulliver's final lodging in the stable. Heightened awareness, by means of contrast with the Houyhnhynms, of what we are rather than the pinpointing of an explicit proposal from Swift (via their nature or some combination of theirs and ours) of what to do about it, can be taken as a satisfactory outcome of reading the Travels. There have certainly been other critical routes to this conclusion. I do not propose it as an exclusive advantage of taking Gulliver's Travels as science fiction. But I suggest that by doing so we can nicely specify not merely the targets of its satire but the effects of its satire upon readers. We can also define its social role in relationship to its aesthetic virtues, which are in fact also the virtues of our best science fiction.

Notes

1. Samuel R. Delany, "Science Fiction and 'Literature' or, The Conscience of the King," Analog 99, no. 5 (May 1979): 59–78; rpt. in Samuel R. Delany, Starboard Wine: More Notes on the Language of Science Fiction (Pleasantville, N.Y.: Dragon Press, 1984), pp. 81–100. Delany's other books of criticism are The Jewel-Hinged Jaw (Elizabethtown, N.Y.: Dragon Press, 1977); and The American Shore: Meditations on a Tale of Science Fiction by Thomas M. Disch—"Angouleme" (Elizabethtown, N.Y.: Dragon Press, 1978). Delany's fiction includes The Jewels of Aptor, The Fall of the Towers, The Ballad of Beta 2, Babel-17, Empire Star, The Einstein Intersection, Nova, Driftglass, Dhalgren, Triton, and Stars in My Pocket like Grains of Sand. If you wish to sample his fiction, I suggest starting with The Einstein Intersection and Babel-17.

2. Mark Rose, Alien Encounters: Anatomy of Science Fiction (Cambridge: Harvard University Press, 1981), p. 5.

3. For the accepted usage of this terminology, see the article "New Wave" in Peter Nicholls, ed., The Science Fiction Encyclopedia (Garden City, N.Y.: Doubleday, 1979).

4. Samuel Holt Monk, "The Pride of Lemuel Gulliver," The Sewanee Review 63 (1955): 48.

5. Kingsley Amis, "Starting Points," in Mark Rose, ed., Science Fiction: A Collection of Critical Essays (Englewood Cliffs, N.J.: Prentice-Hall, 1976), p. 21. The discussion is taken from the published version of the Gauss seminar at Princeton: Kingsley Amis, New Maps of Hell: A Survey of Science Fiction (New York: Harcourt, Brace, 1960).

6. For example, in Neil Barron, ed., Anatomy of Wonder: A Critical Guide to Science Fiction, 2d ed. (New York: R. R. Bowker, 1981), p. 80, the entry for Gulliver's Travels concludes: "Of its seventeenth- and eighteenth-century contemporaries, Gulliver's Travels probably remains the most important to contemporary science fiction from Wells onward because of the bitterly critical tone it takes toward humanity."

7. Robert M. Philmus, *Into The Unknown: The Evolution of Science Fiction From Francis Godwin to H. G. Wells* (1970; rpt. Berkeley: University of California Press, 1983), p. 12.

8. Brian W. Aldiss, *Billion Year Spree: The True History of Science Fiction* (Garden City, N.Y.: Doubleday, 1973; rpt. New York: Schocken Books, 1975), p. 72. If you wish to sample science fiction by Aldiss, I suggest starting with his *Frankenstein Unbound* if you are lucky enough to obtain a copy.

9. Jonathan Swift, *The Annotated Gulliver's Travels*, ed. Isaac Asimov (New York: Clarkson N. Potter, 1980). Subsequent citations of Asimov's commentary in this edition will appear in my text.

10. C. S. Lewis, "On Science Fiction," in *Of Other Worlds: Essays and Stories*, ed. Walter Hooper (London: Geoffrey Bles, 1966), pp. 59–73. See the article "Hardcore SF" in Nicholls, *The Science Fiction Encyclopedia*. See also Peter Nicholls, ed., *The Science in Science Fiction* (New York: Alfred A. Knopf, 1983).

11. Delany, *Starboard Wine*, p. 89.

12. *Gulliver's Travels*, in *The Prose Works of Jonathan Swift*, ed. Herbert Davis et al. (Oxford: Basil Blackwell, 1939–68), 11:21–22. Subsequent references to *Gulliver's Travels* will appear within the text.

13. For the context of the sentence from "Angouleme" see Thomas R. Disch, "Angouleme," in *Fundamental Disch* (New York: Bantam Books, 1980), pp. 207–23; the sentence is on pp. 207–8. "Angouleme" first appeared in *New Worlds* 1 (1971).

14. For a more detailed account of the examples from twentieth-century science fiction mentioned in this paragraph, and of related issues, see Delany's "Science Fiction and 'Literature' " and the other essays in *Starboard Wine*, esp. "Some Presumptuous Approaches to Science Fiction," pp. 46–55, and "Dichtung und Science Fiction," pp. 165–96.

15. See Delany's *The American Shore* for an extensive analysis of such lexical shifts in one story.

16. Raymond Trousson, *Voyages aux pays de nulle part: histoire littéraire de la pensée utopique*, 2d ed. (Brussels: Éditions de l'Université de Bruxelles, 1979), p. xxvii.

17. Bertolt Brecht, "Kleines Organon für das Theater," in his *Gesammelte Werke* 16 (1973), trans. in John Willett, ed., *Brecht On Theatre* (New York: Hill and Wang, 1964); cited in Darko Suvin, *Metamorphoses of Science Fiction: On the Poetics and History of a Literary Genre* (New Haven: Yale University Press, 1979), p. 6.

18. Suvin, *Metamorphoses*, p. 8.

19. Suvin, *Metamorphoses*, pp. 9–10.

20. In fairness I should remark that perhaps neither Suvin nor Delany would thank me for stressing what I take as a convergence of their views. Delany doubts the utility of applying concepts such as cognitive estrangement to science fiction. He also objects to those who would describe early works like *Frankenstein* according to the reading conventions that *must* be applied to make sense of recent science fiction: see especially *Starboard Wine*, pp. 173–74 and 186–92, as well as the discussion of "generic history" and "originary assumptions" in *The American Shore*, pp. 231–43. I believe it is nevertheless true, if only a partial and partially misleading truth, that Suvin's approach both resembles and logically extends that of Delany. For my present purposes the resemblances are most important. Anyone who goes for the first time to Suvin

and Delany from this essay will soon enough appreciate the contexts in which their differences must also be taken into account.

21. Suvin, *Metamorphoses*, p. 113.

22. Patrick Parrinder, *Science Fiction: Its Criticism and Teaching* (New York: Methuen, 1980), p. 74.

23. See Asimov, *The Annotated Gulliver's Travels*, p. xix.

Gulliver's Account of Houyhnhnmland as a Philosophical Treatise

William Bowman Piper

Jonathan Swift's *Travels into Several Remote Nations of the World* is not, as Philip Pinkus has warned us, a philosophical treatise, although its putative author, Lemuel Gulliver, once calls it one.[1] Gulliver, who adheres to no categorical literary design beyond that of always telling the truth, also describes his composition here and there with such common terms as "book," "story," history," "work," and "volume." Different parts of his travels Gulliver labels variously "description," "passage," "relation," "adventure," "extract," "discourse," "representation," "account," and "digression." Certain of these terms, notably "description," "account," and "discourse," all of which occur many times, have a close affinity with *treatise*.

Gulliver often acknowledges, moreover, the proximity to a treatise, that is, to a discussion having abstract philosophical value, of those descriptive and discursive passages in his work by which he especially hopes "to inform and instruct Mankind."[2] "Although I intend to leave a Description of this [Lilliputian] Empire to a particular Treatise," he once asserts, he is "content . . . in the mean time . . . to gratify the curious Reader with some general Ideas"; and he goes on immediately to do so for the next several pages (p. 57). Gulliver likewise interrupts himself on another occasion: "But I shall not anticipate the Reader with farther Descriptions of this Kind, because I reserve them for a greater Work, which is now almost ready for the Press; containing a general Description of this Empire . . ." (p. 47). As "farther Descriptions of this Kind" suggests, Gulliver has just been writing in the treatise vein. This kind of generic overlap between the *Travels* and a treatise proper, which occurs throughout the book, is also acknowledged in part 4: "I could with great Pleasure enlarge further upon the Manners and Virtues of this excellent People; but intending in a short time to publish a Volume by itself expressly upon that Subject, I refer the Reader thither" (p. 275). This statement interrupts a passage of several pages, spanning a chapter break, devoted to an abstract, general exposition of Houyhnhnm ways, an exposition that was formally introduced: "Having already lived three Years in this Country, the Reader I suppose will expect, that I should, like other Travellers, give him some Account of the Manners and Customs of its Inhabitants" (p. 267). As Irvin Ehrenpreis has remarked, part 4, "A Voyage to the Country of the Houyhnhnms," has much more such discursive, philosophical matter than any of the earlier three parts of the Travels.[3]

Swift's own awareness of the closeness between the Travels and a philosophical treatise was as strong as these practices of Gulliver suggest that it would have been. When Thomas Tickell wrote Swift a letter asking to see the manuscript a few months before the work was to be published, he described it as "an Account of imaginary Travels." Swift, in putting Tickell off, echoed his description with the phrase "an imaginary Treatise," allowing the word "Treatise," partly perhaps because of alliteration, to force its way into the generic formula.[4] Swift's insistence in his letter to L'Abbé des Fontaines, however, that the Travels "draws its merit . . . from a series of observations on the imperfections, the follies, and vices of man"—by which he means, as he makes clear, man in general, justifies this substitution of treatise for travels.[5]

The term "treatise" also occurs in Swift's letter of September 1725 to Alexander Pope. He reports in this letter that he has just finished preparing the Travels for the press and insists, contrary to a good-humored suggestion his friend made in a previous letter, that all his labors are calculated "to vex the world rather than divert it." Then after the famous passage on hating mankind and all human activities in general and loving only particular people such as "John, Peter, Thomas and so forth," he writes: "I have got Materials Towards a Treatise proving the falsity of that Definition of man as animal rationale; to show it should be only rationis capax." That the Travels itself constitutes "Materials Towards a Treatise" on such an abstract philosophical subject it would be rash to insist. But Swift goes right on in this letter to assert: "Upon this great foundation of Misanthropy (though not in Timons manner) the whole building of my Travells is erected."[6] In spite of Swift's normal skepticism toward philosophical speculation on such abstract, general topics, we may nevertheless infer from this letter to Pope that he viewed the *Travels*, somewhat like Gulliver, as a preliminary account, the elements of which have, at least potentially, an abstract philosophic import such as a treatise would openly develop.[7] Or we may infer, rather, that this work is not a preliminary study for an argument that man is only *rationis capax* but the literary consequence of this general point's firmly established certainty. In either case, the *Travels* stands shoulder-to-shoulder with a philosophical treatise that Swift, of course, never composed.

1

Critics have shown that part 4, to which I am chiefly devoted in this essay, is more philosophical, more of a treatise, than any other part of the book. David Leigh finds in this voyage an intensification of Swift's "lifelong debate with various types of rationalists"; Louis Landa has descried in it a "rejection of a basic assumption of the [materialistic] mercantile philosophy"; and J. M. Treadwell argues that in being confronted by the Houyhnhnms, Gulliver becomes "converted into a . . . projector with a program for the reform of the world."[8] Each of these arguments has considerable substance, isolating within part 4 a serious strain of general, abstract significance. Claude Rawson has also acknowledged the strongly philosophical flavor of this voyage, describing in the Houyhnhnm landscape, as distinguishable from the shiftier scenes preceding it, "a stark world of moral absolutes."[9] Although he emphasizes Swift's characteristic "indirection" of style and insists that Swift denies the reader of the *Travels* "the solace of definite categories" (and thus the definitive rigor a philosophical treatise should have), Rawson asserts that the category *Houyhnhnm* constitutes "a statement of what man is not." He finds in the exposition of this equine figure "an insulting exercise in 'logical' refutation."[10] The philosophic force of part 4 Ehrenpreis has enunciated with still greater severity: Swift, Ehrenpreis insists, "remorselessly spells out" the significant parallels between his fabulous figures and humanity; he argues further that Swift "denies the reader the pleasure of interpreting the parallels for himself," not daring in this case to "risk being misunderstood." In part 4, Ehrenpreis says, quite in harmony with Rawson, Swift has practiced "a bleak uniformity of style."[11] By pursuing stylistic qualities described by these two excellent critics, I believe I shall be able to oppose, or at least to modify, the solemnity and the univocal tendency of their judgments.

I recognize the serious moral significance of any identification between Yahoo and Human and of any discrimination between Houyhnhnm and Human. But a satire, like a philosophical treatise, may have moral seriousness; and Swift's *Travels*, as everyone recognizes, is pervasively satiric. Being a satire, however, it cannot be expected to give us, as a treatise would no doubt do, an abstract, general definition of Houyhnhnm or Yahoo or a definition of Human. Swift, who had the same contempt as his friend, George Berkeley, for abstractions and transcendentals, has presented in the Houhynhnms and Yahoos tangles of particular observations that cannot simply be reduced, as Rawson recognized, to rigid categories of Houyhnhnm and Yahoo: both the figures and the terms are volatile; and so, of course, is the authorial apprehension of Gulliver.[12] Swift's traveler, however, did entertain universal ambitions, and he often drew abstract parallels, especially between Yahoo and Human. I shall begin therefore with the abstract philosophical formulae that a scholarly Gulliver, not Swift, might finally have established in a treatise of *his*, hoping by this means to clarify the elusive satiric formulae of Gulliver's creator.

In concluding the introduction of his great *Treatise Concerning the Principles of Human Knowledge*, Berkeley provided an excellent view of a philosophical treatise in general:

> Unless we take care to clear the First Principles of Knowledge from the embarras and delusion of words, we may make infinite reasonings upon them to no purpose; we may draw consequences from consequences, and be never the wiser. The farther we go, we shall only lose ourselves the more irrecoverably, and be the deeper entangled in difficulties and mistakes. Whoever therefore designs to read the following sheets, I entreat him to make my words the occasion of his own thinking, and endeavor to attain the same train of thoughts in reading that I had in writing them. By this means it will be easy for him to discover the truth or falsity of what I say. He will be out of all danger of being deceived by my words, and I do not see how he can be led into an error by considering his own naked, undisguised ideas.[13]

The dedication of a treatise to general questions of "truth or falsity," a concern we have just recognized in "A Voyage to the Country of the Houyhnhnms"; its reliance on a rigorous control of the basic terms, the "First Principles of Knowledge"; its demand of an analytical enlargement of "the naked, undisguised ideas" by which the author would justify his understanding of these terms; and its focus on the mind and the judgment of its reader: all these points, which are evident in Berkeley's peroration, indicate the course I must take in considering part 4 of the *Travels* as a treatise.

I start by clearing the general terms *Human*, *Yahoo*, and *Houyhnhnm*, "from the embarras and delusion of words."

I. Human: a creature
   A. Of anthropoid physique
   B. Of sufficient intellect
      1. To employ a language
      2. To organize a society
      3. To use tools for physical convenience;
II. Yahoo: a creature
   A. Of anthropoid physique
   B. Of insufficient intellect
      1. To employ a language
      2. To organize a society
      3. To use tools;
III. Houyhnhnm: a creature
   A. Of equine physique
   B. Of sufficient intellect
      1. To employ a language
      2. To organize a society
      3. To use tools for physical convenience.

I realize that the negative "insufficient" is questionable definitive form. However, since the Yahoos, like the Houyhnhnms, are mere fictions, and since this negative term, by enforcing the distinction between *Yahoo* on the one hand and both *Human* and *Houyhnhnm* on the other, allows us to keep the categories separate from one another, I have determined to endure it. One might also complain that I have not mentioned clothes in my definition of Human, although I have silently subsumed them, along with wheels, hangers, and boats (other conveniences invented by human kind) under the category "tools." I have not noticed clothes specifically, first, because doing so would blur the physical similarity between Human and Yahoo—as clothing itself did for some time in the minds of the ignorant Houyhnhnms; and, second, because clothes are, after all, not a real or necessary aspect of Human—as the naked savages Gulliver saw on leaving Houyhnhnmland clearly demonstrate. When clothes, like any other human property, become significant, I will of course mention them.

All the elements of these definitions are vividly articulated in the first two chapters of part 4. Gulliver simply carries his anthropoid form, his discursive and social capacities, and his hanger (not to speak of his garments with their various fastenings) into Houyhnhnmland. That the roaring and howling anthropoids soon to be called Yahoos lack the use of what Gulliver describes in the letter to Sympson as "a Sort of Jabber" (p. 8), that they merely "herd" together, and that they lack tools is dramatically declared in Gulliver's first encounter with them. Their "perfect human Figure," admittedly, he is first forced to recognize in the second chapter, in which he is placed experimentally, as it were, in comparative proximity with a Yahoo. In the first chapter, during which the reader may have decided on the strength of Gulliver's meticulous description that Yahoos have an anthropoid physique, Gulliver found their shape "singular"—a key judgment, it seems to me—and "deformed" (p. 223). "Deformed from what?" one might ask. By the middle of the second chapter, at which point Gulliver has declared the physical similarity between Human and Yahoo, the elements of my definition have been assembled. The involvement of the Houyhnhnms, whose experimental efforts were described as "not unlike those of a Philosopher, when he would attempt to solve some new and difficult Phaenomenon" (p. 226), underscores the philosophical, definitive value of these early experiences.

The Houyhnhnms, which Gulliver studies with something like the same intellectual concentration they focus on him, judging them at one point to be sorcerers (p. 226) and modifying this by degrees as Houyhnhnm evidence mounts up, are likewise made philosophical objects in the first two chapters. Gulliver, who has just been through a looking-glass confrontation with a Yahoo, goes through a like experience with Houyhnhnm. In the first case the Yahoo "lifted up his fore Paw" toward Gulliver; in the second Gulliver reached his hand out to stroke the Houyhnhnm's neck (p. 224)—mirroring processes of examination that give the two situations comparable definitive force. Gulliver's raising his hand to stroke the Houyhnhnm, "using the common Style and Whistle of Jockies," declares the Houyhnhnm's equine shape; this had been clear enough, however, from the first moment when Gulliver saw "a Horse walking softly in the Field." The term "softly" may present an intellectual strain, but a horse is a horse. Houyhnhnm sociability and discourse also emerge in the first chapter when a second horse appears, and the two, after a courteous striking of right hoofs, begin "to confer together" as "Friends" in a language that "expressed the Passions very plainly."[14] Gulliver straightway begins to learn the Houyhnhnm language, and significantly the words he first practices are "Yahoo" and "Houyhnhnm" (pp. 226–27), the two new terms he and his reader must chiefly attempt to understand. In the next chapter, Gulliver enters a Houyhnhnm "House" and discovers Houyhnhnms engaged in "domestic Business" (p. 228), notices the "elegant Manner" in which their "Rooms" are furnished (p. 229), and receives some milk "in Earthen and Wooden Vessels" (p. 231)—from all of which we may infer the Houyhnhnm capacity to use tools and begin to discover, perhaps, that in this capacity they lag far behind the human race. The fundamental elements of the definition of Houyhnhnm are evident, therefore, before the end of the second chapter.

To benefit from these definitions we must hold them firm throughout the developing particulars of the discourse that follows, being ready at any time, when one of the basic terms is used, to substitute the definition and thus test any given statement. Beforehand, however, it may be useful to acknowledge the flexibility in our definitions and make sure, by doing so, that the distinctions thus indicated are sufficiently firm and reliable to hold. According to my definitions, then, Human and Yahoo resemble one another physically and not intellectually; Human and Houyhnhnm resemble one another intellectually and not physically.

I begin testing the scope of these likenesses by recalling the young Yahoo female who no doubt found in Gulliver a perfect Yahoo figure. Although Gulliver did not instinctively recognize a perfect human figure in her, he eventually neglected his own sense and took hers as authoritative. His first Yahoo contacts, we may recall, followed the same pattern: immediate, unquestioned discrimination was followed by an expressed identification. When the Houyhnhnms put Gulliver next to a Yahoo, however, he acknowledged the resemblance with horror—surely the sign of some reservation in the identification—and noted certain small differences in face and feet, which suggest vast differences in physical conduct. We may recall that when Gulliver actually descried naked savage people, human beings, that is, of the least sophisticated kind, on the island he visited after leaving

Houyhnhnmland, he immediately identified them as "Men, Women and Children round a Fire" (p. 284). Although his mind can be led to emphasize the physical similarity between himself and all human beings on the one hand and Yahoos on the other, then, these two species of anthropoid nevertheless differ in evident and unmistakable ways. No one who first sees a Yahoo, we may infer, would expect him—like the first human creature Gulliver saw in Lilliput—to have a bow-and-arrows.

The resemblance is there of course in much of the body, the disposition of the limbs, and even the kinds of hair. Humans and Yahoos are also both omnivores. The difference in diet is nevertheless enough to allow Gulliver to maintain some distance at table—as he no doubt does. Yahoos eat roots of all kinds—such as yams and radishes and potatoes, perhaps—but no oats; they devour several kinds of meat: beef, dog, ass, and cat—all quite raw, of course. Although Gulliver catches an occasional fowl or rabbit—with "Springes made of *Yahoos* hairs" (p. 232)—and cooks them for his supper, his main fare is oats and milk, Houyhnhnm food. Soon after seeing an old Houyhnhnm eat a warm porridge of oats boiled in milk, Gulliver makes an oatmeal cake for himself, which he likewise eats warm with milk. Gulliver prepares his food with some care, while the Yahoos merely snatch and gnaw. There is nevertheless enough physical similarity to describe both humans and Yahoos—along with Brobdingnagian monkeys, and even the Brobdingnagians themselves—as anthropoid specimens. But the exact degree of resemblance is indeterminable, seeming sometimes to Gulliver and the Houyhnhnms to be perfect and at other times to Gulliver, if not to the Houyhnhnms, to be almost too slight to acknowledge.

The degree of identity between human and Houyhnhnm intellect is also both various and subject to interpretation. We may best note the closeness by recognizing the remarkable degree to which Gulliver, a relatively normal human being, fit into their society. He quickly learned the Houyhnhnm language, often took part in Houyhnhnm conversations, and in time found a place—if a humble one as "Fellow-Servant" of the Sorrel Nag—in a Houyhnhnm household. He held many close talks with the master, talks from which this model of rationality derived, as the Houyhnhnm assembly complained, "some Advantage or Pleasure" (p. 279). He was admitted into wider reaches of Houyhnhnm society as well—if under somewhat insulting conditions—and, unlike his fellow servants (not to mention the Yahoos), participated in discussions among its more elevated ranks. Gulliver's technological skills were much greater than those of his hosts, of course. The Houyhnhnms had fire to heat their oatmeal, flint knives, clay and wooden bowls, and extremely simple houses (or, as we might call them, stables). They lacked the wheel and were pulled along in sledges. Gulliver, who brought his metal hanger and his complicated clothes along with him to Houyhnhnmland, developed not only "Springes made of *Yahoos* hairs," but "two Chairs"; and he extensively repaired his clothes (p. 276). He both designed and built his own "*Indian* Canoo" and furnished it with four paddles (p. 281). Gulliver, if a Houyhnhnm, seems like a technologically advanced Houyhnhnm. The Houyhnhnms themselves celebrated his departure much as human beings mark the departures of their great explorers, with public honors (of a kind) and personal regrets.

The difference between Houyhnhnm and human intellect can best be indicated by recalling western culture both as it is in our experience and as Gulliver and the master apprehend it. The English language, first of all, is much more complex in form and extensive in diction than the Houyhnhnm tongue, containing as it does ways of expressing doubt, hope, opinion, and passion as well as facts; and requiring terms for an enormously wider range of activities than the Houyhnhnms ever conceived. This difference, or so the convert to Houyhnhnmism would claim, constitutes the measure of human depravity. Speaking with philosophical detachment, however, I would suggest that each language is broadly adequate to the various sociopolitical needs of its users. Since "vast Numbers of our People are compelled to seek their Livelihood by Begging, Robbing, Stealing, Cheating, Pimping, Forswearing, Flattering, Suborning, Forging, Gaming, Lying . . ." (p. 252), not to mention many more respectable activities not acknowledged by Gulliver, we need all these terms. The Houyhnhnms, of course, do not. Both cultures are centered, however, in family life and responsibility; both present sociopolitical hierarchies with upper and lower classes; both depend on large-scale organization with a representative assembly. The two are thus similar enough for a decent person like Gulliver to accommodate himself both to the Houyhnhnm language and Houyhnhnm ways and to describe these to the rest of us so that we can judge and, where relevant, adopt them.

2

Having established my definitions, I now apply them to the tangle of Gulliver's adventures and to his discourse. The traditional notion is that humans are somewhat superior to Yahoos and somewhat inferior to Houyhnhnms—a notion that the placing of Gulliver's domicile in Houyhnhnmland and certain abstract Houyhnhnm judgments seem to support. This notion has recently been challenged by Donald Keesey, who points out several ways in which humans are significantly worse or lower than Yahoos.[15] This would mean, perhaps, that wherever traditionalists came upon the word *Human* or *Gulliver* (taking Gulliver as a fairly representative human being), they would argue for such a Houyhnhnm formulation as "wonderful" or "gentle" Yahoo and that Keesey would substitute something like "odious" Yahoo. Our definitions will not allow either of these moves, of course, since Yahoo does not contain the capacities for speech, tools, or true sociability. No modification, neither "wonderful" nor "odious," can bridge the substantive difference between Human and Yahoo.

No identification, no substitution of our different terms, seems to me to be justified. Although humankind may resemble Yahoos very closely at certain points, as Swift once suggested to Thomas Sheridan, the categories are sufficiently remote so that every substitution must be seriously inexact.[16] When, for example, Gulliver, after "getting upon my Feet," describes himself to the Portuguese seamen—in Portuguese—as "a poor *Yahoo*" (p. 285), he has, by definition, contradicted himself, since Yahoos do not possess the linguistic capacity to say anything: they only howl and roar. One who speaks must be either a Houyhnhnm, as Gulliver's accent and many aspects of his conduct toward the Portuguese seamen proclaim him to be, or a human, "a poor distressed *Englishman*," say, as he had informed the first horses that he met on his arrival in Houyhnhnmland (p. 226). Consider, again, Gulliver's refusal to wear any of Pedro de Mendez's clothing on the grounds that he would abhor "to cover myself with anything that had been on the Back of a *Yahoo*" (p. 288). Gulliver's attitude here reflects that of the Houyhnhnms, who are indignant at the mere proximity of a Yahoo. But as a Houyhnhnm, Gulliver should have simply rejected all clothing whatever—something he never does. He should also do so, of course, if he is the poor Yahoo he just announced himself to be. But taking Gulliver as an articulate anthropoid creature who fastens himself up in garments, what do we make of his statement? That is, since the garments under discussion are those of Pedro de Mendez, what do we make of Gulliver's identifying this gracious Portuguese sea captain as Yahoo? Since Pedro de Mendez has clothes, he is immediately remote from Yahoo: one cannot wear a garment that has been on the back of a Yahoo. One would not even discuss this topic, as Gulliver has done with the Portuguese captain, with a Yahoo. Actually, one could wear something that had been on the back of a Yahoo, it occurs to me, if like Gulliver he had created some of his clothing from Yahoo skins. We need hardly labor the fact that Gulliver eventually accepts, as man from man, two of the captain's clean shirts to see that his use of the term "Yahoo" and his implicit identification of the captain are ridiculous.

Consider one last case, Gulliver's telling the master that "a *Soldier* is a *Yahoo* hired to kill in cold Blood as many of his own Species, who have never offended him, as possibly he can" (pp. 246–47). One doesn't want simply to sacrifice the satiric shock of this identification; one can't. But as a reader absorbs it, he may— he must, if he thinks of himself as reading a treatise—question its discursive propriety. If he simply accepts it, for instance, he must be willing to substitute "his fellow Yahoos" for "his own Species"; and if he does this, the human enormity of the soldier's occupation is destroyed: logically destroyed for the Houyhnhnm master and for Gulliver, who makes shoes and sails out of Yahoo skins; and substantially so for the rest of us. Soldiers, however, do not kill unoffending Yahoos; they kill unoffending human beings. And one thing that makes this horrible is the fact that soldiers are also human beings. In the continuation of this discussion of soldiers, Gulliver himself speaks of princes who hire out their subjects as soldiers "for so much a Day to each Man"— not "to each Yahoo." And the climactic description of war that immediately follows is dreadful only as an exposition of man's inhumanity to man.

This rigorous application of our definition of Yahoo is possible because Swift has preserved its empirical foundation with considerable care. When he extends Yahoo nature at all—as in the master's discourse on certain odd Yahoo practices—he carefully hedges the discourse. In the first place, the master claims merely to have heard about some of these practices—if we can believe him—from "some curious Houyhnhnms" (p. 262). Other odd Yahoo activities were "discovered," he says, by "his Servants" (p. 263). And in all the activities by which the master, having heard about human civilization, draws Yahoo life into an approximation with it, Gulliver himself allows, "my Master might refine a little in these Speculations" (p. 264). This stretch in the concept *Yahoo* is always rendered, finally, so as to preserve my definition:

Yahoos never speak or use tools; and even their most apparently communal activities need not be described as either social or organized. It is thus immediately evident that Gulliver is being illogical when he says such a thing as "I am a poor crature with insufficient intellect to be using a language."

The definition of Houyhnhnm, although it generally clarifies any discussion of the Human-Houyhnhnm equation, will not give us such immediate results—except, of course, in the few but amusing instances when human and Houyhnhnm physiques are at issue. Both humans and Houyhnhnms almost always show sufficient intellect, as the definitions assert, to speak, socialize, and use tools. (Well, the matter of tools is occasionally subject to humorous question.) The issue in studying both human and Houyhnhnm discourse is, how sufficient, how adequate, is this intellect? And this requires somewhat closer analysis than we have made so far.

Such analysis reveals that Houyhnhnm understanding is, like all created intelligence, limited in experience, in sense. Consider, for example, the master's suggestion that Gulliver should make himself a boat: the master "wished," as he put it, that "I would contrive some Sort of Vehicle resembling those I had described to him, that might carry me on the Sea" (p. 279). Having seen no such "Vehicle" nor, except for Gulliver, the sentient anthropoids who might build or sail it, he has no certainty that Gulliver can make such a contraption and very little confidence that the thing will float. The master reveals the same ignorance, the same ignorant skepticism, we may recall, of such human concerns as clothing, weapons, nobility, and horsemanship; and he thus reasons incorrectly—sometimes to Gulliver's amusement—about everyone. The master also has trouble absorbing what he does see. He has seen how clean, how busy, and how picky in his food Gulliver is; he has remarked his aversion to Yahoos. But when the representatives of the Houyhnhnm assembly attack Gulliver because, as Gulliver reports, "I might be able to seduce [the Yahoos] into the woody and mountainous Parts of the Country, and bring them in Troops by Night to destroy the *Houyhnhnms* Cattle, as being naturally of the ravenous Kind, and averse from labour" (p. 279), he apparently has nothing to oppose. The syntax of this charge is fuzzy: is it the Yahoos or Gulliver or both who are being described as "naturally . . . averse from labour"? Is Gulliver, elsewhere in the same passage, being charged with "the natural Pravity of those Animals," or merely with the ability seductively to prey on such pravity? But taking this into account, it is still inconceivable that Gulliver (whose transformation into an anthropoid Houyhnhnm the master has superintended and observed) should act as the assembly infers that he might, and equally inconceivable that a sensible intelligence should not recognize this and, out of sheer Houyhnhnm devotion to truth and honesty, bring up the relevant facts to combat the assembly's charge. But the master does not combat this charge; he merely carries out, if reluctantly, the demand for Gulliver's removal.

Take a simpler case of this Houyhnhnm imperviousness to experience, one in which a number of these creatures were involved:

> The *Houyhnhnms* who came to visit my Master [as Gulliver reports] out of a Design of seeing and talking with me, could hardly believe me to be a right *Yahoo*, because my Body had a different Covering from others of my Kind. (p. 236)

These Houyhnhnms, who came pointedly to see *and* talk with Gulliver, could not know that he had, in fact, exactly the same kind of covering as others of his species since, unlike Gulliver's reader, they had never seen any other such beings. But by conversing with Gulliver, they surely should have recognized that he was capable of talking and thus, clothed or not, that he was crucially remote from any Yahoos they had ever observed. It was the intelligence each Houyhnhnm recognized in the other's speech, after all (and not any covering), that prompted each one to infer rationality in another and in all the Houyhnhnms at large. Not even Gulliver could infer rationality—that source of Houyhnhnm complacency—from the two stone horses (why not one stallion and one mare?) that he purchased when he got back to England; whereas he was forced to recognize and respond to the discursive, argumentative rationality of Pedro de Mendez.[17] And yet the Houyhnhnms, who visited the master expressly to talk with Gulliver, totally neglected the force, the implications, of Gulliver's talk—and his Houyhnhnm talk, at that. Instead, they reasoned about his clothes.

I have now reached the vexing problem of Houyhnhnm reason or, rather, the problem of what I have called its sufficiency and what others, among these the Houyhnhnms themselves, call its perfection.[18] That it is at least sufficient to allow speech, society, and technology, I do not question. I am as willing to believe a horse might have such intelligence as the next fellow. But that

this intelligence as shown in the *Travels* is adequate to pro-
nounce on the central concerns of this treatise, that is, on human
reason, human pride, and human nature in general, I do question. If we practice the minute particularity of attention that Dr.
Johnson described as characteristic of Swift's mind and analyze
the processes of Houyhnhnm discourse, we will have to add to
my complaint aginst their sense a further complaint against their
reasoning. I say "reasoning" and not "reason," because, as Swift
knew, one can reason wrong sometimes and still be prevailingly
reasonable; or be reasonable quite a lot of the time and yet reason
wrong on occasion. Consider, then, the master's reasoning in this
discussion of human capacity:

> He said, if it were possible there could be any Country where *Yahoos*
> alone were endued with Reason, they certainly must be the governing
> Animal, because Reason will in Time always prevail against Brutal
> Strength. But, considering the Frame of our Bodies, and especially of
> mine, he thought no Creature of equal Bulk was so ill-contrived, for
> employing that Reason in the common Offices of Life; whereupon he
> desired to know whether those among whom I lived, resembled me
> or the *Yahoos* of his Country. I assured him, that I was as well shaped
> as most of my Age; but the younger and the Females were much more
> soft and tender, and the Skins of the latter generally as white as Milk. He
> said, I differed indeed from other *Yahoos*, being much more cleanly,
> and not altogether so deformed; but in point of real Advantage, he
> thought I differed for the worse. That my Nails were of no Use either
> to my fore or hinder Feet: As to my fore Feet, he could not properly
> call them by that Name, for he never observed me to walk upon them;
> that they were too soft to bear the Ground; that I generally went with
> them uncovered, neither was the Covering I sometimes wore on
> them, of the same Shape, or so strong as that on my Feet behind. That
> I could not walk with any Security; for if either of my hinder Feet
> slipped, I must inevitably fall. He then began to find fault with other
> Parts of my Body; the Flatness of my Face, the Prominence of my
> Nose, my Eyes placed directly in Front, so that I could not look on
> either Side without turning my Head: That I was not able to feed my
> self, without lifting one of my fore Feet to my Mouth: And therefore
> Nature had placed those Joints to answer that Necessity. He knew not
> what could be the Use of those several Clefts and Divisions in my
> Feet behind; that these were too soft to bear the Hardness and Sharp-
> ness of Stones without a Covering made from the Skin of some other
> Brute; that my whole Body wanted a Fence against Heat and Cold,
> which I was forced to put on and off every Day with Tediousness and
> Trouble. And lastly, that he observed every Animal in this Country
> naturally to abhor the *Yahoos*, whom the Weaker avoided, and the
> Stronger drove from them. So that supposing us to have the Gift of

Reason, he could not see how it were possible to cure that natural Antipathy which every Creature discovered against us; nor conse-quently, how we could tame and render them serviceable. However, he would (as he said) debate the Matter no farther. . . . (pp. 242–43)

The very fact that Gulliver's account of human activity has drawn the master into a highly contentious "debate"—one that is also intellectually speculative—is strictly contrary to the Houy-hnhnm notions of reason as unproblematical and truth as strictly factual.

But the debate itself is laden with difficulties of both sense and reason. We begin, where the Augustans would all advise, with sense.[19] The master's dislike of Gulliver's face, first of all, is very puzzling. In attacking the prominence of his nose, the master may seem to be thinking with satisfaction about his own perfect "Countenance" and its mere nostrils: he is surely remembering his eyes with some complacency when he attacks Gulliver for being able to look straight before himself. But is not a horse's face, in a truer sense, at least from the eyes on down, one great proboscis, a nose so prominent, indeed, that it splits the horse's face? The master's denial that Gulliver's nails are of any use, once again, anyone can contradict who has tried to pick up something when his fingernails were too short or when wearing gloves. But the master's discussion of Gulliver's "fore Feet" is the most bla-tant piece of nonsense in this remarkable debate. The Houy-hnhnm has quite recently been described closely observing Gulliver undress himself, an experience he actually refers to in this passage; as this passage also suggests, he has beheld Gulliver feed himself. And he must have noticed Gulliver's manual dex-terity in trapping and dressing game and in making bread, which his elbows allow him to carry to his mouth. But all that here occurs to the master is how poorly adapted his hands are for walking—and dear, dear! how Gulliver totally neglects to use them for this. He is unable to call Gulliver's hands "fore Feet," not because of what Gulliver does with them, but, he says, be-cause of what he does not do.[20] Moreover, the master's doubts about even entertaining the notion that creatures such as Gulliver might possibly be animals "endued with Reason" is another failure: it shows the master's difficulty in acknowledging the very presence of Gulliver, an obviously rational creature, a creature who uses the same logical forms of speech as the master, and, as their discussions develop, comes to the same deliberate judg-ments about the same intellectual materials.

The errors of reason in the master's statement, in so far as we can separate these from the errors of sense, are equally destructive of Houyhnhnm perfection. How can the master complain both against the prominence of Gulliver's nose—whatever we may judge about the sense of this—and, in almost the same breath, against the flatness of his face and hope to be judged to be logically consistent? His unwillingness to see any reason for the clefts in Gulliver's hind hoofs, furthermore, reminds us of his failure to notice the reasons Gulliver has found for such clefts in his hands. But the master's great failure of reason in this debate occurs at its end, in his enunciating the conclusion, "consequently," that reasonable anthropoids could not "tame and render . . . serviceable" any other animals. Apparently because of his dislike of Gulliver's anthropoid physique, the master rejects his own universal principle, that reason will always prevail: it is not applicable to "us." "So that [how impressively rational] supposing us to have the Gift of Reason, he could not see how it were possible to cure that natural Antipathy which every Creature discovered against us." Even if we allow the master to disbelieve Gulliver's account of human horsemanship (and never to have heard about man's best friend), he has seen with his own eyes a reasonable *and* sociable anthropoid: he is at this moment in a close conversation with one. But the master has fooled himself with his own nonsense into contradicting the premise of this very debate and, with the same stroke, denying the first principle of Houyhnhnm life.

I am not arguing that all Houyhnhnm discourse is nonsensical and irrational; nor will I argue this about all of Gulliver's discourse. Often when he and the master confine themselves to what Gulliver would call the "general ideas" of such topics as Yahoo existence or human life, they present descriptions and judgments that are not only impressive but apparently just. This is so in part, however, because of the discourse's very generality, which provides a tolerance, a neutral intellectual ground between the discourse itself and all particular embodiments. This neutral ground, this intermediate realm between general words and real things, to which the actual experiences of life may be added, sometimes provides merely an intellectual buffer. Such is virtually always the case, of course, in the general expositions of Yahoo modes of conduct. And even the comments on Europe that Gulliver makes, being aimed at the master, who lacks any particular European knowledge, may simply be observed at the distance of broadly relevant generality. Thus when Gulliver describes European conflicts over "whether *Flesh* be *Bread* or *Bread* be *Flesh*," one may leave it at that, as the master must do: in this case, he recognizes the essential triviality of our religious conflicts. Or he may—and probably will—go on to fill in the arguments of transubstantiation and consubstantiation from his own knowledge, preserving, of course, his own opinions of these arguments. This will flavor his primary sense of Gulliver's discourse with a secondary sense—although with a sense that he might be wise to mistrust—and give him a full impression of its propriety. Thus the reader, himself supplying particulars or merely observing broad applicabilities, finds considerable satisfaction in these general discourses. But when Gulliver and the master confront the particulars of Gulliver's Houyhnhnm adventure or Gulliver himself as an example of humanity, their talks are deprived of the tolerance, the vagueness of application, that surrounds and protects their general discussions. Certain of these talks, I am arguing, can be proven to be seriously at fault. And since they are faulty, I would suggest further, everything the Houyhnhnms say should be examined with intellectual caution; and their general claims to perfection should be viewed with serious—or amused?—suspicion.

Gulliver's elaborations on these claims must also draw our doubts, and his rationality must, consequently, be suspect. To consider it in particular—as one always should do—I turn toward his response to the assembly's charge against him. Gulliver fainted, we may recall, when he heard the assembly's decision that he must quit Houyhnhnmland; and when he came to, the master, who had been observing this phenomenon, reported that he had "concluded I had been dead"—another case in which truth turns out to be problematical. Gulliver then responded to the assembly's "Exhortation":

> I answered in a faint Voice, that Death would have been too great an Happiness; that although I could not blame the Assembly's *Exhortation*, or the Urgency of his Friends; yet in my weak and corrupt Judgment, I thought it might consist with Reason to have been less rigorous. That, I could not swim a League, and probably the nearest Land to theirs might be distant above an Hundred: That, many Materials, necessary for making a small Vessel to carry me off, were wholly wanting in this Country, which however, I would attempt in Obedience and Gratitude to his Honour, although I concluded the thing to be impossible, and therefore looked on myself as already devoted to Destruction. That, the certain Prospect of an unnatural Death, was the least of my Evils: For, supposing I should escape with

Life by some strange Adventure, how could I think with Temper, of passing my Days among Yahoos, and relapsing into my old Corruptions, for want of Examples to lead and keep me within the Paths of Virtue. That, I knew too well upon what solid Reasons all the Determinations of the wise *Houyhnhnms* were founded, not to be shaken by Arguments of mine, a miserable *Yahoo*; and therefore after presenting him with my humble Thanks for the Offer of his Servants Assistance in making a Vessel, and desiring a reasonable Time for so difficult a Work, I told him, I would endeavour to preserve a wretched Being; and, if ever I returned to *England*, was not without Hopes of being useful to my own Species, by celebrating the Praises of the renowned *Houyhnhnms*, and proposing their Virtues to the Imitation of Mankind. (pp. 280–81)

Gulliver has sandwiched between the assembly's charge and this response a note on Houyhnhnm "Exortation," explaining that, as the Houyhnhnms see things, a rational creature can never be "*compelled* but only advised, or *exhorted*; because no Person [a lovely term here] can disobey Reason, without giving up his Claim to be a rational Creature." This seems to me to be Swift's hint that we should be especially alert in testing the arguments immediately before us—that is, the Houyhnhnm exhortation, certain aspects of which I have touched on incidentally, and Gulliver's response.

This response seems to me to be Gulliver's unconscious parody of Houyhnhnm reasoning and, more particularly, of the very exhortation to which he is responding. He employs the same paraphernalia of reason as does the master: a series of "that" clauses and a liberal sprinkling of logical terms such as "for," "although . . . yet," "however," and "therefore." He likewise commits the same kind of failures in both sense and reason. If we place our definition of Yahoo in the statement about the "arguments of . . . a miserable *Yahoo*," noting not only the Yahoos' lack of speech but, a fortiori, of any kind of argumentative capacity, we see that Gulliver is practicing in an exaggerated form the kind of nonsense he will soon try on the Portuguese—and something like the same nonsense in the exhortation that underlies the Houyhnhnm fear of a Yahoo's organizing a rebellion. His horror of returning to Europe as an ordeal of "passing my Days among *Yahoos*" is similarly foolish: it is only in Houyhnhnmland that he may—that he must, to some degree—be so accompanied; only there do Yahoos truly worthy of such a name exist. Gulliver's assertion that the Houyhnhnms are "renowned" is also empirically false: the Houyhnhnms may eventually become renowned through Gulliver's authorial exertions (if he can make anyone believe in their existence at all); but at the moment he speaks, they are absolutely unrenowned. His certainty that Houyhnhnmland lacks "many Materials, necessary for making" a boat also proves, finally, to be wide of the facts.

The consideration of possible materials for his boat reveals Gulliver, in line with Houyhnhnm discipleship, to be not only nonsensical but irrational as well. If necessary materials are simply unavailable, as Gulliver asserts, no matter what motives of obedience and gratitude may press him, his attempt to build a boat is foolish. Consider also Gulliver's complaint that the assembly's exhortation was too rigorous. Either they are right in describing Gulliver as a dangerous Yahoo and thus strictly justified in expelling him, or they are wrong and thus silly to do so: reason cannot be too rigorous. If the Europeans are Yahoos, again, as Gulliver insists, his plan to teach them is strictly irrational, for as he knows, Yahoos are quite unteachable. This whole discourse, finally, shows the same kind of intellectual flip-flop we discovered in the master's debate. It begins in abject despair: "Death would be too great an Happiness." But as Gulliver discusses the perils of travel and the horrors of life on the other side, his mind shifts about; and it does so, moreover, against the extremely negative tendency of his discourse. He was "not without Hopes," he concludes, of a useful life back home where he would not merely live in the corrupting environment of Yahoos but, although officially an unteachable Yahoo himself, teach those unteachables. The fact that the master made a "very gracious Reply" to this effusion should remind us that, in respect to discursive rationality, the perfect Houyhnhnm and his miserable human disciple are just about on a par.

3

By thus identifying Gulliver's central terms, applying them analytically to the details of his discourse, and focusing judgment upon *Yahoo, Houyhnhnm* and *Gulliver,* a reader can draw from part 4 of Swift's *Travels,* I would suggest, not one "train of thought" but two: one for "the World," to the effect that human nature deprived of moral restraint is, as Keesey argued, worse than *Yahoo;* the other for "the courteous Reader," to the effect that he himself is not an *animal rationale* but only *rationis capax.* The first of these trains, to which the king of Brobdingnag gave preliminary utterance, has something like the explicitness and the firmness that one expects to find in a treatise; the second, however, does not: it presents, rather, a lurking possibility, a continuous satiric threat, that the reader endures, often without recognizing it, as he or she goes along. We may encounter the *Travels*, correspondingly, either as members of the human race in general, whom Swift hated and whom Gulliver pronounced "Yahoo," in which case we will chiefly notice the first "train of thought"; or as individual human beings, in which case we will proceed in constant danger of the second.

Thackeray read as a member of human society, and the *Travels* often prompted him to do so. Gulliver's attention is often directed at the public, the race, Europe, England, or the world. He sometimes thinks of this general audience as an enemy to his reputation but more characteristically as the object of his zeal for reform. Swift spoke sarcastically of achieving general reform by means of the *Travels*: they were "admirable things," he wrote in a letter to Charles Ford, "and will wonderfully mend the world."[21] Gulliver, on the other hand, although at least he bitterly disowned all "visionary Schemes," often represents himself in the *Travels* at large as a universal reformer. One who reads his work as a member of mankind in general becomes a candidate for such reforms and implicitly acknowledges in him or herself the bad human qualities that Gullliver wishes to change. We thus accept a share in all the imperfections, the follies, and vices of mankind, general follies and vices that no doubt deserve Gulliver's general reprehension; and having done so, we take what mankind gets and either subscribe *Yahoo*—as Dogberry subscribed *Ass*—or struggle like Thackeray to save all mankind from the taint of such a label. In short, we take Gulliver's way and get daubed in the same mire. I do not deny that we may all be in part subject to Gulliver's categorization and thus to some extent to his general judgment; but we can, on the contrary, preserve our own separate identities, each one his own, and avoid much of it—all of it, that is, except for the bit that actually sticks.

The *Travels* often addresses not "the World," but the "gentle" or "candid" or "curious" or "courteous" or "judicious" reader, and thus prompts an actual reader to maintain his or her own moral and intellectual identity. Doing so, one will be able to apply to the unfolding particularities of Gulliver's discourse his or her personal sense and reason. This seems to me to be the special benefit in coping with the *Travels* as a treatise. In testing terms and striving to penetrate the process of argument for oneself, a reader has the chance (to use Berkeley's words) to grasp "his own naked, undisguised ideas" and thus achieve an understanding both of the *Travels* and one's own mind.

Keeping thus on what Rawson calls "an intimate footing" with Swift's imaginary treatise of human nature or his materials toward such a treatise is neither safe nor easy.[22] Even the simplest appeal to "the Reader" may get one into trouble. When Gulliver describes his first contact with the Houyhnhnms and suggests "the Reader will easily believe I did not much like my present Situation" (p. 225), one may pause to consider that he does not believe any such thing; that he chooses, at least with part of his mind, to remain skeptical of the whole imaginary affair. Or one may take this language as just a storyteller's conventional way of talking and pass on. If one simply passes on, he intensifies the danger, which is omnipresent in this work, of conniving with Gulliver unconsciously, and in the process, of often conniving not merely with fiction but with folly. I myself read through the following pair of explanations for the flat faces of Yahoos and savages a dozen times or more, quite satisfied with Gulliver's offered parallelism: the flatness of such faces comes, Gulliver remarks comfortably, "by the Natives suffering their Infants to lie grovelling on the Earth, or by carrying them on their Backs, nuzzling with their Face against the Mother's Shoulders" (p. 230). By the time I responded sufficiently to "nuzzling" and "Mother's" and thus both recognized the rich tissue of maternal nurture in the second item and decided that I must discriminate, whether Gulliver did or not, finding in the second item what was quite lacking in the first—the signs of human nature and human society that cancelled any equation between Yahoo and Human; by the time I reached this personal judgment, I say, I had also to realize that I had often before passed by this statement without making such a judgment. I enjoyed at once, then, a present pleasure in my new discrimination between *Human* and *Yahoo* and a present chagrin at my tardiness in making it, at my own recalcitrant if finally corrected lack of sense. Such a mixed pleasure, repeated almost inexhaustibly, is the benefit of reading *Gulliver's Travels* with one's own two eyes, of sifting and testing it as materials toward a treatise.

The reader accepts for himself "the role of interpretation left vacant," as Clive Probyn has acutely pointed out, "by the author's dereliction." He thus accepts this position, not as the target of Gulliver's universal pronouncements but as "the target of Swift's satirical strategies."[23] The most vexatious of these strategies is, as

Probyn suggests, the putative author, Gulliver himself. The intellectual unreliability of this figure forces us to recognize again and again that Gulliver's Travels is a faulty treatise; but when we feel that we must question or reject Gulliver, we are broaching this outer generic shell of Swift's work. In treading on the thin ice of treatise, we have broken into the bracing waters of satire. "What a fool I was not to have noticed until now the crucial difference between a creature that grovels and one who nuzzles!" In reading the Travels as a treatise, then, one presents himself in the right attitude to discover again and again his foolish pride in believing, as Probyn has described it, "that he alone is comfortably above and beyond implication" in the shifting designs of Swift's work[24]—or in believing, as Swift himself might have said, that he is an *animal rationale*. In even understanding the language of Gulliver's assertion that he was "a poor *Yahoo*" (p. 285), in entertaining as an object of study the pretensions to rationality with which the Houyhnhnms discuss Gulliver, in unraveling the tangle of significance in Gulliver's using Yahoo tallow to caulk his boat, the judicious reader finds him or herself involved in Gulliver's complacent exposition and implicated in the full meaning of his performance.

This vexatious involvement—with its many incidental diversions—is the special joy that occurs to the reader who judges these imaginary materials against a few rigorously held definitions. By taking on such intellectual demands and perils, one preserves himself as John, Peter, or Thomas and earns the chance of becoming, here and there, the worthy companion of a most exacting and valuable man.

Notes

1. This sentence, or, rather, this whole essay, is an echo of a fragment from Philip Pinkus, Swift's Vision of Evil (Victoria, B. C.: University of Victoria, 1975): "The Travels is not a philosophic treatise. But" (2:102).

2. Gulliver's Travels, in The Prose Works of Jonathan Swift, ed. Herbert Davis et al. (Oxford: Basil Blackwell, 1939–68), 11:293. Subsequent references will be to this edition and will be included within the text.

3. Literary Meaning and Augustan Values (Charlottesville: University of Virginia Press, 1974), pp. 102–6.

4. The Correspondence of Jonathan Swift, ed. Harold Williams (Oxford: Clarendon Press, 1963), 3:133–36 and 137–38.

5. Swift, Correspondence, 3:225–27. A translation of this letter is produced in the Norton Critical Edition of the Travels, ed. Robert A. Greenberg, rev. ed.,

(New York: W. W. Norton, 1970), p. 271. Perhaps we should notice explicitly that Swift is here describing a treatise with a powerful satiric undercurrent.

6. Swift, *Correspondence*, 3:102–5. I have emended the spelling of "Treatis" for the sake of consistency.

7. See *A Tale of a Tub*, ed. A. C. Guthkelch and D. Nichol Smith, 2d ed. (Oxford: Clarendon Press, 1958), p. 56: "the Philosopher's Way in all Ages has been by erecting certain *Edifices in Air.*"

8. Leigh, "Wollaston and Swift," *Philosophy and Literature* 4 (1980): 92–106; Landa, "The Dismal Science in Houyhnhnmland," *Novel* 13 (1979): 38–49; and Treadwell, "Jonathan Swift: The Satirist as Projector," *Texas Studies in Literature and Language* 17 (1975): 439–60.

9. *Gulliver and the Gentle Reader* (London: Routledge and Kegan Paul, 1973), p. 18; references immediately following occur on pp. 17 and 29–32.

10. This is an allusion to R. S. Crane's exposition of contemporary logic's use of the definition *animal rationale* for humankind and of the common use of a *Man-Horse* opposition to expound this definition.

11. Ehrenpreis, *Literary Meaning and Augustan Values*, pp. 102–9.

12. See Clive Probyn, *The Art of Jonathan Swift* (New York: Barnes and Noble, 1978), pp. 8–10, on "the author's dereliction."

13. For convenience I have used a popular edition of the *Principles* (Lasalle, Ill.: Open Court, 1957), pp. 26–27.

14. This early description of the Houyhnhnms' tongue may present a problem even more troublesome than their walking "softly," since, as Gulliver learns later, Houyhnhnms have no passions to express.

15. Keesey, "The Distorted Image: Swift's Yahoos and the Critics," *Papers on Language and Literature* 15 (1979): 320–32.

16. Swift, *Correspondence*, 3:94.

17. Like others before me, I sense the shadow of Locke and his *Essay Concerning Human Understanding* playing across the surface of the *Travels*, especially, during part 4, in the use of such terms as *Man, Human,* and *Person.* Locke insisted that by *Man* we mean only a certain kind of living body; whereas with *Person* we are referring to a continuous, identifiable consciousness. Locke's rigorous definition of these terms, with which, or rather, against which Swift's discourse seems to work, illuminates Gulliver's usages. For the pertinent passages in Locke, see the Pringle-Pattison edition of the *Essay* (Oxford: Clarendon, 1950), pp. 186–200.

18. Even critics who seem, like F. R. Leavis, to swallow the Houyhnhnms' impressive claims usually show some doubts, doubts that I am seeking herein to intensify. In his essay on Swift in *The Common Pursuit* (New York: New York University, 1952), p. 84, Leavis says, with revealing equivocalness, "Swift did his best for the Houyhnhnms, and they may have all the reason." That Swift did his best, in Leavis's sense, I deny, just as I deny that they have anything like all the reason.

19. A number of scholars have explained the necessary subordination of reason to sense in the inductive procedures that Augustans both advocated and practiced. See especially Harold Kelling, "Reason in Madness: *A Tale of a Tub*," *PMLA* 69 (1954): 198–222.

20. I acknowledge the validity of the master's suggestion that Gulliver walks with relative insecurity (although how often, in fact, has he seen Gulliver fall down?); but this is such a tiny grain of understanding in such a mountain of nonsense.

21. Swift, *Correspondence*, 3:87.

22. Rawson, *Gulliver and the Gentle Reader*, p. 28.

23. Probyn, *The Art of Jonathan Swift*, pp. 7–10.

24. Probyn, *The Art of Jonathan Swift*, p. 12. Probyn also refers significantly, pp. 66–72, to "the dichotomy between the individual and the group," a point with which I am concerned.

Reading "with Conviction": Trial by Satire

Janet E. Aikins

1

During the long period when Swift was writing and revising *Gulliver's Travels*, his close friend Pope was composing his own commentary on the follies of mankind, the *Essay on Man*.[1] Although the *Essay* is not a satire but, in Swift's words, an "Ethick System," it resembles Swift's "Travels" in attempting to alter the reader's behavior by adjusting his view of himself in relation to others.[2] Both works tease out an analogy between visual perception and moral awareness. On 14 September 1725, shortly before the *Travels* appeared, Pope wrote a letter to Swift in which he not only mentioned Swift's narrative but alluded to his own plans for the *Essay* as if it, too, were a set of "Travels":

> Your Travels I hear much of; my own I promise you shall never more be in a strange land, but a diligent, I hope useful, investigation of my own Territories. I mean no more Translations, but something domestic, fit for my own country, and for my own time.[3]

By implication, both sets of "travels" shared a common mission; nevertheless, a month later, in a letter of 15 October, Pope described a contrast in temper between himself and Swift that would be reflected in their writings. Pope yearned for "peace," respite from the political strife of the time, and he felt "content to enjoy the Kingdome of the Just in Tranquillity"; of Swift, however, he remarked, "I find you would rather be employ'd as an Avenging Angel of wrath, to break your Vial of Indignation over the heads of the wretched pityful creatures of this World; nay would make them *Eat your Book*, which you have made as bitter a pill for them as possible."[4]

Here Pope craftily implies an affinity between Swift and Um-

briel, the "Swift . . . Gnome" of *The Rape of the Lock* who flitted
down to the Cave of Spleen to obtain the "Vial whence the
sorrows flow," which he then broke over Belinda's unfortunate
head. Swift wants his readers, the "wretched pityful creatures of
this World," to "eat the bitter pill" of his book as administered by
the ship's physician and surgeon, Lemuel Gulliver. The pill is not
a simple curative; rather, it is a bitter agent of "wrath" intended
as much to make us feel our moral illness as to heal it. Indeed, as
I shall show, Swift's changes in the 1735 edition grimly highlight
the text's expected failure to amend us through its "vile" power.

Pope's medical metaphor is especially apt, for Swift himself
associated the composition of *Gulliver's Travels* with his own
experience of disease. His letters reveal that ill health was a
continual concern as he was writing it. In his first recorded
mention of the Gulliver project he tells us, for example, "I am
now writing a History of my Travells, which will be a large
Volume, and gives Account of Countryes hitherto unknown; but
they go on slowly for want of Health and Humor." Swift also uses
disease as a metaphor when, for instance, he describes his reluc-
tance to write letters as a "Malady." Moreover, he hints that he
views physicians as healers not only of the body but of the mind
when he remarks that his friend Dr. Arbuthnot is better able to
control his emotions because he is "a Philosopher and a Physician, & can overcome by [his] Wisdom and [his] Faculty those
Weaknesses which other men are forced to reduce by not thinking on them." Indeed, Swift seems to anticipate the "bitter pill"
metaphor for *Gulliver's Travels* when he comments to Pope, "O, if
the World had but a dozen Arbuthnetts in it I would burn my
Travells," as if the wisdom of his physician friend were somehow
equivalent to the curative influence of his book. It is clear that
Swift thinks of Gulliver as a physician rather than a sailor, for in
a letter to his French translator he identifies the writer of the
Travels as a "chirurgien de vasseau."[5] As we read the doctor's
narrative, Swift frequently invites us to ponder the possible
connection between reading and spiritual healing; for example,
he illustrates the sorrowful plight of the Struldbruggs by pointing
out that at ninety they lose their ability to read, while "the
Diseases they were subject to [throughout life], still continue."[6]

Pope's "bitter pill" comment is of double importance, for in
addition to its suggestive equation of Swift's book to "physick," it
hints that the reader was as vividly pictured within Swift's mind
during the composition of *Gulliver's Travels* as were the worldly
ills that the book mocks. That is, we will better apprehend the

genre of the *Travels* if we approach it as a structured response to a
certain type of reader: one who, according to Pope, would best
profit from having a "Vial of Indignation" broken over his head or
"eating" a bitter book. A reexamination of Swift's narrative from
such a perspective reveals a feature of its satiric method that we
have not yet understood: that it sketches its "reader" as a curious
multiple. Robert Uphaus rightly observes that the "manifest fictions" in *Gulliver's Travels* transform the reader from an observer
to a participant, and Alain Bony argues persuasively that
Gulliver embodies a curious fusion of narrator and reader, a
"narrateur-lecteur" within the text.[7] What I wish to demonstrate,
however, is that Swift actually posits not one but at least three
separate kinds of "readers" within the narrative, who are all
different in their implied responses. Each of these figures performs a unique function for actual readers by modifying our
reactions as we proceed.

As I shall show, this curious device adds a special force to the
satiric thrust of *Gulliver's Travels*. Swift recognized that while
satire is a useful means of making us see the world differently, it
is also a treacherous form of discourse because it urges a peculiar
sort of complacency.[8] As we progress through such a work we
develop a confident allegiance to either the narrator or the author, since our ability to comprehend the satiric point encour-
ages a feeling of superiority within us. Swift saw this tendency as
a danger and employed his multiple "Reader" as a vehicle for
counteracting it; moreover, Swift's text importantly links its medical theme with the curious plight of its reader. Pope's laughable
metaphors thus rightly identify the implied reader as a determi-
nate difference between the genres of *The Essay on Man* and
Swift's "Travels."[9] By taking this feature into account, it is possible to explain why critics have argued so furiously over the
genre of *Gulliver's Travels*, for its variant addresses to "the
reader" constitute a series of contradictory generic signals.

2

Obviously, every author contemplates his reader as he writes,
but as we shall see, *Gulliver's Travels* is a special case. Evidence
from Swift's letters and other writings shows that he regarded the
reader not merely as a passive respondent but as a curiously
active force in the creation of a text, an agent whose capacities are
awesomely beyond those of the author himself. In the publisher's

address "To the Reader" of the 1762 collection of Swift's works, George Faulkner recorded an anecdote about Swift's editorial procedure. He tells us that in 1726, when Swift agreed to Faulkner's printing his writings, he insisted:

> That the Editor should attend him early every Morning, or when most convenient, to read to him, that the Sounds might strike the Ear, as well as the Sense the Understanding, and had always two Men Servants present for this Purpose; and when he had any Doubt, he would ask them the Meaning of what they heard? Which, if they did not comprehend, he would alter and amend, until they understood it perfectly well, and then would say, *This will do; for, I write to the Vulgar, more than to the Learned.*[10]

Although the remark applies to much of what Swift wrote, its bearing on *Gulliver's Travels* is especially suggestive. First, it reveals that Swift valued the immediate impact of a work on its hearers. Not only did its aural reception matter, but the sequential experience of a text was as central to its "meaning" as the "point" that it made.[11] Faulkner's anecdote also hints at a concept of satire as a vehicle for instantaneously affecting readers' emotions and judgments rather than for communicating complex ideas, which can only be understood upon reflection. Instead of merely comparing ourselves to Yahoos or Houyhnhnms, we should examine the startling experience of coming upon such strange beings. In one of his letters of 1726, Swift himself remarked the striking quality of such sudden encounters: "I have often reflected in how few hours, with a swift horse or a strong gale, a man may come among a people as unknown to him as the Antipodes."[12] Whether or not "a swift horse" was an intended allusion to the "Travels," Swift's point is that the impact of a confrontation with alien beings is as important as the equivalencies or parallels we can discover between those beings and ourselves. What is perhaps most significant about the Faulkner anecdote is that it shows that Swift thought deeply about his readers and not only valued their reactions but credited their responses with complexity.

Throughout his correspondence, Swift recognizes "reader identity" as an inevitable issue for every writer. He was intensely lonely for his friends in England during the years that he was writing *Gulliver's Travels*, and his letters reveal that a particularized image of the reader was vivid in his mind whenever he wrote. For example, in a letter to Dr. Arbuthnot of 16 June 1714, he makes the anguished comment, "Writing to you much

would make me stark mad; judge his condition who has nothing
to keep him from being miserable but endeavoring to forget those
for whom he has the greatest Value, Love, and Friendship." Nine
years later, as he was working on part 4 of the *Travels*, he observed:

> there is not a more universall Malady than an unwillingness to write
> Letters to our best Friends and a Man might be philosopher enough
> in finding out Reasons for it. One thing is clear that it shews a mighty
> difference betwixt Friendship and love; for a Lover (as I have heard)
> is allways Scribling to his Mistress.[13]

Writing letters to dear friends is unbearable because of the memory of the reader that the process conjures up. By contrast, the
ease of "Scribling" to one's mistress is evidence that love is less
powerful than friendship.

Swift apparently believed that a sense of the reader's vital
presence and probable response is what determines not only the
author's mental state but also the success of his composition. He
states this idea quite explicitly in the introduction to his edition
of the letters of Sir William Temple:

> *how great a Master* [Temple] *was of* [the English tongue], *has I think,
> never appeared so much, as it will in the following Letters; wherein
> the Style appears so very different, according to the difference of the
> Persons, to whom they were address'd; either Men of Business, or
> Idle; of Pleasure, or Serious; of great or of less Parts or Abilities, in
> their several Stations. So, that, one may discover, the Characters of
> most of those Persons, he writes to, from the Stile of his Letters.*[14]

Temple's mastery of "our English Tongue" is apparent to the
degree that we can "discover" or infer the "Characters" of the
persons to whom he writes merely by analyzing his style of
writing to them. Although these remarks refer to a letter-writer's
address to specific people, Swift applied similar principles to the
"general reader" whom a novelist or satirist must imagine.[15]

Swift's tendency to write as if to a particularized portrait of the
reader is perhaps most clearly revealed in one of his remarks
about the *Travels*: "I tell you after all that I do not hate Mankind,
it is vous autres who hate them because you would have them
reasonable Animals, and are Angry for being disappointed. I
have always rejected that Definition and made another of my
own."[16] These words are often quoted as evidence either for or
against the supposed misanthropy of Swift's satires, yet they also

hint at an important aesthetic principle: a satirist has the power
of attributing to mankind and to his readers whatever traits he
wishes as he writes. In fact, he has an obligation to do so, since
his own mental peace as well as the success of his satire will be
determined by the choices he makes. Some men might indeed be
"reasonable Animals," but nothing is lost by treating them as if
they were not and basing a satire on such a view, even when you
know it to be an exaggeration.

Here Swift suggests that literal truth is not a matter of central
importance in satire and can even be a liability; it is preferable to
expect little of particular men, even if you are aware that they are
virtuous, for you will then be pleasantly surprised at their behavior. After all, a misanthropy that is directed against an admittedly hypothetical "mankind" is far less upsetting than an anger
at actual human beings. Swift articulated this principle in a letter
of advice to his friend Sheridan:

> expect no more from Man than such *an Animal* [my emphasis] is
> capable of, and you will every day find my Description of Yahoes
> more resembling. You should think and deal with every Man as a
> Villain, without calling him so, or flying from him, or valuing him
> less.[17]

As we shall see, Gulliver often applies this approach to the
readers of his narrative; in his mind he exaggerates the attributes
he assumes that readers might possess, knowing all the while
that he is making false or tenuous assumptions. More often than
not, he treats the reader according to his imagined and only
partially conceived vision. If we can understand the confusion of
a man who is treated "as a villain" without being called so, we
can similarly fathom the perplexed response of the reader of
Gulliver's "Travels."[18]

This odd strategy is remote from the most frequently discussed
features of satire, yet John Dryden's "Discourse Concerning the
Original and Progress of Satire" asserts a strikingly similar idea.
Describing the inborn genius of the best satirists, Dryden remarks, "How easy it is to call rogue and villain, and that wittily!
But how hard to make a man appear a fool, or a blockhead, or a
knave, without using any of those opprobrious terms!"[19] The
most skillful satires attack by seeming not to; they deal with men
as villains but without calling them so. Here Dryden locates the
satiric mechanism not in the correspondences between the literary work and the object of its attack but in the language and style

of address to its object. Whether or not Swift drew this notion from Dryden's essay, his technique of attributing imagined traits to the reader powerfully accomplishes the very aim that Dryden recommends.

In the address "to the Reader" at the start of the *Travels*, the "Publisher" uses this strategy of imagining the reader's attributes. He explains that in his abridgment of the nautical passages, "I was resolved to fit the Work as much as possible to the general Capacity of Readers," as if he were certain what such capacities might be. As we read this sentence we assume that the publisher knows us and is on our side. However, in the very next sentence he withdraws his assurance, and when he does, we feel an inexplicable uneasiness:

> if my own Ignorance in Sea-Affairs shall have led me to commit some Mistakes, I alone am answerable for them: And if any Traveller hath a Curiosity to see the whole Work at large, as it came from the Hand of the Author, I will be ready to gratify him. (p. 10)

The first sentence had assumed the "general Capacity" of readers to be of a clearly identifiable nature, while the second sentence modestly acknowledges such assumptions to be mere hypotheses. Further, the passage refers to the reader as a "Traveller" through the "Work," while only a few paragraphs earlier the publisher referred to Gulliver's "Papers" themselves as if they were the "Travellers": "I now venture to send them into the World," he declares. The text and the imagined reader are thus voyaging toward a confrontation, and we remain in doubt about which party, text or reader, is more in control. By this direct address to "the Reader" Swift draws actual readers into the struggle since we must either accept or reject the publisher's characterization of us, and yet the moment we have done so he undermines our assurance.[20]

The letter to Cousin Sympson, added in 1735, multiplies the complication. Within it, Gulliver says that he has sent his cousin certain corrections to be inserted "if ever there should be a second Edition," and he adds a peculiar qualification: "I cannot stand to them, but shall leave that Matter to my judicious and candid Readers, to adjust it as they please" (p. 7). We realize that Swift is being facetious in a style that anticipates Tristram Shandy's calling attention to the artifice of his "life"; nevertheless, by the action of speaking these words Gulliver creates a hypothetical "judicious and candid Reader" whose presence all actual readers must confront, just as they must deal with the various voices of Gulliver himself. We are forced to consider what it would indeed mean to "adjust" *Gulliver's Travels* "as [we] please." Obviously there is no answer to the question, and Swift eagerly invites our perplexity.

One fact is clear about Swift's attitude toward the "literal" readers of *Gulliver's Travels:* he believed that "civilized Europeans" were all capable of understanding his book. He vehemently expressed this idea to his French translator, the Abbé des Fontaines, who worried that cultural differences would prevent the French people from enjoying the *Travels* as much as the English. Swift protested:

> les memes vices, et les memes follies regnent par tout, du moins, dans tous les pays civilises de l'Europe, et l'auteur qui n'ecrit que pour une ville, une province, un Royaume, ou meme un siecle, merite si peu d'etre traduit qu'il ne merite pas d'etre lû.[21]

Not only will the French understand *Gulliver's Travels*, but the author who aims at too narrow an audience does not deserve to have a readership at all. We may assume from these words that actual readers of a wide variety are expected to enjoy *Gulliver's Travels;* but what are we to make of the imagined readers that Gulliver calls into being?

3

It is apparent in the very language of *Gulliver's Travels* that the book pulls in different directions generically and that it thereby makes a special demand on the reader to remain flexible enough to adjust his or her response as appropriate. Sentence by sentence, Swift elicts variant and often contradictory reactions from us, but without acknowledging the confusion. He does so by inviting three distinct modes of reading and thereby positing, in effect, three kinds of "implied readers." Moreover, it is essential to acknowledge the differences among them, for until we recongize their incompatibility, we continue to treat *Gulliver's Travels* like other books. Typically, when we read we assume that an author or narrator addresses the "reader" as a consistent entity. The very concept of "narration" assumes that variations in the tale will arise from shifts in the point of view of the speaker and not from changes in the listener. *Gulliver's Travels* oddly reverses this assumption, and for this reason it is inappropriate to classify the work with other narratives.

The first of the three modes of reader response prompted by *Gulliver's Travels* is that most readily recognized by critics who accept Edward Rosenheim's definition of satire as *"an attack by means of a manifest fiction upon discernible historic particulars."*[22] The text forces such readers to perceive implied connections between events described within the *Travels* and recognizable events in the real world. Through such a process we identify Flimnap as a satiric portrait of Walpole and we notice that the conflict between Lilliput and Blefuscu alludes to the historic rivalry and warfare between England and France. By spelling out the implications of such responses, critics have rightly although not exhaustively accounted for part 1 as a political allegory. We can explain much of what goes on in the first voyage by this approach, yet it is important to recognize that the allegory is not perfect, consistent, or complete. Analysis of the allegory is only one of three distinct modes of response that the text explicitly invites, and our awareness of the others can free us to explore the allegorical implications as far as they go without worrying that they do not explain everything about the book as a whole.

Indeed, the recent trend among critics has been to acknowledge that the allegorical features of the *Travels* are not wholly adequate. Phillip Harth, for example, cautions:

> At certain points in Swift's narrative, though not consistently, some of the characters and events suggest analogies to the alert reader. . . . Such details are not symbols but allusions suggesting parallels in the reader's own experience which confirm the truth of Gulliver's generalizations from what he has observed in Lilliput.[23]

Swift clearly hoped that readers would recognize such parallels to a greater or lesser degree and draw appropriate conclusions from them. Doing so always involves our eager criticism of our world, independent of Gulliver's judgment. Furthermore, when we respond in this mode we tacitly assume that Gulliver does not really exist but that he is a persona or a tool of the satire. Our mood is such that we laugh at Swift's blatant artifice when Gulliver pretends to talk to us by directly addressing us as readers. We lightly dismiss such unnecessary phrases as, "The Reader may please to observe" (p. 44), "I shall not trouble the Reader" (p. 54), "I . . . shall not interrupt the Reader with the Particulars" (p.

54), and "The Reader may remember, that" (p. 55). These words call attention to the book's artifice; they distance actual readers from the text. At such moments our emotional or empathetic response to Gulliver is of a minimal intensity.

Swift's method is treacherous, however, for at other points the same sort of phrase used in a slightly different context calls for a second, radically different mode of reader response. For example, after describing his capture by the Lilliputians, his arms, legs, and hair fastened to the ground and small human creatures running up and down his body, Gulliver says, "I lay all this while, as the Reader may believe, in great Uneasiness" (p. 22). The phrase "as the Reader may believe" is as artificial and stylized as those I pointed to earlier. Yet precisely because we can "believe" or relate to Gulliver's uncomfortable situation our response is of a fundamentally different order. Here we feel in league with Gulliver. The visual image of having one's hair and limbs tied down and small creatures crawling over one's body creates an undeniable uneasiness in all of us, and we can relate to the fictional character who reacts to the situation as we would.

In this instance, because we can confirm the fictional Gulliver's assessment of the situation, we are willing to be included in his use of the pronouns "we" and "us." The phenomenon occurs repeatedly throughout the *Travels*. For example, after his description of the people of Lagado, Gulliver speaks of his view of the mathematicians of Europe and concludes that both suffer "from a very common Infirmity of human Nature, inclining us to be more curious and conceited in Matters where we have least Concern, and for which we are least adapted either by Study or Nature" (p. 164). Here we readily accept the use of "us" because we can assent to the truth of Gulliver's generalization. Sometimes, however, we feel a distinct oddity in the sense of allegiance that Gulliver creates. For example, we find ourselves accepting a designation as Englishmen when Gulliver expresses indignation at the king of Brobdingnag's contempt for human grandeur: "my Colour came and went several Times, with Indignation to hear our noble Country, the Mistress of Arts and Arms, the Scourge of *France*, the Arbitress of *Europe*, the Seat of Virtue, Piety, Honour and Truth, the Pride and Envy of the World, so contemptuously treated" (p. 107). Here, whether or not we are English, we tacitly assent to a shared perspective with Gulliver while at the same time disagreeing with his blind admiration for "our" country. We sense that the king's assessment of the English people as "diminutive Insects" is justly based on Gulliver's "too copious" account of "us" as a people who "fight," "dispute," "cheat," and "betray," but we can only do so if we are willing to claim a knowledge of England equally as full as that of Gulliver, its inhabitant. Admittedly, these responses are not considered views that we hold with any seriousness, for the illusion is dispelled the moment that we consider it; nevertheless, the pressure of Gulliver's sentence quietly elicits from us a response something like the one that I have sketched.

Sometimes Gulliver's use of the collective "us" is more simple, as for example when he says, "I was at the Mathematical School, where the Master taught his Pupils after a Method scarce imaginable to us in *Europe*" (p. 186). This direct use of the collective "us" and "ours" also runs throughout Gulliver's account of mankind to his Houyhnhnm master. He explains, for instance, "I . . . told my Master, that in the Country from whence I came, those of my Kind always covered their Bodies with the Hairs of certain Animals prepared by Art, as well for Decency, as to avoid Inclemencies of Air both hot and cold" (p. 236), and we readily identify ourselves as part of "my Kind." At still other moments he attributes a collective vision to us through a sly use of metaphors. Thus we will only understand Gulliver's comparison between the cable in Lilliput and a packthread (p. 51) if we are familiar with packthreads; if we happen never to have seen one, we tend to assume that the comparison makes sense. I would argue that this explains why we do not flinch when we notice the inconsistencies in Gulliver's measurements, as for example when he says that in Blefuscu he "drew fifty of the Enemy's largest Men of War after me" (p. 52), even though such a feat would be physically impossible if all human creatures in Blefuscu are indeed six inches high, like those in Lilliput, and the ships of appropriate proportion. With a similar eagerness to overlook the facts, we tend to agree when Gulliver says that the Lilliputians write "aslant from one Corner of the Paper to the other, like Ladies in *England*" (p. 57), as if we had personally shared Gulliver's observation of an affected style of writing among English women. The comparison is an amusing one, and to feel the pleasure we are forced to assume an allegiance with Gulliver. Even if we find we cannot sympathize with his attack on female affectation, we at least acknowledge that a certain type of male will indeed hold such an opinion of women's writing and will make fun of it.

Our willing inclusion in Gulliver's "us" involves us in extreme reactions, however momentary, of either sympathy with or alienation from Gulliver himself. Each such response draws us into the fiction by forcing us to judge the truth or falsehood of the "manifest fiction's" depiction of the actual world. That is, if we react at all to Gulliver's portrayal of "our" world, as he calls it, we have by implication assented to the "truth" of the *Travels* themselves and to the existence of Gulliver, fictional though we know him to be. Our response is similar to our feeling of the "reality" of characters within novels, yet with an important difference. Unlike most such characters, Gulliver aggressively asserts his particularized relationship with his readers so that we ourselves become part of his fictional world as we assent to his reality. Thus, the vital difference between the first and second response of the implied reader is that while the first tacitly assumes that Gulliver is a mere fictional character, a "manifest fiction" that serves as a tool of the satire, the second is tantamount to accepting Gulliver as an actual person.[24] This second phenomenon is fleeting and temporary, for Gulliver is merely a literary construct; nevertheless, to react at all to the "us" is to act as if he were not. If we doubt Swift's conscious use of this technique, we have only to remember the fierce hostility of the dwarf in Brobdingnag on whom Gulliver got a very powerful revenge merely "by calling him *Brother*" (p. 108); the man's rage prompted his attempt to drown Gulliver in a dish of cream. Clearly, Swift recognized and exploited the vicious power of the collective "us."

The third mode of implied response differs from the first two since it is prompted by a "character" whose existence is posited within the text through Gulliver's direct address to him as the "Reader." This figure is not a true "character" within the narrative, however, for his identity changes radically from moment to moment, depending on the descriptive adjectives that Gulliver employs. Gulliver's choices expose a distance between himself and his "Reader" unlike the collective "us," which implies our allegiance with him. Moreover, Gulliver's adjectives reveal his assumptions about "human nature."

Our reaction to these "Readers" constitutes a third "reading mode" that contrasts importantly with the other two that I have described. Every actual reader of Swift's text practices all three, and the differences among them appear most clearly if we think of them as three sorts of implied readers that the text forces us to become. The first is a bodiless figure whose one identifiable trait is his capacity to recognize allusions and parallels between the lands Gulliver explores and the actual world. The second is a slightly less shadowy figure whose existence is implied by

Gulliver's use of the pronoun "us" and who thereby appears to share the same cultural and national heritage as the narrator himself. Unlike either of these two, the third implied reader defines himself or herself in relation to the "Reader" who possesses a series of ever-changing but highly specific traits. For example, the "Reader" is at various points described as male ("him," p. 10), "candid" (p. 29), good at understanding the ideas of the Lilliputians even when Gulliver himself "could not very perfectly understand them" (p. 37), "curious" about "the Style and Manner of Expression peculiar to" the Lilliputians (p. 43) or simply "curious" in general (p. 57), possessed with a capable imagination (p. 41), likely to be "diverted" by details of Gulliver's domestic life in Lilliput (p. 63), someone who does not always wish to be "troubled" with "particular Accounts" (pp. 74, 78, 79, etc.), "indulgent" (p. 90), "gentle" (p. 94), "courteous" (p. 127), "judicious" (p. 162), and so forth. When all adjectives are considered together, a complete or coherent description of the "Reader's character" does not emerge, yet the specificity of these adjectives is such that we cannot merely dismiss them as jokes exposing the artifice of the text.

Each of these miniatures demands a local response from actual readers. For example, when Gulliver assumes that the reader will be "curious" about the exact size, shape, and look of the nursing mother's breast in Brobdingnag, we are forced to consider whether or not he is right about us. He says, "I must confess no Object ever disgusted me so much as the Sight of her monstrous Breast, which I cannot tell what to compare with, so as to give the curious Reader an Idea of its Bulk, Shape and Colour" (p. 91). By the delayed placement in his sentence of the term "curious Reader" Gulliver gives us sufficient time to become curious about the details of the breast so that we are then embarrassed when he attributes a curiosity to us rather than to himself. Swift does not call us prurient; instead, he simply assumes that we are and behaves accordingly. To recall his advice to Sheridan, he treats us as if we were villains but without calling us so. By this technique Swift draws our attention to our own curiosity, and he causes us to blush. At each of our encounters with Gulliver's address to the "Reader" a dual process occurs. We partially own up to Gulliver's accuracy in guessing our thoughts, and we simultaneously disown at least a portion of the attributed traits. Gradually throughout the text, the "Reader" becomes an object of our derision and/or disdain, for our impulse is to distinguish ourselves from the reader whom Gulliver claims to know so well.

Because all three of the implied reader responses come into play for actual readers of the *Travels*, critics have understandably felt a certain generic confusion in the work. Robert Scholes and Robert Kellogg once argued that the interpretive disputes about part 4 stem from "assumptions by critics that Gulliver himself must be regarded either as a 'real' and developing character or as a mere tool of allegorical satire"—when in fact he represents a "fusion" of these two kinds of "fictional images of reality."[25] My point is that this error has also been made with regard to the reader's response, insisting that it be single and consistent rather than seeing that the implied reader's identity is multiple and that the actual reader's reaction is thereby shifting and unstable. At times we do indeed break though the "manifest fiction" of the text, but at other moments Gulliver remains for us a crucially realistic and even moving character.[26]

4

While it is true that there is a range of fluctuation in the reader's reaction to *Gulliver's Travels*, the sequential experience of the text is also vitally important in light of Swift's heightened awareness of his readers.[27] As I have argued, his expressed attitudes toward the experience of reading indicate that he arranged the four sections of *Gulliver's Travels* not according to the "satiric message" or the "ideas" they were to convey but to intensify their power to manipulate us. Swift wrote part 3 last, after completing the other three voyages, and his ordering of the books thus suggests that their sequence was a considered choice.

As we progress from part 1 to part 4, we gradually gain experience in dealing with our fluctuating response. That is, we develop skills in reading Swift's satire, and each new voyage gives us a fresh chance to practice them. We can thereby see why Swift inserted the voyage to Laputa after parts 1 and 2, for it contains the largest mass of satiric allusion to the scientific, intellectual, and political worlds. It is the section of *Gulliver's Travels* in which the reader most fully and diversely tests his skill as an experienced interpreter of Swift's satire, and it thereby prepares us for the trap that Swift lays for the confident reader in part 4. In part 3, we recognize allusions to the actual world, and we also waver between trusting and questioning Gulliver's reliability as a narrator, ultimately feeling secure in our own skill in asking such questions about narrators. The "Voyage to the Country of the

Houyhnhnms," however, presents a new and unusual challenge. To see that this is so, we have only to compare the first sentences of each of the four voyages.

The opening lines of parts 1, 2, and 3 all convey essentially the same kind of information and do so whether they are read in the context of the whole work or out of it:

1. My Father had a small Estate in *Nottinghamshire;* I was the Third of five Sons.
2. Having been condemned by Nature and Fortune to an active and restless life; in two Months after my Return, I again left my native Country, and took Shipping in the *Downs* on the 20th day of *June* 1702, in the *Adventure,* Capt. *John* Nicholas, a *Cornish* Man, Commander, bound for *Surat.*
3. I had not been at home above ten Days, when Captain *William Robinson,* a *Cornish* Man, Commander of the *Hope-well,* a stout Ship of three Hundred Tuns, came to my House.

These sentences tell us external facts, many of which turn out to be superfluous, either about who Gulliver is, the people he is with, or what he is doing or about to do. They forecast that the formal structure of each voyage will involve an accurate listing of details selected by the sort of encyclopedic principle that dominates many travel narratives. Read in context, the opening lines of parts 2 and 3 are enriched by our external knowledge that Gulliver has traveled before and that he has had many strange adventures and has survived. This awareness leads us to expect that in parts 2 and 3 he will have similarly instructive but ultimately harmless experiences, which of course he does. Yet there is no "plot" in any of the first books, in the sense that E. M. Forster uses the term. Within each book the mock travel narrative easily coexists with and helps convey the satiric purpose, and we tend to accept the additive structure of the narrative as Gulliver proceeds from one adventure to the next.

However, the opening sentence of part 4 presents us with a peculiar dilemma. Gulliver says, "I continued at home with my Wife and Children about five Months in a very happy Condition, if I could have learned the Lesson of knowing when I was well"— and for the first time we are confronted with an opening line that demands interpretation.[28] It is not immediately clear what Gulliver means by the foreboding lamentation, "if I could have learned the Lesson of knowing when I was well."[29] Taken in its most obvious sense it seems to imply that Gulliver should have known to stay at home. Yet eventually we realize that the narrator of part 4 is the Gulliver who so much preferred life among the Houyhnhnms and that it is impossible to believe that he should wish to have stayed home and never met them. As students continue to demonstrate, all readers have trouble accounting for the mood of Gulliver as the narrator of part 4 who reveals for the first time, suddenly and unexpectedly, his bitter attitude toward mankind upon his forced exile from the land of the Houyhnhnms. On a first reading the opening sentence is especially confusing, for the only hint that we should notice the narrator's new attitude has been the letter to Sympson where we hear the same despairing voice; it would take an exceptionally alert reader to connect the tone of the letter with the voice in part 4, since we tend to forget the letter as we read parts 1, 2, and 3. Moreover, of all the four opening sentences, that of part 4 is the only one that seems to warn of an instability or serious threat to Gulliver's well-being to be brought on by travel. The placement of this voyage at the end makes a radical difference, since our prior experience of parts 1, 2, and 3 allays the seriousness of our expectations for part 4—and in doing so it dangerously although intentionally misleads us.

Our sequential encounter with the first three voyages and our growing adeptness at the three modes of reading determine our approach to the final journey; while we feel that misfortune is ahead, we assume that it will be an external disaster, which will yield knowledge, wisdom, and pleasure for the reader. This benefit will compensate for any of the hardships Gulliver goes through in the process. We are predisposed to think that we will join in the laughter with or at Gulliver or at whatever object of satire Swift will next attack.[30] Here we smugly expect to be able for a fourth time to recognize the foolishness of others. However, in part 4 Swift does not simply point at recognizable evils in the world or implicate his readers through comparison; instead, he prompts us to an act of prideful folly and then forces us to recognize our error. Gradually we realize that Gulliver himself is not who we think he is.

In part 4, Gulliver is an alien in disguise, like a Houyhnhnm who seems to be only a horse, and the disorientation and humiliation we thus experience at the discovery of his true temperament structurally parallels Gulliver's "Horror and Astonishment" at discovering a "perfect human Figure" in the features of a Yahoo (pp. 229–30). We feel glimmerings of the realization as we hear Gulliver describe humankind with less and less sympathy, but we are absolutely aghast when we watch Gulliver's final response to the kind Don Pedro and especially to his family. Here Swift perfected a strategy that he was to use again at the end of *A Modest Proposal*. In the latter work we are reduced to surprised silence in horrified respect for mothers who would insist that their children would be better off eaten; in the *Travels* we feel a terrifying and unanticipated pity for the misanthropic voyager who cannot stand the stench of his own family. In both works Swift slyly manipulates us until we uneasily assent to the rightness of the very attitudes that seemed such obvious objects of ridicule at the beginning. At the end of *A Modest Proposal*, it makes a grizzly sort of sense that babies would be better off eaten, and we shudder at this discovery. At the end of the *Travels*, we are forced to admit that Gulliver's rudeness to Don Pedro and to his family are inevitable responses in the wake of the voyage of self-discovery and painful exile that he and we have undergone. Just when we have become most smugly confident in our knowledge of Gulliver and in our ability to interpret Swift's satires, Swift makes us extremely uncomfortable with the character who Gulliver turns out to be.[31]

In *Gulliver's Travels* Swift uses this clever device to expose the treachery of satire as discourse. As if to call even further attention to the problem, he focused on it within Gulliver's letter to Cousin Sympson.[32] The letter attacks the reader for his failure to correct the world's ills in direct response to Swift's text. Captain Gulliver complains that the "Reformations" that were "plainly deducible from the Precepts delivered in my Book" have not been put into practice:

> I cannot learn that my Book hath produced one single Effect according to mine Intentions: I desired you would let me know by Letter, when Party and Faction were extinguished; Judges learned and upright; Pleaders honest and modest, with some Tincture of common Sense; and *Smithfield* blazing with Pyramids of Law-Books; the young Nobility's Education entirely changed; the Physicians banished; the Female *Yahoos* abounding in Virtue, Honour, Truth and good Sense: Courts and Levees of great Ministers thoroughly weeded and swept; Wit, Merit and Learning rewarded; all Disgracers of the Press in Prose and Verse, condemned to eat nothing but their own Cotton, quench their Thirst with their own Ink. (p. 6)

In these last words we see a twisted version of Pope's comment to Swift that readers should *"Eat your Book."* Gulliver not only uses his letter to attack the ineffectual reader but also to comment on the veracity of his tale; he remarks that no Yahoo has ever been so "presumptuous" as to dispute its sincerity, since "the Truth immediately strikes every Reader with Conviction" (p. 8).

With these words, Swift creates an interpretive problem, for we clearly do not think of *Gulliver's Travels* as literally true. As we read about the people of Lilliput, Brobdingnag, and Laputa we accept that we are in a realm of satire that employs fiction to refer to actual situations, people, events, and human traits. Moreover, in the final chapter of part 4, the same embittered Gulliver complains that travel narratives easily abuse the "Credulity" of the "unwary Reader" and expresses his "great Disgust against this Part of Reading" (p. 291), as if the truth did *not* possess the power to "strike" us with conviction in the way that he first suggested. What then does it mean to be Captain Gulliver's "Reader with Conviction"? Is this a good or a bad trait? And why in the letter to Sympson does Swift introduce this doubt about Gulliver's consistency in close juxtaposition with Gulliver's complaint that his book has failed to "amend" its readers because they have not responded to it as a clear, truthful, and explicit directive to action?[33] Swift's purpose in raising the problem is to force us as readers to be not merely active, as Uphaus argues, but vigilant—unlike the unfortunate "maid of honour" who fell asleep while reading a romance (p. 55).

The very sentence with which Swift brings up the issue of reader response is itself maddeningly difficult to interpret: "the Truth immediately strikes every Reader with Conviction." Does the prepositional phrase, "with Conviction," define the noun "Reader" or the verb "strikes"? Must a reader possess "Conviction" in order to perceive truth, or does truth itself contain sufficient force to overwhelm all readers? Puzzling over this question of meaning calls attention to the phrase itself so that we notice its recurrence throughout the *Travels*. In part 1, for example, it occurs in a context that reverses its expected sense. Gulliver tells us in chapter 7, that a "considerable Person at Court" (p. 67) came to him with his articles of impeachment and the news that "his sacred Majesty, and the Council, who are your Judges, were in their own Consciences *fully convinced* [my emphasis] of your Guilt; which was a sufficient Argument to condemn you to death, without the *formal Proofs required by the strict Letter of the Law*" (p. 71). In the eyes of the reader, Gulliver is by no means condemned by these words; rather, the sentence convicts the Lilliputians of injustice for condemning Gulliver to death merely on the strength of their "convictions." We also are aware that the Lilliputians are great readers and interpreters of texts, for they possess "Many hundred large Volumes" on the Big- and Little-Endian controversy, yet their folly is once again clear when they conclude that there simply cannot be a whole race of men of the size of Gulliver because their "Histories of six Thousand Moons make no Mention of any other Regions" (p. 49).[34] Far more sensible is the attitude of Peter Williams, who meets Gulliver shortly after his escape from Lilliput and at first believes him mad until the tiny sheep and cattle in his pockets "clearly convinced him of [Gulliver's] Veracity" (p. 79). All of these examples show that "immediate convictions" are often seriously misleading.

Gulliver next alludes to this problem in part 2 where he himself is "produced" as "evidence" of the "Truth" of his own, minute existence (pp. 86–97). After leaving Brobdingnag, Gulliver tells his fantastic story to the Captain who rescues him and says, "as the Truth always forceth its Way into rational Minds; so, this honest worthy Gentleman, who had some Tincture of Learning, and very good Sense, was *immediately convinced* [my emphasis] of my Candor and Veracity" (p. 146). Despite the Captain's willingness to believe, Gulliver again "confirms" his truth by another display of souvenirs, an action that prompts him to comment on the evils of travel books that divert "ignorant Readers" by straying from exact truth (p. 147). In part 3, when in the school of political projectors, Gulliver remarks that "there is nothing so extravagant and irrational which some Philosophers have not maintained for Truth" (p. 187), as if even the most outrageous propositions could be made to "seem" true in certain contexts. Indeed, when Gulliver first sees a Yahoo he tells us, "I never beheld in all my Travels so disagreeable an Animal" (p. 223), yet upon another viewing of the same features, he exclaims, "I observed, in this abominable Animal, a perfect human Figure" (p. 230). Gulliver does not account for his perception of a double truth in a single reality.[35] In part 4, when Gulliver offers to expose his unclothed body to his Houyhnhnm master, he says, "as to my own Person I would give him immediate Conviction" (p. 236), again as if truth itself were powerful and immediately clear. When Gulliver discusses the Houyhnhnms' lack of a conception of "what is evil in a rational Creature," he tells us:

Neither is *Reason* among them a Point problematical as with us, where Men can argue with Plausibility on both Sides of a Question;

but *strikes you with immediate Conviction* [my emphasis]; as it must needs do where it is not mingled, obscured, or discoloured by Passion and Interest. (p. 267)[36]

In this instance, both parts of the proposition seem true: truth itself is potent, but it is so only if man has developed his reason sufficiently. The very word "Conviction" occurs so often, and in so many forms, that it becomes a central conundrum in the text. When we first hear the phrase, "Reader with Conviction," its positive connotation urges us to accept the idea that the truth *does* seem immediately clear to a virtuous reader, especially one who has "some Tincture of Learning, and very good Sense" (p. 146, echoing p. 8). Yet at the same time Swift continually subverts our best efforts at reading with such immediate awareness of truth.

The letter to Sympson itself displays a curious illogic that confounds even readers of the greatest "Conviction." For example, Gulliver claims that "Reformations" can be "plainly deduced" from "Precepts." On the surface this statement assumes a kind of mathematical clarity; the notion seems meaningful because the sentence echoes the language of logicians. Yet "Reformations," if we are to take the term in the usual sense, are not "deduced" directly from precepts that have been "delivered" in books; rather, they are conceived of through an application of precepts to specific situations in the world.[37] Furthermore, Swift's text itself never "delivers" precepts at all but instead implies them through its satiric structures. The precepts must be deduced from the book by the reader.

We see other instances of such logical disjunction in part 4, for example in the long passage that describes Gulliver's first view of the Yahoos. It seems "novelistic" in its sequential and descriptive structure; however, on close examination we discover phrases that merely appear to inform us of causal relations and facts while in actuality they disarm and disorient us, apparently without any final purpose. For example, why does Gulliver bother to tell us that "The Land was divided by long Rows of Trees, not regularly planted, but naturally growing" (p. 223)? His careful observation of the curious regularity in "naturally growing" trees invites us to draw significant conclusions or to read this descriptive detail as more than mere description. Yet it is impossible to articulate exactly what information the sentence conveys. By its form the sentence suggests a design or purpose, which it ultimately belies. Again and again we notice ways in which Swift places us in such quandaries. When Gulliver triumphantly tells us that he "escaped pretty well" from the rain of Yahoo excrement, he adds the contradictory afterthought that he "was almost stifled with the Filth" (p. 224). By its orderly structure the passage seems at first to describe a closed form: Gulliver encounters the Yahoos, a conflict develops, and it is resolved to Gulliver's satisfaction. Nevertheless, we are left with the vague feeling that the narrative has failed to offer the sort of assurance and closure that we would expect because of its shape. We strongly sense that Gulliver's apparent triumph or control of the situation is not unqualified, but we are uncertain why we intuit this. We are having difficulty being readers with conviction.

The presence of Robert Purefoy ("pure faith") in Gulliver's doomed vessel of part 4 is Swift's crucial warning to the "unwary Reader" to pay attention to what he is doing. Purefoy is the young physician whom Gulliver enlists to replace himself on his last voyage because he has "grown weary of a Surgeon's Employment at Sea" (p. 221). Following this suggestive detail, we cannot help but think that "pure faith" in oneself or strength of conviction is dangerous when we hear, a few lines after the mention of Purefoy, the story of the tragic drowning of Captain Pocock. We are told he was "an honest Man, and a good Sailor, but a little too positive in his own Opinions, which was the Cause of his Destruction." Gulliver prompts our curiosity about the details of this story, yet he refuses to satisfy us with an account of the causal connection between strong opinions and drowning. Nevertheless, the presence of both Robert Purefoy (the surgeon) and Captain Pocock warns us that although we have become experienced readers of *Gulliver's Travels* and of Swift's satire by the time we began part 4, we would do well to reexamine our own "conviction" in assessing the narrative.[38]

By making Robert Purefoy a physician, Swift signals us to take the allegorical name seriously, for Gulliver himself is a physician. Whether or not the title page was designed by Swift, from the first edition in 1726 to that of Faulkner in 1735 it consistently describes Lemuel Gulliver as "first a Surgeon, and then a Captain of several Ships."[39] Oddly, critics tend to ignore or discount this detail, yet both Robert Purefoy and Pope's comment that the "Travels" were a "bitter pill" for readers suggest that there is significance in the choice of Gulliver's profession.[40] Physician Purefoy urges the moral healing of the reader. The symbolism of his name is a clue that like Captain Pocock, we are about to be drowned by being "a little too positive in our opinions" even within the context of Swift's "amending" satire. As I suggested at the outset, if we are cured at all, it will be a secondary effect of our bitter and violent experience within Swift's text.

The very word "strike" occurs not only in Gulliver's statement of how the truth should affect us but also in a number of important moments throughout the *Travels* in which the truth "strikes" Gulliver and, by implication, us. Gulliver tells us that he "was struck with the utmost Grief and Despair" at his Houyhnhnm Master's "Exhortation" to leave the country (p. 280). He tells us that it "struck" him with "utmost Shame, Confusion and Horror" to imagine that he had been the parent of Yahoos (p. 289). Although he does not always use the word "struck," various other critical passages capture the same sense of violence and bitterness at a realization that comes from a new sight or insight. For example, when Gulliver tells us about the moment he realized the affinity between Yahoos and men, he says, "My Horror and Astonishment are not to be described" (pp. 229–30). The Yahoo himself has had the analogous experience a few pages earlier, for as Gulliver tells us, "The ugly Monster, when he saw me, distorted several ways every Feature of his Visage, and stared as at an Object he had never seen before" (p. 224). In response to this gesture, Gulliver "strikes" the Yahoo "a good Blow with the flat Side" of his "Hanger." Other moments of mutual shock and horror occur in parts 2 and 3, as for example, when Gulliver in "Astonishment" observes the flying island, while a crowd gathered upon it and "[he] found by their pointing towards [him] and to each other, that they plainly discovered [him]" (p. 157). The same shock occurs when Gulliver sees himself: "When I happened to behold the Reflection of my own Form in a Lake or Fountain, I turned away my Face in Horror and detestation of my self; and could better endure the Sight of a common *Yahoo*, then of my own Person" (p. 278).

Perhaps the most blatant hint that Swift feels he must awaken his readers by literally striking them comes in part 3 when Gulliver gives us first an elaborate description of the action and function of the flappers in Laputa and then calls attention to his own function as a flapper of his reader: "It was necessary to give the Reader this Information, without which he would be at the same Loss with me, to understand the Proceedings of these People" (p. 160). In writing his book, Swift is concerned, as Faulkner suggests, about the force with which "the Sounds might strike the Ear, as well as the Sense the Understanding" of the reader. At the ultimate moment when Gulliver is "struck . . . with the utmost Shame, Confusion and Horror" at being the father of Yahoo children, we are struck with horror at him and at the dangerous tendency of satire to lure us into a sympathy with Swift's cynical narrator.

Pope was oddly astute in his remark that Swift wished to "break [his] vial of Indignation over the heads of the wretched pityful creatures of this World, nay would make them *Eat* [his] *Book*, which [he has] made as bitter a pill for them as possible." Swift believed that readers typically come away unaffected by satire. Therefore, Gulliver, the ship's surgeon, will heal us or at least shock us through our own bitter experience of the text. Swift sets a trap for us in part 4 so that we are quite literally "struck" with astonishment at the moment we realize that Gulliver's voice is no longer what we thought it to be. Our realization that our narrator is an alien in disguise parallels his own horror at seeing a "perfect human Figure" in a Yahoo. We must take our lesson from the unwary maid of honor who fell asleep while reading a romance. Gulliver drowned the fire that she started, and Swift warns his readers to be careful lest the treacherous undertow of the satire drown us for being "a little too positive in [our] own Opinions."

Terry Castle has asserted that "Grammophobia, or fear of the written word, is at least potential within the Swiftian text"; yet close examination of the text of *Gulliver's Travels* shows her argument to be incomplete, for it blurs the distinction between the tasks of the writer and the reader.[41] Swift is not inadvertently revealing a fear of written language but advancing his respect for its generic powers. He is training us to be wary of an excessive faith in our capacity for linguistic or literary analysis. Gulliver may insist that "the Truth immediately strikes every Reader with Conviction," but Swift ultimately warns us that as "readers with conviction" we should be cautious since "Precepts" do not necessarily translate into "Reformations" or effective action. Pride continually threatens to cloud the vision, even when we think we are most vigilant.

Notes

1. According to evidence from Swift's correspondence, he began composing *Gulliver's Travels* in the early 1720s. For a persuasive argument that Swift's changes for the 1735 edition were revisions rather than corrections see F. P.

Lock, "The Text of 'Gulliver's Travels,'" *Modern Language Review* 76 (1981): 513–33.

2. *The Correspondence of Jonathan Swift*, ed. Harold Williams, 5 vols. (Oxford: Clarendon Press, 1963; rpt. with corr. 1965), 3:376 and 383.

3. Swift, *Correspondence*, 3:96. Williams quotes George Sherburn, who accepts Warburton's view that this is Pope's first mention of the *Essay on Man*.

4. Swift, *Correspondence*, 3:108.

5. Swift, *Correspondence*, 2:381; 2:464; 3:117; 2:36–37; 3:104; and 3:226.

6. *Gulliver's Travels*, in *The Prose Works of Jonathan Swift*, ed. Herbert Davis et al. (Oxford: Basil Blackwell, 1939–68), 11:213. All future references will be cited by page number within the text. W. B. Carnochan explores the connection between moral and physical sickness in *Gulliver's Travels* in "Some Roles of Lemuel Gulliver," *Texas Studies in Language and Literature* 5 (1964): 520–29.

7. See Robert Uphaus, *The Impossible Observer: Reason and the Reader in Eighteenth-Century Prose* (Lexington: University Press of Kentucky, 1979), pp. 16–17; and Alain Bony, "Call me Gulliver," *Poétique* 4 (1973): 202. See also "Preface: Swift and the Reader's Role" in Clive T. Probyn, ed., *The Art of Jonathan Swift* (London: Vision Press, 1978); and Frederik N. Smith, "The Danger of Reading Swift: The Double Binds of *Gulliver's Travels*," *Studies in the Literary Imagination* 17 (Spring 1984): 35–47.

8. See W. B. Carnochan, "The Complexity of Swift: Gulliver's Fourth Voyage," *Studies in Philology* 60 (1963): 23–44, for an essay that explores related ideas. My argument resembles that of Robert Uphaus; however, Uphaus obscures the complexity of the experience of reading *Gulliver's Travels* in his effort to demonstrate the single point that the text transforms the reader from an observer to a participant.

9. W. B. Carnochan has also detected an affinity between the *Essay on Man* and *Gulliver's Travels*. See *Lemuel Gulliver's Mirror for Man* (Berkeley: University of California Press, 1968), pp. 2 and 120.

10. *The Works of the Reverend Dr. Jonathan Swift*, 11 vols. (Dublin, 1762), 1:vii.

11. Irvin Ehrenpreis says that Swift's decision to locate part 4 at the end of the *Travels* is also evidence of his "desire for the sequence of parts to have its own power." See *Swift: The Man, His Works, and the Age* (Cambridge: Harvard University Press, 1962–83), 3:444. See also Michael V. DePorte, *Nightmares and Hobbyhorses: Swift, Sterne, and Augustan Ideas of Madness* (San Marino: The Huntington Library, 1974), p. 94. For an essay exploring the often-slighted distinction between the voiced and the written texts of *Gulliver's Travels*, see Terry J. Castle, "Why the Houyhnhnms Don't Write: Swift, Satire and the Fear of the Text," *Essays in Literature* 7 (1980): 31.

12. Swift, *Correspondence*, 3:158.

13. Swift, *Correspondence*, 2:36 and 464. Ehrenpreis mentions that exile and banishment are persistent themes in Swift's letters during the years in which he wrote *Gulliver's Travels*. See *Swift: The Man, His Works, and the Age*, 3:471–72.

14. "The Publisher to the Reader" in *Letters Written by Sir W. Temple*, 2 vols. (London, 1700). Cf. the *Journal to Stella*, ed. Harold Williams, 2 vols. (Oxford: Clarendon Press, 1948): "Pshaw, what's all this I'm saying? methinks I am talking to MD face to face" (2:409).

15. Ehrenpreis argues that a similar skill distinguishes Swift's own letters. See "Swift's Letters" in C. J. Rawson, ed., *Swift* (London: Sphere Books, 1971),

pp. 197–215. He also suggests that *Gulliver's Travels* is better understood as a work addressed, almost like a letter, to a "core of enlightened readers" whom Swift equated in his mind with a select group of his personal friends. As Ehrenpreis explains, Swift expected these readers readily to distinguish the moments of frivolous clowning from the moments of serious satiric attack within his narration. See *Swift: The Man, His Works, and the Age*, 3:447. See also Paula R. Backscheider, "Swift's Harley and the Nature of Biography," *Biography* 5 (1982): 284–96.

16. Swift, *Correspondence*, 3:118.

17. Swift, *Correspondence*, 3:94.

18. This peculiar feature of *Gulliver's Travels* is particularly evident if we compare Swift's narrative to the other travel narratives that it presumably imitates or even borrows from, for they do not contain the frequent references to the "Reader" that pepper Swift's book. Captain William Symson's *A New Voyage to the East-Indies* (London, 1715) does begin with a statement about the reader that resembles similar remarks in the *Travels*. The preface announces that the book "has nothing in it of the Romantick Strains of Travellers, who very often discredit their Works by stuffing them with Things altogether incredible, which are ever disagreeable to judicious Readers, tho' they may happen with their Novelty to please the Ignorant." In general, however, Symson's book leaves the reader to fend for himself, unlike the intrusive Gulliver. For an argument that Swift recognized that Symson borrowed material from both John Ovington's *A Voyage to Surat* (London, 1696) and from the works of Sir William Temple, and that Swift parodied this literary fraud in *Gulliver's Travels*, see Mackie L. Jarrell, "The Handwriting of the Lilliputians," *Philological Quarterly* 37 (1958): 116–19.

19. "A Discourse Concerning the Original and Progress of Satire" in W. P. Ker, ed., *The Essays of John Dryden*, 2 vols. (Oxford: Clarendon Press, 1900), 2:92–93.

20. Uphaus importantly describes the first phase of this experience, but he overlooks the second, "undermining" tendency of Gulliver's technique.

21. Swift, *Correspondence*, 3:226. "The same vices, and the same follies rule everywhere, at least in the civilized countries of Europe, and the author who writes only for a city, a province, a kingdom, or even a century, deserves as little to be translated as to be read."

22. Edward W. Rosenheim, Jr., *Swift and the Satirist's Art* (Chicago: University of Chicago Press, 1963), p. 31.

23. Phillip Harth, "The Problem of Political Allegory in *Gulliver's Travels*," *Modern Philology* 73 (1976): 545. See also F. P. Lock, *The Politics of Gulliver's Travels* (Oxford: Clarendon Press, 1980); Carnochan, *Lemuel Gulliver's Mirror for Man*, p. 66; and Ehrenpreis, *Swift: The Man, His Works, and the Age*, 3:454.

24. Sheldon Sacks makes a similar distinction between fully realized characters in novels and those in satire by arguing that character consistency is simply not important to the success of satire. See *Fiction and the Shape of Belief* (Berkeley: University of California Press, 1967), p. 32.

25. Robert Scholes and Robert Kellogg, *The Nature of Narrative* (London, Oxford, New York: Oxford University Press, 1966), p. 115.

26. Even Uphaus gives in to the tendency to see the reader's response as a unified whole through his eagerness to argue that a consistent device of the text is the reader's breaking through the manifest fiction. By contrast, Ehrenpreis asserts that *Gulliver's Travels* is "a machine designed not to advance a set of doctrines but to start readers on the way to reflection, self-doubt, and fresh

thought." See *Swift: The Man, His Works, and the Age,* 3:454. See also David Oakleaf, "*Trompe l'Oeil:* Gulliver and the Distortions of the Observing Eye," *University of Toronto Quarterly* 53 (1983–84): 166–80.

27. Stanley Fish has argued that critics of literature should more frequently attempt to analyze "*the developing responses of the reader in relation to the words as they succeed one another in time*" and that the application of such an approach would result in the "rehabilitation of works like *The Faerie Queene* which have been criticized because their poetic worlds lack 'unity' and consistency." Fish, "Literature and the Reader: Affective Stylistics," *New Literary History* 2 (1970–71): 126–27.

28. The title of the fourth voyage also stands apart from the others since it names, for the first time, the inhabitants of the country Gulliver visits, while the others name the countries themselves: Lilliput, Brobdingnag, Laputa, Balnibari, Luggnagg, Glubbdubdrib, and Japan.

29. W. B. Carnochan suggests that the word "well" here is to be taken in the double sense, " 'well-off' and 'sound of body and mind.' " See "Some Roles of Lemuel Gulliver," p. 522. Hugo M. Reichard calls the Gulliver of part 4 a "double-dealer" who deliberately hides the facts from us. See "Gulliver the Pretender," *Papers on English Language and Literature* 1 (1965): 316–26. See also C. J. Rawson, "Gulliver and the Gentle Reader" in *Imagined Worlds: Essays on Some English Novels and Novelists in Honor of John Butt,* ed. Maynard Mack and Ian Gregor (London: Methuen, 1968), p. 59.

30. See Everett Zimmerman, *Swift's Narrative Satires: Author and Authority* (Ithaca: Cornell University Press, 1983), pp. 18–19.

31. See Uphaus, *The Impossible Observer,* p. 26.

32. Although it is written by "Gulliver," the letter has sometimes been said to echo Swift's own disappointment in his work's effect on its readers, and yet it seems clear that he expected to be disappointed from the outset. For example, in 1725 he wrote the facetious statement that the *Travels* "are admirable Things, and will wonderfully mend the World" (*Correspondence,* 3:87). I disagree with A. E. Dyson who fails to detect irony in this remark. See "Swift: The Metamorphosis of Irony," *Essays and Studies* 11, n.s. (1958): 55.

33. W. B. Carnochan also analyzes this passage in his discussion of the *Travels* as a satire on Lockean epistemology. His reading of the passage accords with mine, for he points out that within it Gulliver has inadvertently implied "a difference between the reality of his first three voyages and that of the voyage to the Houyhnhnms." See *Lemuel Gulliver's Mirror for Man,* p. 119.

34. Sir William Temple discussed this form of Lilliputian folly in *An Essay upon Ancient and Modern Learning.* He wrote, "In the growth and stature of Souls as well as Bodies . . . there are or have been, sometimes Dwarfs and sometimes Gyants in the World, yet it does not follow, that there must be such in every Age nor in every Country; This we can no more conclude, than that there never have been any, because there are none now, at least in the compass of our present Knowledge or Inquiry" (p. 31). This essay was one of several of Temple's works that Swift copied in his youth, and there are echoes of his ideas throughout *Gulliver's Travels.* For example, the tone of Gulliver's praise of "our" country echoes Temple's tone in the Preface to *An Introduction to the History of England,* which was printed, interestingly, for Richard and Ralph Simpson in 1695. Ehrenpreis goes so far as to call Gulliver a "humorous reincarnation of Sir William" (*Swift, The Man, His Works, and the Age,* 3: 456).

35. Sir William Temple also explored this notion in the third part of his *Miscellanea* (London, 1701), edited by Swift. Temple remarked the tendency of

human beings to insist on "similitudes" between themselves and baboons when in fact their facial features and hair made them look very different not only from baboons, but from each other. See "Of Popular Discontents," pp. 1–2. Here again Swift may perhaps have drawn inspiration from Temple.

36. This passage is highly reminiscent of Sir William Temple's remarks about the life and thought of the Chinese. In fact, Temple's essays anticipate several of the features of society that Swift describes throughout Gulliver's four voyages including the absence of letters among the Houyhnhnms, their reliance on reason, their attitude toward physicians, the absence of beggars in Lilliput, and the idea that "Reward and Punishment" are the "two great hinges of all Government." See *Miscellanea*, part 2 (London, 1692) and *Miscellanea*, part 3 (London, 1701).

37. Swift revealed his awareness of the proper relation between "premises" and "conclusions" when he wrote, in a letter of 1714, "I thought myself twenty times in the right, by drawing conclusions very regularly from premises which have proved wholly wrong. I think this, however, to be a plain proof that we act altogether by chance; and that the game, such as it is, plays itself." *Correspondence*, 2:22.

38. Frank Brady argues that Swift's repetition of key words and his techniques of "underlining" are evidence that Swift expected readers of *Gulliver's Travels* to look very closely at the text. See "Vexations and Diversions: Three Problems in *Gulliver's Travels*," *Modern Philology* 75 (1978): 348–50. See also William Kinsley, "Gentle Readings: Recent Work on Swift," *Eighteenth-Century Studies* 15 (1981–82): 442–53.

39. See *Travels into Several Remote Nations of the World*, 2 vols. (London, 1726); *Travels into several Remote Nations of the World* (Dublin, 1726); *Travels into Several Remote Nations of the World*, 2d ed., 2 vols. (London, 1727); and *Travels into Several Remote Nations of the World*, vol. 3 of *The Works of Jonathan Swift*, 4 vols. (Dublin, 1735).

40. Robert C. Elliott, for example, writes, "The fictive premise controlling *Gulliver's Travels* is that Gulliver, a retired sea captain, writes his memoirs," and Charles Peake pragmatically asserts that Gulliver "is a ship's surgeon in order that he may be sent on voyages and possess sufficient education to compare his own nation's institutions with those of other nations." See "Gulliver as Literary Artist," *ELH* 19 (1952): 49, and "The Coherence of *Gulliver's Travels*," in *Swift*, ed. C. J. Rawson (London: Sphere Books, 1971), p. 172. For an essay that explores the importance of Gulliver's medical profession, see W. B. Carnochan, "Some Roles of Lemuel Gulliver."

41. Castle, "Why the Houyhnhnms Don't Write," p. 31. Grant Holly makes a similar argument to Castle's but in doing so incorporates the reader. He suggests that "Swift's text makes signifying its subject, by implying a vast textuality which incorporates the reader" ("Travel and Translation: Textuality in *Gulliver's Travels*," *Criticism* 21 [1979]: 135).

Deconstructing *Gulliver's Travels:* Modern Readers and the Problematic of Genre

1

Reading a literary text is a learned behavior applied to a recognized situation, an act that takes place within a particular cultural and individual context. As readers, we are no more monolithic entities than we are in other facets of our lives: we choose the role of reader for a variety of purposes and bring different frames of reference, degrees of attention, expectations, and evaluative standards to the texts that we encounter. At one end of the theoretical spectrum of reading behavior a casual frame of reference causes attention, expectation, and evaluation to be minimal; the experience is used to stave off insomnia, to relax on the beach, to pass time in the dentist's waiting room—the text is primarily a means to that end. At the other end of the spectrum, the critical reading of literature is a more demanding act: "One must bring to it an implicit understanding of the operations of literary discourse which tells one what to look for."[1] It further implies serious attention, well formulated expectations, and a fairly complex set of evaluative determinations. Here the text as an aesthetic construct, an end-in-itself, is of major importance, and the experience of reading is a means to its comprehension and appreciation. To understand more fully a historical text that we wish to read critically, we often approach it by recreating ourselves as earlier readers, a process that means more than acquaintance with the kind of knowledge that provides basic intelligibility—vocabulary, literary conventions, and cultural context. Such re-creation seeks the specific goal of a meaning identified as the author's or the text's "intentions," or an

230

approximation of the original (not present) readers' experience of the work.

If we forego this re-creation and read an early eighteenth-century text from the vantage point of today; we will undoubtedly discover that many of the responses of earlier readers are irrelevant to our own. Reading *Gulliver's Travels*, for instance, we will not, as did one reader in Swift's day, rush to a map in search of Lilliput; nor will we react like the bishop Swift wrote to Pope about, who thought the book to be "full of improbable Lies, and for his part, he hardly believed a word of it."[2] We could not recover that kind of innocence as readers even if it seemed desirable: much that struck earlier readers as "new and strange," according to Dr. Johnson, will be neither to us, any more than our own first glimpse of the Pacific Ocean will be of the same order as Balboa's. Such earlier loci of critical attention as the machinations of Augustan political factions and the satire on scientific investigation will sustain our interest today little more than will the geographical location of Lilliput. Similarly, we are less inclined to attribute perceived peculiarities of the book to Swift's "madness" or "depravity." The temper of our own age prefers other theoretical bases. Yet in less obvious ways than is suggested by these examples, modern critics stubbornly continue to recreate themselves as earlier readers.

Genre is central to these interpretations since readers invariably bring generic assumptions to texts.[3] Reading *Gulliver's Travels* as a reader of the 1980s, however, requires that we abandon the long history of categorizations that fit the book only partially or fit according to the interests of another time; it also requires that we relinquish the security of genre itself, its authority to confer and name coherence. Jacques Derrida reminds us that the concept of genre already contains its own antithesis, or the seeds of its own deconstruction—the present and implicit assumption that genre may be transgressed or transformed.[4] This is an established dialectic, one that readily adapts to the tension between synchronic and diachronic forces in a given genre. What is difficult to tolerate when we approach a work through genre is plurality, a degree of latitude that obliterates generic boundaries entirely rather than merely emphasizing their existence by overstepping them.

The present-day uncertainty about the genre of *Gulliver's Travels* has its origin in the book's initial reception. In the words of Dr. Johnson, critics were "lost in wonder; no rules of judgment were applied to a book written in open defiance of truth and regularity."[5] This suspension of critical activity was only momentary, but it reflects a problematic that has persisted. As Sir Walter Scott writes: "Perhaps no work ever exhibited such general attractions to all classes. It offered personal and political satire to the readers in high life, low and coarse incident to the vulgar, marvels to the romantic, wit to the young and lively, lessons of morality and policy to the grave, and maxims of deep and bitter misanthropy to neglected age, and disappointed ambition."[6] *Quot lectores tot genera:* every subgenre of fictive travel narrative has seemingly been applied to *Gulliver's Travels* by now, determining which aspects of the text are foregrounded and which ignored. It has been variously regarded as philosophical tale à la *Candide,* real-seeming adventure à la *Cyrano de Bergerac,* picaresque narrative à la *Lazarillo de Tormes.* It has also been included in such categories of contemporary interest and definition as children's literature and science fiction and even had the genre of Menippean satire revived more or less to accommodate it.[7] "The history of genre theory," as Gérard Genette observes, "is everywhere marked by these fascinating schemas that inform and deform the often irregular reality of the literary field and claim to discover a natural 'system' when they construct a factitious symmetry with a great supply of blind windows.[8] The history of reading *Gulliver's Travels* is a series of such genre decisions that attempt to cope with the text's polyvalence and indeterminacy by means of this principle—the implicit assumption that genre confers coherence and stability, that is, the text read monologically.[9]

Efforts to deal with the genre of *Gulliver's Travels* continue to appear, and I would like to place mine in the company of two recent readings in order to examine the problematic of genre from several different perspectives.

2

When a system is superimposed upon a text, there can never be a perfect match between the paradigm, which is abstract, and the text, which is real: "The kinds are only *ideas* of form, established by custom and consensus . . . adumbrations of an idea of order, shapes for content, as well as the shadows cast by solid, individual works of literature."[10] The delicate balance so well described by Rosalie Colie is especially subject to strain when a text is

polyvalent: the better the fit achieved in one direction by imposing a monologic reading, the more troublesome aporias open in
other directions.

As a case in point I should like to apply the idea that Gulliver
is a picaro to the evidence that Frederick J. Keener presents for
his interpretation of *Gulliver's Travels* as a philosophical tale, a
reading that consists almost entirely of a critique of Gulliver as a
philosophical protagonist intentionally manqué—inconsistent,
self-centered, insensitive, superficial.[11] For Keener, Gulliver is a
character who is always at fault: first, in not being as complicated
a character as he should be, and then, in not being particularly
likeable. If he were the ideal philosophical protagonist, Gulliver
would remain at home devoting himself to family, country, and
introspection. Instead, he shows "a violent inclination not to stay
put and examine what he is and the way he thinks . . ." (p. 126).
Next best, Keener's remarks suggest, would be a reflective narration of his adventures, one that gave others "credit for having a
history of thought and feelings" (p. 103).

If, however, we approach *Gulliver's Travels* with another frame
of reference, the picaresque, all of the above-mentioned qualities
that make Gulliver a parodic philosophical hero contribute to
defining him as a prototypical picaro.[12] The essential picaresque
situation, as Ulrich Wickes defines it, "is that of a protagonist,
worse than we, caught up in a chaotic world, worse than ours, in
which he is on an eternal journey of encounters that allow him to
be alternately both victim of that world and its exploiter." For
Richard Bjornson, picaros are "invariably confronted by a choice
between social conformity (which is necessary for survival) and
adherence to what they have learned to consider true or virtuous." The ending of a picaresque narrative, according to
Claudio Guillén, confirms the picaro's apartness by a "final with-
drawal from society."[13]

Examples from picaresque criticism that suit *Gulliver's Travels*
could be multiplied, and it is worth noting that those given
above, taken as descriptions of what occurs in the text divorced
from generic attribution, could readily be assimilated by Keener's
reading. While Keener sees Gulliver's failure to examine his
values as a fault in a philosophical character, the picaro is *properly* reactive and unanalytical, the passive experiencer of marvelous adventures. So, for example, when Gulliver says that the
Lilliputian admiral Skyresh Bolgolam "was pleased, without any
Provocation, to be my mortal Enemy," Keener comments: "It
never occurs to Gulliver that the arrival of a superman would

cause resentment in Lilliput or anywhere, especially resentment by those whose station and power the newcomer threatens" (p. 103).[14] *Should* it occur to Gulliver? Not if he is a picaro, whose fictive role is simply to survive and record his experience with only the rudimentary evaluation appropriate to his naïveté. According to the requirements of one genre, Gulliver is a typical character, successfully realized; according to another, he is atypical, a parodic figure although no less successfully realized.

This does not mean that Gulliver can be both straightforward picaro and philosophical protagonist at the same time. In the larger terms of genre, "that sense of the whole by means of which an interpreter can correctly understand any part of its determinacy," there can be no reconciliation.[15] Although Gulliver$_1$ and Gulliver$_2$ share some traits (naïveté and humorlessness, for example), they belong to systems, whether conceived of as prescriptive or descriptive, that resist intermingling. "As soon as genre announces itself," Derrida writes, "one must respect a norm, one must not cross a line of demarcation, one must not risk impurity, anomaly, or monstrosity."[16] This is the *law* of genre. To read *Gulliver's Travels* as picaresque narrative is to emphasize a series of adventures centered upon satiric interaction. To read it as philosophical tale is to emphasize a series of ideas that are embodied in these adventures and interactions.

Arriving here, we are apt to think of some version of a familiar refrain of *Gulliver* criticism: "The most immediate problem is that of genre." For Robert C. Elliott the issue is posed in a question and answer: "Is *Gulliver* a novel? Probably not, although it is not easy to say (except by arbitrary stipulation) why it is not."[17] This formula could serve for any number of genres and reader responses, including the two outlined above. It is easy enough to marshal evidence for a particular classification, yet the question and answer, with their attendant difficulties, remain. The text escapes encompassing rubrics and the kind of centering that such rubrics impose.

It is this sense of the text as elusive and indeterminate that governs the second reading I wish to examine, Robert W. Uphaus's reader-response approach.[18] Uphaus posits and rejects a reader whose commitment to "objective" criticism obscures a basic affective response. Since his purpose is to explore this affective experience, he constantly eschews as its inimical antinomy any sort of classification: "An obsession with generic distinctions and rules often blunts the powerful affective appeal of literature" (p. 7). Not surprisingly, Uphaus concludes: "The variety of effects Swift's text produces . . . seems to me strong evidence that *Gulliver's Travels* is not written with any one effect in mind, other than to violate or vex the reader's expectations of coherent, rationally formulable meaning. Rather than reading *Gulliver's Travels* as if it were proceeding toward some one coherent and unifying goal, it may be truer to the reader's experience of the text to speak of a succession of moments that yield varying effects" (pp. 17–18). Thus, Uphaus feels that the very premise of genre, that of nameable form, is inappropriate. Instead of the homogeneous reading experience producing the stable, authoritative text necessary to a generic interpretation, Uphaus finds a diversity that resists the imposition of pattern and must simply be taken as a series of discrete moments.[19]

Neither this dynamic nor the concept of genre is necessarily at odds with the affective response Uphaus values, although "an obsession with generic distinctions and rules" may very well be. But just as the danger of genre criticism is a monologic coercion of the text, so the danger of the genreless stance is a rejection of aesthetic form. In approaching one of the standard problems of *Gulliver's Travels*, the sequence of voyages, Uphaus writes: "Book 3, we know, was written last, and yet Swift does not place it in this position. The fact that Swift does not place it last may tell us something about his attitude to formal coherence—namely, that there never was a developing pattern or an evolving plan which would explain the sequence of books 1–4, other than the general intention to vex the reader" (p. 19). Surely another possibility (which Uphaus does not consider) is that the departure from the order of composition expresses an artistic intention, one that has been confirmed over the centuries by the affective responses of readers who find the last voyage climactic.

Uphaus therefore acknowledges the problematic of genre, only to dismiss it as irrelevant to the reader-critic's real job or else beyond resolution, a determination that may leave as much to be desired as traditional readings that impose inadequate labels upon the text. Is *Gulliver* a genreless text? Probably not, although it is not easy to say (except by arbitrary stipulation) why it is not. Such literary institutions as genre transcend individual relation, and even the generic blind window that Genette refers to "can on occasion let in a true light, and reveal the importance of a misapprehended term."[20] We do not have to agree with E. D. Hirsch, Jr. that "all understanding of verbal meaning is necessarily genre-bound" in order to feel the legitimacy of generic expectation, a shaping convention shared by writer and reader.[21]

3

There is a general consensus among interpreters of *Gulliver's Travels* that the book is puzzling in various ways but nevertheless a classic work of art. A satisfactory generic approach would speak to both of these attributes, neither ignoring the heterogeneity of the text as would a monologic reading nor embracing indeterminacy to the exclusion of formal meaning entirely. Such a reading can be attempted through deconstruction, for like all of Swift's greatest works, *Gulliver's Travels* proffers forthrightly the contradictory energies, marginal peculiarities, and generic aporias that characterize a text's own deconstructive potential.[22] Considering *Gulliver's Travels* as deconstructors *and* as modern readers leads to a dislodging of a number of earlier concerns: among them the literal voyage in whatever form—picaresque, fantastic, philosophical—and, in this post-Darwinian age, the idea that Yahoos are the shocking creatures they once seemed to be.

Now let us go back to Elliott's question, "Is *Gulliver* a novel?" and this time answer it yes, in terms of our own experience as readers of postmodernist fiction, whose authors routinely abuse their characters more flagrantly than Swift does Gulliver. For critical readers of today there can be little doubt that any extended prose fiction with as much character and incident as *Gulliver's Travels* will be experienced as a novel; indeed by our standards it may even seem more conventional than experimental. That it is not a novel according to the conventions of Swift's time does not enter into our experience of the text when we are not pretending to be readers of that time or readers of Swift's mind.

Gulliver, the same ordinary Englishman that most interpretations agree upon, will continue to serve as the protagonist of a deconstructive reading, but it may seem that an abandonment of the "earlier reader" posture has already ruled out a great deal for him to do. Deprived of those literal adventures, which I have already suggested cannot sustain the interest of contemporary readers, he must be translated to a metaphoric level where the text engages human experience in spiritual terms as valid now as when *Gulliver's Travels* was written. Generically, then, the work is a spiritual bildungsroman in which humankind—Gulliver and the reader—must confront a reality that admits of only a pessimistic construction, a condition desperate enough to drive even a more intellectually resourceful person than Gulliver to the madness he ultimately exemplifies. The text may dissociate itself from Gulliver's final extremism, but it does not repudiate the dilemma that brings it about: namely, that the Houyhnhnms are an ideal that can never be realized by man, that the humanlike Yahoos are disgusting brutes, and that man, abusing his mere tincture of reason, is much worse than even a Yahoo.[23] For modern readers these propositions do not seem as extraordinary as they once did, but what remains puzzling is the ending—Gulliver's unbearable awareness of this condition without the possibility of salvation. Deconstruction can illuminate the way the text arrives at this denouement through an examination of Gulliver's apprenticeship to life/death, a typical Derridean opposition.

Given this almost cosmic sense of human inadequacy, religion would appear to be the great absence that haunts the text and calls to mind *Gulliver's* antitype, *The Pilgrim's Progress*. At the end of Gulliver's education there is awareness but no salvation. Far from being open-ended, *Gulliver's Travels* allows no way out of this impasse, whose unpalatable corollaries emerge in Swift's correspondence with close friends. To Pope he wrote that we are only *rationis capax*, analogous not only to Yahoos but to the kite that flew off with one of Swift's chickens and was later, to Swift's satisfaction, shot dead.[24] There is no reason to question the seriousness of his counsel to Sheridan: "Expect no more from Man than such an Animal is capable of, and you will every day find my Description of Yahoes more resembling." Or, his assertion to Pope: "I hate and detest that animal called man."[25] Like *Gulliver's Travels* itself, all of these pronouncements posit a flawed human nature ineluctably mired in its animal character. Swift's satire is hardly "corrective," for, as John Traugott remarks, "one cannot correct one's being."[26]

We may further recall from Swift's letters that even the most excellent women were only "bestes en juppes" (animals in skirts) compared to Vanessa, whom he could scarcely believe to be of the same species.[27] Although here the satire is turned to compliment, such animal imagery often recurs in Swift's writings as a standard satiric strategy given effective variation in the idea of the Yahoos. Additionally, as Roland M. Frye has pointed out, "the very words used by Swift in describing the Yahoo are throughout strikingly like—and frequently identical with—those used by the theologians in treating 'the flesh' and the sins to which it incites man."[28] Flesh/animal/man/sin: this conjunction, common in Swift's other writings, assumes its most effective form in the Yahoo, a creature both animal and man, whose flesh, because it is human rather than animal, is sinful.[29] Unreferred to and unacknowledged, sin is everywhere implicit in the exotic but still human or human-resembling worlds of *Gulliver's Travels*, either in the culpability of the beings Gulliver encounters or in his explanations of practices in his native land.

What is overtly inscribed in the text is death, the wages of sin. In a letter to Archbishop William King Swift once divided the world into "two Sects, those that hope the best, and those that fear the worst. . . . the former . . . is the wiser, the nobler, and most pious Principle; and although I endeavour to avoid being of the other, yet upon this Article I have sometimes strange Weaknesses."[30] Death exposed the aporia of fearing the worst in its most intense form, the situation where religion and temperament clashed most poignantly and irreconcilably in Swift. In the first two books Gulliver moves from one adventure to another under the ever-present threat of sudden death, first as a helpless giant in Lilliput, subject to human treachery, then as a truly powerless homunculus, vulnerable to careless destruction. In the narrative paradigm Gulliver must always meet some test of survival in a strange and dangerous place, but in the first two books the pattern is simply repeated without any growth of insight on Gulliver's part. Meaning is deferred in keeping with Derrida's idea of *différance*.[31] The hierarchical opposition life/death seems to be affirmed by the voyages to Lilliput and Brobdingnag, for in spite of threats to his life Gulliver survives. Death emerges, startlingly for many readers, out of the fragmented and decentered episodes of the third voyage. By means of the Struldbruggs, the power relation of life/death is changed in keeping with Derrida's assertion that "to deconstruct the opposition, first of all, is to overturn the hierarchy at a given moment."[32]

The play of *différance* in the Struldbrugg episode can be located in an inconspicuous remark produced by Gulliver's innocence before the revelation that redefines the word *Struldbrugg* more accurately for him. When Gulliver's audience of knowledgeable Luggnuggians draws him out concerning what his own scheme of living should be were he a Struldbrugg, Gulliver prefaces his dizzying chronicle of lifetimes lived profitably and pleasurably with a clause given little syntactical weight: "As soon as I could discover my own Happiness by understanding the Difference between Life and Death, I would first revolve . . ." (p. 209). The happiness that Gulliver thought to discover was to have been an affirmation of life through the absence of death, but in the first movement of *différance* the terms of the binary opposition life/death reveal that death is the desirable presence in the Struldbruggian, and by extension, the human economy. Learning the real condition of the Struldbruggs seems to bring about Gulliver's enlightenment as nothing else on his voyages has done. He writes: "The Reader will easily believe, that from what I had heard and seen, my keen Appetite for Perpetuity of Life was much abated. I grew heartily ashamed of the pleasing Visions I had formed; and thought no Tyrant could invent a Death into which I would not run with Pleasure from such a Life" (p. 214). After his initial raptures over the imagined benefits of immortality, Gulliver now envisions death as a desideratum to be pursued actively ("run with Pleasure") in preference to a lifeless life.

At the moment this is only an intellectually apprehended horror. Gulliver himself is so far removed from a personal sense of menace that his next chapter eclipses the horror of the Struldbruggs with a matter-of-fact beginning: "I thought this Account of the *Struldbruggs* might be some Entertainment to the Reader, because it seems to be a little out of the common Way . . ." (p. 215). "Account," "Entertainment": this uncharged language reflects Gulliver's desire to distance the trauma of his earlier reaction while at the same time it becomes charged with the anomaly of its inadequacy to the experience. Gulliver does not in fact come to understand the difference between life and death; the Struldbrugg exemplum is immediately turned into a text directed outward to the reader.

The play of *différance* continues in the fourth voyage where life/death is further deconstructed to elaborate upon the convertibility inherent on the periphery of the Struldbrugg episode. The text demythologizes death by overdetermining the web of relationship uniting the living and the dying so that there is no violent rupture between the two states. In the Houyhnhnm language "to die" is "to retire to his first Mother," the reinstatement of the primordial tie, with all of its accruing positive values. Similarly, the dying Houyhnhnm feels as if he were "returning Home from a visit to one of his Neighbours." The dying "take a solemn Leave of their Friends, as if they were going to some remote Part of the Country, where they designed to pass the rest of their Lives" (p. 275). This controlling metaphor of the visit or interaction of the dying with relatives and friends is supported by an anecdote Gulliver tells:

> I remember, my Master having once made an Appointment with a
> Friend and his Family to come to his House upon some Affair of
> Importance; on the Day fixed, the Mistress and her two Children
> came very late. . . . Her Excuse for not coming sooner, was that her
> Husband dying late in the Morning, she was a good while consulting
> her Servants about a convenient Place where his Body should be laid;
> and I observed she behaved herself at our House, as chearfully as the
> rest. . . . (pp. 274–75)

Death, like life, is natural, appropriate, acceptable, even positive.
The distinction between them is ultimately obliterated in terms
of affect because Houyhnhnms have no different feelings about
these two states. For humans, in contrast, only the horrific effects
of life—the age and decay embodied in the Struldbruggs, for
instance—can bring about an acceptance of death.[33]

Ties of affection are the chief vehicle of meaning, both metaphorically and literally, in Gulliver's account of the
Houyhnhnms' attitude toward death since the death of loved
ones would naturally be the most difficult test of acceptance. In
his correspondence Swift remarks repeatedly that he cannot bear
the death of friends.[34] When Lady Ashburnham died, he wrote to
Stella, "I hate Life, when I think it exposed to such Accidents
and to see so many thousand wretches burthening the Earth
while such as her dye, makes me think God did never intend Life
for a Blessing."[35] When he believed Stella herself to be dying, he
confessed to Thomas Sheridan, "All my Preparations will not
suffice to make me bear it like a Philosopher, nor altogether like a
Christian."[36] Throughout Swift's writings "nor altogether like" is
the mark of différance, the undermining bent of temperament
that deconstructs so many Swiftian positions.

What Gulliver finally comes to feel is that the life he is condemned to lead is a kind of death like that of the Struldbruggs,
now that he knows what a life of perfect reason can be.[37] When
his Houyhnhnm Master informs Gulliver that he must leave the
country, his reaction is that "death would have been too great an
Happiness" (p. 280). Having experienced both enlightenment
and bliss, Gulliver cannot willingly go back to a grossly imper-
fect existence in spite of the pressure exerted by the conventional
human/equine hierarchy that the fourth voyage has so perversely
deconstructed. But rather than dying, he goes mad: in England
he clings to "Houyhnhnm" in a context that recognizes only
"horse" and insists upon "Yahoo" for his own species—substitutions that create conflicting demands in readers between their

own (human) perspective and the involvement of first-person narration. Gulliver in the stable communing with his horses perfectly illustrates Diderot's definition of madness: "To deviate from reason knowingly, in the grip of a violent passion, is to be weak, but to deviate from it confidently and with the firm conviction that one is following it, is to be what we call *mad*."[38] The madman is engulfed by his own fiction, whereas Swift's fiction allows us to imagine ourselves through Gulliver in fantastic contexts without demanding that we actually experience or valorize these phenomena.

By continuing at home the disjunction between Gulliver and society that obtained in the lands he visited, the epilogue unexpectedly extends the by-now-familiar structure of the *Travels*. Yet the repetition entails *différance*. Gulliver is no longer the reassuring, earnest Englishman confronting a fantastic world; the world is now the familiar place and Gulliver fantastic. Once again, a hierarchical opposition has been subverted, not through a process of mechanical reversal but through a probing of its internal differences. "Familiar" and "foreign" lose their sharp polarity since the world Gulliver returns to—one of wives, children, and decent individuals like Pedro de Mendez—is also the world of the terrible list of book 4: "Gipers, Censurers, Backbiters, Pickpockets, Highwaymen, House-breakers," etc. (pp. 276–77)—a catalogue whose ruthless energy is authoritatively Swiftian. That powerful voice speaks the validity of Gulliver's realization that by a standard of *perfect* rationality man is without hope, and the weight of that message overshadows its vehicle, that is, Gulliver's madness. As Shoshana Felman writes, "Every novel contains simultaneously the temptation of madness and the negation of this temptation, in a reflexive narrative system, where the 'novelesque' at once discloses and denounces its own madness."[39] Conventionally, the madness of a Gulliver reassures us of our own sanity, but a satirist is particularly apt to subvert these categories, to deconstruct sanity to reveal madness. Gulliver discloses the madness of accepting the unsavory world of the epilogue, yet his own behavior offers no viable alternative.

Gulliver's cloying speech on the virtues of British imperialism includes a mention of "devout and able Pastors to propagate *Christianity*" (p. 296), but there is no evidence that religion is any solace to *him* for the loss of the secular paradise of Houyhnhnmland. We might remark that the world Gulliver returns to has need of Christian redemption, but within the boundaries of the text religion remains a felt absence, one that moves the work closer to a twentieth-century sensibility. Without establishing Christianity as explicit or implicit presence, *Gulliver's Travels* nevertheless partially deconstructs the binary opposition of life/death according to its tenets. Life is the sinful negative term, is in fact death, while death becomes positive.[40] Yet the essential part of the Christian transvaluation is obviously missing. Death loses its sting in the Christian belief-system because it opens the way to everlasting spiritual life; in *Gulliver's Travels* it contains no such promise. Fear of death is not mitigated by Christianity but by the perfect rationality of the Houyhnhnms, which strips it of pain, grief, and regret.

Since man cannot achieve this perspective on death, what Gulliver has learned among the Houyhnhnms is useless: the generic pattern of the Bildungsroman, the acquisition of wisdom, is thus deconstructed to produce a ~~Bildungsroman~~, in Derridean terms a critique of the Bildungsroman pattern undertaken within the work itself. As readers, we recognize this combination of fictive structure and its violation as postmodernist, a rubric that will readily accommodate *Gulliver's Travels*. Such an approach not only conforms to our present-day critical sensibility; it fits the shape of the text more accurately. The reader can hold opposing impulses without subjecting them either to the constraints of a monologic reading or to the amorphousness of an appraoch that denies generic validity completely. The (provisional) last word that describes this condition of simultaneous generic fulfilment and transgression belongs to Derrida: "There is no genreless text . . . yet such participation never amounts to belonging."[41]

Notes

1. Jonathan Culler, *Structuralist Poetics: Structuralism, Linguistics, and the Study of Literature* (Ithaca: Cornell University Press, 1975), p. 114.

2. John Arbuthnot to Swift, 5 November 1726, *The Correspondence of Jonathan Swift*, ed. Harold Williams, 5 vols. (Oxford: Clarendon Press, 1963–65), 3:180; Swift to Alexander Pope, 27 November 1726, 3:189.

3. Ralph W. Rader, "The Concept of Genre and Eighteenth-Century Studies," in *New Approaches to Eighteenth-Century Literature, Selected Papers from the English Institute*, ed. Phillip Harth (New York: Columbia University Press, 1974), p. 90, states that "readers are always aware to some degree of making generic assumptions," a process he traces back to the nature of mental activity itself.

4. "The Law of Genre," trans. Avital Ronell, *Critical Inquiry* 7 (1980): 57. Rpt. in *On Narrative*, ed. W. J. T. Mitchell (Chicago: University of Chicago Press, 1981), 51–77.

5. *The Lives of the Most Eminent English Poets*, 2 vols. (Charlestown: S. Ethridge, 1810), 2:193.

6. *Life of Swift*, in *The Miscellaneous Prose Works of Sir Walter Scott*, 6 vols. (Boston: Wells and Lilly, 1829), 2:219.

7. Northrop Frye, *The Anatomy of Criticism* (Princeton: Princeton University Press, 1957), pp. 308–12.

8. "Gérard Genette, "Genres, 'types,' modes," *Poétique* 32 (1977): 408, my translation: "L'histoire de la théorie des genres est toute marguée de ces schémas fascinants qui informent et déforment la réalité souvent hétéroclite du champ littéraire et prétendent découvrir un 'système' naturel là où ils construisent une symétrie factice à grand renfort de fausses fenêtres."

9. See Murray Cohen's pleas for the application of modern critical theory to eighteenth-century texts, "Eighteenth-Century English Literature and Modern Critical Methodologies," *The Eighteenth Century* 20 (1979): 5–23. He writes, "In response to problems and complexities, we create more categories so that every assertion signifies a clear meaning; and at the evident inadequacy of the traditionally few genres, we invent new ones, for formalist critics abhor a text without a classification" (p. 5).

10. Rosalie L. Colie, *The Resources of Kind: Genre Theory in the Renaissance*, ed. Barbara K. Lewalski (Berkeley: University of California Press, 1973), pp. 127–28.

11. Frederick J. Keener, *The Chain of Becoming: The Philosophical Tale, the Novel, and a Neglected Realism of the Englightenment: Swift, Montesquieu, Voltaire, Johnson, and Austen* (New York: Columbia University Press, 1983), pp. 89–126. Further references will be given parenthetically in the text. It is not my purpose to take issue with Keener's reading; arguments against such an interpretation have long been in print. See Edward W. Rosenheim, Jr., *Swift and the Satirist's Art* (Chicago: University of Chicago Press, 1963), p. 157: "Gulliver . . . is above all a *character* whose experiences—rather than postures, beliefs, or literary habits—constitute the major fiction of the work." See also C. J. Rawson, *Gulliver and the Gentle Reader: Studies in Swift and our Time* (Boston: Routledge and Kegan Paul, 1973), p. 27: "The emphasis is so preponderantly on what can be shown through him (including what he says and thinks) than on his person in its own right, that we are never allowed to accustom ourselves to him as a real personality despite all the rudimentary local colour about his early career, family life and professional doings."

12. The standard discussion of *Gulliver's Travels* as picaresque fiction can be found in Ronald Paulson, *The Fictions of Satire* (Baltimore: Johns Hopkins University Press, 1967), pp. 162–69.

13. Ulrich Wickes, "The Nature of Picaresque Narrative: A Modal Approach," *PMLA* 89 (1974): 242; Richard Bjornson, *The Picaresque Hero in European Fiction* (Madison: University of Wisconsin Press, 1977), p. 11; Claudio Guillén, *Literature as System: Essays toward the Theory of Literary History* (Princeton: Princeton University Press, 1971), p. 88.

14. Jonathan Swift, *Gulliver's Travels*, in *The Prose Works of Jonathan Swift*, ed. Herbert Davis et al. (Oxford: Basil Blackwell, 1937–68), 11:42. Further references will be to this edition and will be given parenthetically in the text.

15. E. D. Hirsch, Jr., *Validity in Interpretation* (New Haven: Yale University Press, 1967), p. 86.

16. Derrida, "The Law of Genre," p. 57.

17. *The Power of Satire: Magic, Ritual, Art* (Princeton: Princeton University Press, 1960), p. 184.

18. *The Impossible Observer: Reason and the Reader in Eighteenth-Century Prose* (Lexington: University Press of Kentucky, 1979), pp. 9–27. Further references will be given parenthetically in my text.

19. What Uphaus finds to be true of reading Swift, the fragmentary nature of the process, Wolfgang Iser finds to be true of reading in general. In *The Implied Reader: Patterns of Communication in Prose Fiction from Bunyan to Beckett* (Baltimore: Johns Hopkins University Press, 1974), p. 288, he writes: "We look forward, we look back, we decide, we change our decisions, we form expectations, we are shocked by their nonfulfillment, we question, we muse, we accept, we reject. . . ." While some texts will clearly require more of these operations than others, reading, Iser suggests, is always a spatial and temporal activity that demands constant readjustment—not an instantaneous mastery of an indivisible entity. It is always, in other words, a "succession of moments that yield varying effects."

20. Genette, p. 408, my translation: "La fausse fenêtre peut en l'occurrence donner une vraie lumière, et révéler l'importance d'un terme méconnu. . . ."

21. Hirsch, *Validity in Interpretation*, p. 76.

22. Most of what I draw on as theory comes from the writings of Jacques Derrida, from whom I take the basic assumption of deconstruction: "The reading must always aim at a certain relationship, unperceived by the writer, between what he commands and what he does not command of the patterns of the language that he uses. This relationship is not a certain quantitative distribution of shadow and light, of weakness or of force, but a signifying structure that critical reading should *produce*." *Of Grammatology*, trans. Gayatri Chakravorty Spivak (Baltimore: Johns Hopkins University Press, 1976), p. 158. For the idea of the text's self-deconstructive activity, see J. Hillis Miller, "Deconstructing the Deconstructors," *Diacritics* 5 (1975): "The text performs on itself the act of deconstruction without any help from the critic" (p. 31).

23. A number of critics have already argued for these premises. See, among others, George Sherburn, "Errors Concerning the Houyhnhnms," *Modern Philology* 56 (1958): 92–97; W. B. Carnochan, "The Complexity of Swift: Gulliver's Fourth Voyage," *Studies in Philology* 60 (1963): 23–25; and Rosenheim, p. 163.

24. Swift to Pope, 29 September 1725, *Correspondence*, 3:103, and 26 November 1725, 3:118.

25. Swift to Sheridan, 11 September 1725, *Correspondence*, 3:94; Swift to Pope, 29 September 1725, 3:103.

26. "*A Tale of a Tub*," *Focus: Swift*, ed. C. J. Rawson (London: Sphere Books, 1971), p. 114.

27. Swift to Esther Vanhomrigh, 12 May 1719, *Correspondence*, 2:326.

28. "Swift's Yahoos and the Christian Symbols for Sin," *Journal of the History of Ideas* 15 (1954): 215–16.

29. Swift often satirizes people in animal terms in his poetry. See, for example, "The Salamander," "The Legion Club," "Wood, an Insect," "The Character of Sir Robert Walpole," "Dick, A Maggot," and "Epistle to a Lady."

30. Letter of 6 Janaury 1709, *Correspondence*, 1:117. Swift's admitted preoccupation with death is notable. He wrote to Bolingbroke, 31 October 1729, *Correspondence*, 3:354: "I was 47 years old when I began to think of death; and the reflections upon it now begin when I wake in the Morning, and end when I am going to Sleep." Scott's anecdote, *Life of Swift*, may well be unreliable, but its existence suggests a propensity associated with Swift: "For many years he used to bid his friends adieu with these melancholy words: 'God bless you, I hope we shall never meet again'" (p. 224).

31. "Différance," *Margins of Philosophy*, trans. Alan Bass (Chicago: University of Chicago Press, 1982), p. 7. See also the definitions of *différance* in *Positions*, trans. Alan Bass (Chicago: University of Chicago Press, 1981), pp. 8–10, especially the following: "The movement of *différance* . . . is the common root of all the oppositional concepts that mark our language, such as . . . sensible/intelligent, intuition/signification, nature/culture, etc." (p. 9).

32. Derrida, *Positions*, p. 41.

33. As Swift wrote to John Gay, 10 November 1730, *Correspondence*, 3:417–18: "God hath taken care . . . to prevent any progress towards real happyness here, which would make life more desirable & death too dreadfull." To Bolingbroke and Pope, 5 April 1729, 3:329, he wrote: "I never wake without finding life a more insignificant thing than it was the day before: which is one great advantage I get by living in this country, where there is nothing I shall be sorry to lose. . . ."

34. See, for example, Swift's letter to Rev. John Worrall, 15 July 1726, *Correspondence:* "I am of Opinion that there is not a greater Folly than to contract too great and intimate a Friendship, which must always leave the Survivor miserable" (3:142). See also 3:145, 234, 236, 311, and 435 for similar sentiments.

35. *Journal to Stella*, ed. Harold Williams, 2 vols. (Oxford: Clarendon Press, 1948), 2:595; letter of 27 July 1726.

36. Swift, *Correspondence*, 3:147.

37. While human beings have passions that make it impossible for them to achieve perfect rationality, as Charles Peake discusses in "Swift and the Passions," *Modern Language Review* 55 (1960): 169–80, Swift tends to present the passions as a necessary evil, in need of subordination to reason and discipline, rather than as a desirable component of human nature. For example, Swift advises a young lady that what a husband wants is "a reasonable Companion, and a true Friend." Her match is one of "Prudence and common Good-liking, without any Mixture of that ridiculous Passion which hath no Being, but in Play-Books and Romances" ("A Letter to a Young Lady, on her Marriage," *Prose Works*, 9:86, 89). In his sermon "On the Trinity," in *Prose Works*, 9:166, Swift asserts: "*Reason* itself is true and just but the *Reason* of every particular man is weak and wavering, perpetually swayed and turned by his Interests, his Passions, and his Vices." Writing to Reverend James Stopford, 20 July 1726, about Stella's approaching death, Swift claimed that "violent friendship is much more lasting, and as much engaging, as violent love" (*Correspondence*, 3:145). His poetry to Stella offers other evidence of an attempt to substitute a more rational form of attachment for a passionate one.

38. *Encyclopédie, ou dictionnaire raisonné des sciences, des arts et des métiers* (Lausanne and Berne: Société Typographique, 1781), 14:341–42, my translation.

39. *Writing and Madness* (Ithaca: Cornell University Press, 1986), p. 135.

40. John Wesley, *The Doctrine of Original Sin according to Scripture, Reason, & Experience* (1757), *The Works of John Wesley*, 14 vols. (Grand Rapids: Zondervan, n.d.), 9:259, quotes another divine's reply to the assertion that death is a benefit: "On the contrary, it is the king of terrors to them [men], the burden of their lives, and bane of their pleasures. To talk, therefore, of death's being a benefit . . . is to talk against the common sense and experience of the whole world."

41. Derrida, "The Law of Genre," p. 65.

Afterword:
Style, Swift's Reader, and the Genres of *Gulliver's Travels*

Frederik N. Smith

Each of the above essays has looked at *Gulliver's Travels* through the eyes of one or more genres. Nonetheless, and forgive the tautology, in spite of its allusion to, borrowing from, and participation in a whole array of genres, the book is one book. The text we hold in our hands must be processed and comprehended by a single reader. How, then, does such a reader deal with the multiplicity of genres he or she finds in *Gulliver's Travels*? Given the continual frustration of our generic expectations, why don't we condemn Swift for perversity and throw the book in the fire? Like *Don Quixote*, *Tristram Shandy*, and *Ulysses*, Swift's volume threatens on every page to come apart at the seams, but it holds together somehow, challenging the attentive reader, urging him or her not to surrender but to play with its author his discomfiting rhetorical game. Finally, a good reader comes to recognize that Swift's many genres are not mere hoops to jump through but means to an end: the fuller understanding of the text Swift has written.

Gulliver's Travels alludes on its first page (the initial sentence of the 1735 "Letter from Captain Gulliver to His Cousin Sympson") to William Dampier and the genre of the travel book, and then, within its seemingly calm, untroubled prose, proceeds to scramble genres quite irresponsibly. C. J. Rawson refers to the "teasing fluctuation" of genre in Swift:

> The tense hovering between laughter and something else, the structural indefiniteness of genre and the incessantly shifting status and function of the parodic element, the ironic twists and countertwists, and the endless flickering uncertainties of local effect suggest that one of Swift's most active satiric weapons is *bewilderment*.[1]

Thus the uncertainty is not only in how different readers have seen *Gulliver's Travels* but also in how any single reader might view the book at any given moment. Travel literature is only nominally Swift's genre (just as nominally his narrator is a retired sea captain), but he does not so much parody the form as use it for his own purposes; he attempts neither a travel book nor an antitravel book but rather explores through allusion, an echo, or, most importantly, through the fleeting adoption of a particular style, a range of literary allegiances inside the superstructure of his chosen genre.[2] A reader's prevailing impression of Captain Gulliver's plain, declarative style never really wanes, but Swift is nonetheless able, working always within this malleable prose, to shift emphases and slip for a moment into this or that recognizable generic style.

That allusion in Gulliver's letter to the *New Voyage Round the World* calls up not only Dampier but the whole genre of the travel book—a favorite of Swift's. The first page of the voyage to Lilliput, however, makes this connection more ambiguous than might be suggested by the pat parallel between Gulliver's supposed editing of Dampier and his request to Sympson for similar assistance with his own travels. This page appears to be a self-conscious echo (not a parody) of the first page of *Robinson Crusoe*, published only seven years earlier:

> Being the third son of the family, and not bred to any trade, my head began to be fill'd very early with rambling thoughts. My father, who was very ancient, had given me a competent share of learning, as far as house-education and a country free-school generally goes, and design'd me for the Law; but I would be satisfied with nothing but going to sea. . . .[3]

Gulliver is introduced as a somewhat more educated young man who similarly disagrees with his father about his future and suffers from the same wunderlust:

> My Father had a small Estate in *Nottinghamshire*; I was the Third of five Sons. He sent me to *Emanuel-College* in *Cambridge*, at Fourteen Years old, where I resided three Years, and applied my self close to my Studies: . . . my Father now and then sending me small Sums of Money, I laid them out in learning Navigation, and other Parts of the Mathematicks, useful to those who intend to travel, as I always believed it would be some time or other my Fortune to do.[4]

The effect of echoing one of the most popular travel books within recent memory—but one of dubious authenticity—is immediately to shake the earlier allusion to *A Voyage Round the World*. Is Gulliver's volume a real travelogue or a fictional travelogue along the lines of *Robinson Crusoe*? Answering that question is more difficult than one might imagine. In this particular instance, Swift's ambivalent allusions to the travel book would seem to be a deliberate attempt to undermine the genre of *Gulliver's Travels* right from the start.

In the text proper, Swift's reader is confronted by a wide range of temporary but isolatable snatches of genres—each recognizable by its appropriate style. Two pages into part 1, we come across this account of the sensory experience of a first-person narrator, a passage that reminds us of an excerpt from a novel, or perhaps an adolescent adventure story:

> I could only look upwards; the Sun began to grow hot, and the Light offended mine Eyes. I heard a confused Noise about me, but in the Posture I lay, could see nothing except the Sky. In a little time I felt something alive moving on my left Leg, which advancing gently forward over my Breast, came almost up to my Chin; when bending mine Eyes downwards as much as I could, I perceived it to be a human Creature not six Inches high. . . . (p. 21)

The influence of Locke is apparent here. Notice how each sense comes into play—sight, touch, hearing—as if one is literally awakening to the world; the effect is not unlike the opening paragraph of Joyce's *Portrait of the Artist of a Young Man*. Swift reproduces Gulliver's immediate experience by writing in a plain, unobtrusive style that is neutralized even more than usual in order to let the sensations themselves predominate. The passage is marked by nouns, words of few syllables, and simple subject-verb-object constructions.

Without abandoning his unmodulated prose, Swift in the following passage from part 2 introduces an element of mock-epic or mock-romance. Here Gulliver is no longer static but very much the protagonist; nonetheless, as in *Hudibras*, *The Rape of the Lock*, or passages of *Tom Jones*, the heroic style is not congruent with the situation, quite wrong for the description of this miniature man in a hurry to urinate but unable to climb down off a high bed, attacked by a couple of rats:

> I rose in a Fright, and drew out my Hanger to defend my self. These horrible Animals had the Boldness to attack me on both Sides, and one of them held his Fore-feet at my Collar; but I had the good Fortune to rip up his Belly before he could do me any Mischief. He

fell down at my Feet; and the other seeing the Fate of his Comrade, made his Escape, but not without one good Wound on the Back, which I gave him as he fled, and made the Blood run trickling from him. (p. 93)

The scene hints at St. George and the dragon. Swift never mentions heroes and dragons, but his phraseology assumes heroical proportions: "the Boldness to attack me on both Sides," "the good Fortune to rip up his Belly before he could do me any Mischief," and "the other seeing the Fate of his Comrade, made his Escape." This reads like an account of the Christians and Saracens in *The Song of Roland.* The proud grotesquerie in the last sentence, however, only underscores the discrepancy between subject and style, for although Gulliver has for a brief, melodramatic moment become a hero (typically untroubled by bodily functions), in the next paragraph he confesses that "I was pressed to do more than one Thing, which another could not do for me. . . ."

The following passage from part 3 could well have been lifted from a report in the *Philosophical Transactions.* Again the diction is simple and subdued, but Swift has adopted a few rhetorical tricks characteristic of scientific writing in his day:

By this oblique Motion the Island is conveyed to different Parts of the Monarch's Dominions. To explain the Manner of its Progress, let *A B* represent a Line drawn cross the Dominions of *Balnibarbi;* let the Line *c d* represent the Load-stone, of which let *d* be the repelling End, and *c* the attracting End, the Island being over *C*; let the Stone be placed in the Position *c d* with its repelling End downwards; then the Island will be driven upwards obliquely towards *D.* (p. 168)

The series of "let" clauses, the use of letters of the alphabet (both capitals and lower case) to refer to points on the accompanying diagram, plus a few words associated with physics—"oblique Motion," "repelling End," "driven upwards," etc.—lend the passage at least a superficial credibility. Of course Swift's reader knows by this point in the text that he or she is not reading a scientific report, but the momentary authenticity of style forces us *inside* the technology of the day, making it more difficult to snicker from afar at the likelihood of this sort of scientific contraption out of Jules Verne. Like the old man mentioned by John Arbuthnot, who "went immediately to his Map to search for Lilly putt," there are probably few among us who have not poured over the diagram of the Flying Island in order to find out how the loadstone manages to make it move.[5]

In the following single sentence from part 4, however, Swift abandons all pretence of objectivity in order to mock lawyers, who (as he said above) use language to prove that white is black and black, white. Indirection gives way to invective:

> It is likewise to be observed, that this Society hath a peculiar Cant and Jargon of their own, that no other Mortal can understand, and wherein all their Laws are written, which they take special Care to multiply; whereby they have wholly confounded the very Essence of Truth and Falshood, of Right and Wrong; so that it will take Thirty Years to decide whether the Field, left me by my Ancestors for six Generations, belong to me, or to a Stranger three Hundred Miles off. (p. 250)

The simplicity of the earlier passages is here abandoned. The verb "hath," archaic in 1726, suggests the archaisms of legal language. Moreover, in attacking the "peculiar Cant and Jargon" of the legal trade which the ordinary person finds it impossible to comprehend, Swift's own tangled syntax—"It is likewise," "that this," "that no other," "and wherein," "which they," "whereby they," and "so that it will take Thirty Years to decide . . ."—is itself an imitation (here we might say parody) of exactly the sort of thing he is talking about. Swift ridicules the language of the law by attacking it head-on *and* by giving his reader a taste of its typical convolutions. The directness of the final clause exposes the verbosity of what has preceded.

Adolescent adventure story, mock-heroic tale, scientific report, parody of the law—the examples might be continued almost indefinitely. Sir Walter Scott praised Swift for his "faculty of transfusing his own soul into the body of any one whom he selected,—of seeing with his eyes, employing every organ of his sense, and even becoming master of the powers of his judgment."[6] I have always felt uneasy with this statement, which seems to me to praise Swift for a quality he did *not* have and did *not* strive for. What we *can* say is that Swift possessed a remarkable ability to emulate fragments of generic styles for his own immediate purposes; indeed the fluctuation of genre referred to by Rawson is a result of his unwillingness to commit himself wholeheartedly to any one character, or even to the consistency of the text his character is supposedly writing, but rather to what he senses as the local demands of the text.[7] Swift's attention to temporary effects is quite at odds with generic reading. One would be sorely misled—and maybe driven stark mad—if one were to assume genre was a trustworthy compass for making one's way through *Gulliver's Travels*; as we have seen, travel literature is only superficially Swift's genre, and his fleeting allegiances to various other genres are likewise unreliable, or reliable for only a short time, or reliable in ways different from one another. Thus in the above examples, the genre of mimetic fiction is used to establish the protagonist's reality, as a way of getting the reader involved, and in order to suggest Gulliver's childlike awakening to a totally new world; mock-heroic is used to tease Gulliver for his western pretentiousness and also to emphasize how far modern man has fallen from the epical days of yore; scientific or technical prose is introduced in order to underscore the supposedly advanced science of the Balnibarbians and as a way of making us realize how little modern, technical style depends on image-making; finally, the jargon of lawyers is employed in the service of Swift's invective and is intended to tie us in the same syntactic knots we would experience in reading a legal document. *Note that there is no single role played by these various generic styles.* Throughout the text, Swift's reader is confronted by a panoply of such styles, and his sensitivity to a variety of generic cues would seem to be part of the game; yet those cues steadfastly refuse to function as ready-made guides to Swift's meaning.

The examples we have looked at so far are more or less uncontaminated by other genres (although mock-heroic is itself a mixed form); frequently, however, Swift's characteristic instability of genre can be observed within a single passage. For example, in one page-long section of part 4 we come across the following sequence of paragraphs:

1. A description of the Yahoos' strength, and also their insolent, mischievous, and libidinous natures—in all of which the red-haired of both sexes exceed the norm;
2. A description of their living habits (they claw out kennels for themselves) and eating habits (roots, herbs, carrion, wild rats);
3. A description of the swimming and fishing abilities of the Yahoos; then, without transition, Gulliver says: "And upon this Occasion, I hope the Reader will pardon my relating an odd Adventure";
4. A recounting of Gulliver's near-rape by a female Yahoo,

along with his dramatic rescue by his friend and protector
the Sorrel Nag; and
5. A paragraph describing Gulliver's embarrassment as a result
of this occurrence, especially since the sexual advances of
the female Yahoo make his own Yahooism undeniable.

Paragraphs 1, 2, and 3 are nonfictional in nature, giving us the
sort of information we would find if we were able to look up
"Yahoo" in the encyclopedia. Paragraph 4—the new direction is
signposted by Gulliver's apology for this "odd Adventure"—
jumps deductively from the general to the particular, from information to narrative. Paragraph 5 then jumps back to the general,
inductively drawing a conclusion from the foregoing narrative—
not about the Yahoos but about Gulliver himself.
    Such switching between scene and sermon is characteristic of
Defoe's fiction. But whereas Defoe often employs this format
rather mechanically, Swift's genre-switching is marvelously subtle, as in the two last paragraphs of the sequence:

> Being one Day abroad with my Protector the Sorrel Nag, and the
> Weather exceeding hot, I entreated him to let me bathe in a River that
> was near. He consented, and I immediately stripped myself stark
> naked, and went down softly into the Stream. It happened that a
> young Female *Yahoo* standing behind a Bank, saw the whole Pro-
> ceeding; and inflamed by Desire, as the Nag and I conjectured, came
> running with all Speed, and leaped into the Water within five Yards
> of where I bathed. I was never in my Life so terribly frighted; the Nag
> was grazing at some Distance, not suspecting any Harm: She em-
> braced me after a most fulsome Manner; I roared as loud as I could,
> and the Nag came galloping towards me, whereupon she quitted her
> Grasp, with the utmost Reluctancy, and leaped upon the opposite
> Bank, where she stood gazing and howling all the time I was putting
> on my Cloaths.
>   This was Matter of Diversion to my Master and his Family, as well
> as of Mortification to my self. For now I could no longer deny, that I
> was a real *Yahoo*, in every Limb and Feature, since the Females had a
> natural Propensity to me as one of their own Species: Neither was the
> Hair of this Brute of a Red Colour, (which might have been some
> Excuse for an Appetite a little irregular) but black as a Sloe, and her
> Countenance did not make an Appearance altogether as hideous as
> the rest of the Kind; for, I think, she could not be above Eleven Years
> old. (pp. 266–67).[8]

The anecdote is presumably introduced as a sample of Yahoo
primitivism. But the reader has difficulty maintaining his or her

footing; under the broad canopy of the travelogue, Swift discovers a remarkable number of other genres. The tone remains as
earnest as Dampier or Crusoe; it is the loosening of categories
that is so disconcerting. Details (not so numerous as elsewhere)
such as "the Weather exceeding hot," "within five Yards of the
Place where I bathed," and "could not be above Eleven Years old"
are in the style of the travel book. The strong sense of a first-
person narrator, however, coupled with the emphasis on sensory
detail, carries this passage beyond the travel book and into the
realm of mimetic fiction; thus the reference to the inclement
weather is not simply a documentary detail but serves to explain
the physical pleasure Gulliver enjoys (note the diction) on entering the cooling waters of the river: "He consented, and I immediately stripped myself stark naked, and went down softly into
the Stream." On the other hand, and quite obviously, while this
passage tugs toward the mimetic, it also has important associations with myth or allegory. As the context makes clear, the
Yahoos are to be equated with the raw, physical, incorrigible
libido, and thus this particular Yahoo is only a representative of
the less attractive aspect of human nature and the scene an image
of humanity's rationality victimized by humanity's animalism.
The "enflaming" of this she-Yahoo and her "fulsome" embrace
are part of the palpable drama as well as emblematic of the
Yahoos' behavior in general; moreover, such details serve as the
basis of Gulliver's horrible realization (as individual and as type)
that he is himself of the same species as the Yahoos. And this
realization is (depending on one's point of view) either a "Diver-
sion" or a "Mortification." Swift underscores the comic by pick-
ing up the red-haired joke introduced four paragraphs above and
also by hinting at Gulliver's middle-aged pride in being the object
of *someone's* affections: he tells us that the she-Yahoo quits her
grasp "with the utmost Reluctancy" and admits, at the end of the
last paragraph, that she was indeed not so unattractive as most of
her sisters. Like the aloof Houyhnhnms, we as readers can afford
to laugh at Gulliver. As Europeans and as human beings, however, we have been too closely identified with Gulliver to see his
identification with the Yahoos as altogether humorous.

This passage—in no way unique in the book—contains distinct elements of travelogue, novel, adventure story, allegory,
comedy, tragedy, and of course satire. But here as elsewhere
Swift's reader is caught in a paradox: the borrowings from the
language and tone of various genres would seem to suggest some-
thing; at the same time, however, the author's repeated violations
of generic convention refuse to let the reader utilize those cues

confidently in interpreting the text.[9] To look yet more closely at our example: "It happened that a young Female *Yahoo* standing behind a Bank, saw the whole Proceeding; and inflamed by Desire, as the Nag and I conjectured, came running with all Speed, and leaped into the Water within five Yards of the Place where I bathed." This single sentence functions mimetically but is also an ironic echo of the myth of Acteon secretly observing Artemis as she bathed in the river. Simultaneously, the conventional "as I conjectured" (used elsewhere in this travel book quite straightforwardly) is employed here to ironic effect, for Swift has Gulliver conjecturing with a *horse* and interpreting the Yahoo's actions in such a way that they compliment Gulliver's male body. Vanity, thy name is Gulliver! The rest of the sentence reads like a melodramatic adventure story or perhaps as the crisis-point in a love triangle, a response encouraged by the phrases "came running with all Speed" and (in what follows) terribly frighted," "I roared as loud as I could," and "the Nag came galloping towards me." This single sentence, then, compels Swift's reader to read from several different generic perspectives at the same time.

A more complex example—also from part 4—is the famous description of Gulliver's departure from Houynhnmnland. At stake here is nothing less than the nature of the book we have been reading. Is this paragraph excerpted from a Royal Society travelogue or is it a novelistic, sentimental good-bye in the key of Richardson?

> When all was ready, and the Day came for my Departure, I took Leave of my Master and Lady, and the whole Family, mine Eyes flowing with Tears, and my Heart quite sunk with Grief. But his Honour, out of Curiosity, and perhaps (if I may speak it without Vanity) partly out of Kindness, was determined to see me in my Canoo; and got several of his neighbouring Friends to accompany him. I was forced to wait above an Hour for the Tide, and then observing the Wind very fortunately bearing towards the Island, to which I intended to steer my Course, I took a second Leave of my Master: But as I was going to prostrate myself to kiss his Hoof, he did me the Honour to raise it gently to my Mouth. I am not ignorant how much I have been censured for mentioning this last Particular. Detractors are pleased to think it improbable, that so illustrious a Person should descend to give so great a Mark of Distinction to a Creature so inferior as I. Neither have I forgot, how apt some Travellers are to boast of extraordinary Favours they have received. But, if these Censurers were better acquainted with the noble and courteous Disposition of the *Houyhnhnms*, they would soon change their Opinion. (p. 282)

This paragraph reflects the style of the travel book, the nominal genre of *Gulliver's Travels*. In addition, however, it represents the culmination of the allegory which Swift has been developing throughout part 4 (Yahoo = humanity's animal nature, Houyhnhnm = humanity's rational nature), and it likewise contains elements of a number of other genres, including mimetic fiction, tragedy, and comedy or farce. The paragraph appears immediately after the technical description of the building of a canoe out of oak wattles and the skins of the Yahoos, and the scientific tenor persists here, at least in phrases such as "When all was ready, and the Day came for my Departure," "observing the Wind very fortunately bearing towards the Island," and "I am not ignorant how much I have been censured for mentioning this last Particular." Nonetheless, there is a great deal more to the passage, which focuses not on accurate, supposedly objective description but on an uncharacteristic exchange of sympathies between the captain-surgeon and his noble master. There is of course a contradiction between the emotion inherent in the situation and Gulliver's typically analytical style, but Swift's subtle departures from the conventional diction of the travel book lend a surprising intensity to the scene.

The entire paragraph is dominated by an odd ambivalence between the technical and the fictional, the aloof and the emotional, the comic and the serious. To try to capture all this under the heading "satire" would be greatly to oversimplify Swift's art. Mimetically speaking, the scene is the culmination of Gulliver's visit to Houyhnhnmland and therefore demands no less than a plain, unadorned style; however, the triteness of the initial wording ("mine Eyes flowing with Tears, and my Heart quite sunk with Grief") tends to undermine the sincerity of the feelings involved. A similar doubleness is suggested by Gulliver's reference to "my Master and *Lady*," "the whole *Family*," and "his neighbouring *Friends*" (my italics), which tend either to humanize the situation and thus highlight the fellow-feeling, or else mock it by drawing attention to the absurdity of using these words in reference to *horses*, albeit admirable horses; even Swift's clever pun on "neighbouring" reflects his typical inclusion of more meaning or a greater tonal range than the literal situation would seem to require. So too Gulliver's guess that his master came to see him out of "Kindness" as well as "Curiosity" (a word with scientific import) effectively juxtaposes two quite different interpretations of the same scene.[10]

The ambivalence of this paragraph is especially clear in that simple, complex reference to Gulliver's farewell gesture: when he is about to "prostrate" himself (strong language) before his master, his master instead does him the "honour" of raising his "Hoof" (the *only* word in the passage reminding us that he is a quadraped) to Gulliver's mouth; but note that the Houyhnhnm lifts his hoof "gently," a word used positively in the *Travels*.[11] Now, having presented this detail with a complexity far greater than one would expect in a travel book, in a way that novelistically enwraps a number of perspectives, Swift lets Gulliver slide into his habitual, irksome, apologetic tone, admitting that he has been censured for including this "Particular"; but even Gulliver's apology seems calculated to squeeze as much as possible from this single image, for most readers would probably assume he has been criticized for mentioning that he demeaned himself before a *horse* ("that so illustrious a Person should descend to give so great a Mark of Distinction"), whereas it turns out that he is speaking of the unlikelihood of a horse deigning to lift his hoof to one as lowly as *himself* ("to a Creature so inferior as I"). By the end of this paragraph things are so topsy-turvy that the Houyhnhnm Master, a horse, can be called a "Person," while Gulliver, at least what we used to refer to as a person, can be called a mere "Creature." Moreover, in this surrealistic context Gulliver (Swift!) has the gall to insist on *his* telling of the truth as opposed to the improbable descriptions one has come to expect in the travelogue; this all-too-neat separation of *Gulliver's Travels* from the conventions of the travel book is a nice joke for the reader who has been catching Swift's quite various generic cues.

Such cues put tremendous demands on Swift's reader, who must seemingly decide upon one generic perspective or another or must set aside, if this is possible, the temptations of genre altogether. Thus if I were to approach the above as a scene from a travel book, or even a parody of such a scene, then what I would discover is an exaggeration of similar moments in travel literature—Gulliver having chosen here not just to give a few trinkets to the natives but his very identity. If I were to interpret the passage as mimetic fiction, then I would view this pathetic moment as the denouement to the four preceding parts, the sorrowful farewell of a shipwrecked sailor to the "Person" he has learned to respect the most, who has unintentionally betrayed him. Again, if I were to approach the passage with the assumptions of allegory in mind (as surely would be appropriate by the end of part 4), then I would read this as a scene in which Gulliver, *animal rationale*, dutifully pays obeisance to this embodiment of Reason, pure and simple. Or, finally, if I were to read the paragraph from a comic perspective, what would emerge is the *finale* to the slapstick adventures of a two-dimentional figure (a sort of eighteenth-century Charlie Chaplin), who, venturing into a herd of horses, imagined them to be the perfection of nature, worked hard at *becoming* a horse, but was at last expelled by them for having neither hoof nor horse sense. Surely one of the sources of the frustration experienced by two and a half centuries of critics is the interplay of genre in this and other passages of the book. What's a reader to do? Jonathan Culler advises:

> Citing or opposing conventions of genre brings about a change in the mode of reading. We are forced to cast our net wider so as to . . . allow the dialectical opposition which the text presents to result in a synthesis at a higher level where the grounds of intelligibility are different.[12]

Reading *Gulliver's Travels* is a more complex activity than reading a travel book, a novel, an allegory, or a comedy. Swift's text defamiliarizes itself, making it clear that no one genre is the key to its interpretation. As readers we are forced to ascend to a higher level. On that higher level Gulliver is a legitimate descendant of Dampier, a realistic character like Crusoe or Tom Jones, an abstract representation of *animal rationale*, and, in addition, a lovable, gullible buffoon.

Gulliver's Travels raises important questions about literary norms, and not coincidentally the book is itself about norms— about whether or not they exist. "Understanding is itself genre-bound," argues E. D. Hirsch.[13] This is where Gulliver fails: his understanding is *too* genre-bound. In jumping to the conclusion (on the basis of a few months' acquaintance) that the Houyhnhnms are perfect creatures, Gulliver has misread the situation. It would perhaps not be too far-fetched to say that Gulliver misreads his own text; in part 4 he interprets his experience as clear-cut allegory, although Swift has time and time again demonstrated that things cannot be so easily pigeonholed. On the other hand, the reader's experience has been (as with any well-written text) one long education in how to read the book he or she is reading, and Swift has taught us how to deal with increasing degrees of complexity, how to accept ambiguity, and how we need not always look at either literature or life through the restrictive eyes of any one genre. By the time the Houyhnhnms reach the conclusion that Gulliver is indeed a Yahoo and by the time Gulliver accepts this of himself and accepts the Houyhnhnms as the Perfection of Nature, we as

readers have been prepared to remain more skeptical. The judgments made by both Gulliver and the Houyhnhnms are only
partly true. There is a remarkable integrity to Swift's book: the
difficulty we have in fixing its genre is parallel to the difficulty
we *should* experience in arriving at a neat definition of either
"Houyhnhnm" or "Human." For Swift—as for most of his contemporaries—categories were suspect if taken too absolutely. The
shifting generic connections of *Gulliver's Travels* are themselves
an argument in favor of a less single-minded interpretation than
many readers and critics have attempted. "It seems to me," says
Irvin Ehrenpreis, "that Swift found life and human nature pene-
trated by polarities which only God could resolve, and that
instead of transcending them, he tried to infuse them into the art
of his masterpiece."[14]

Notes

1. *Gulliver and the Gentle Reader: Studies in Swift and Our Time* (London:
Routledge and Kegan Paul, 1973), p. 17; see also p. 5. Cf. Herbert Davis, "Recent
Studies of Swift: A Survey," *University of Toronto Quarterly* 7 (1938): 277, who
aptly describes Swift's satiric practice as "something which varies between
parody and imitation."
2. See Percy G. Adams, *Travel Literature and the Evolution of the Novel*
(Lexington: University Press of Kentucky, 1983), p. 143: "Swift did not, however, in *Gulliver's Travels* satirize travel literature any more than in *A Tale of a
Tub* he satirized religion or learning. There, as he says more than once, he was
attacking only the 'abuses' in religion and learning; and one can show that his
attacks on travel literature were not directed at it as a form but rather at certain
of its features and certain faults of its writers."
3. In *Robinson Crusoe and Other Writings*, ed. James Sutherland (Boston:
Houghton Mifflin, 1968), p. 5.
4. *Gulliver's Travels*, in *The Prose Works of Jonathan Swift*, ed. Herbert
Davis et al. (Oxford: Basil Blackwell, 1939–68), 11: 19. Subsequent references
will be to this edition and will be included within the text.
5. Letter to Swift, 5 November 1726. *The Correspondence of Jonathan Swift*,
ed. Harold Williams (Oxford: Clarendon Press, 1963), 3:180.
6. Scott's most important comments on Swift are collected in *Swift: The
Critical Heritage*, ed. Kathleen Williams (New York: Barnes and Noble, 1970),
pp. 283–314. For the above quotation, see p. 300.
7. On Swift's lack of interest in developing a full-bodied narrator, see my
"Vexing Voices: The Telling of Gulliver's Story," *Papers on Language and Literature* 21 (Fall 1985): 383–98.
8. Cf. Chaucer's description in *The Miller's Tale* of promiscuous Allison's
eyebrows: "Full smale ypulled were hired browes two,/ And tho were bent and
blake as any sloo."
9. Cf. Jonathan Culler, *Structuralist Poetics: Structuralism, Linguistics, and
the Study of Literature* (Ithaca: Cornell University Press, 1975), p. 148: "What is

made intelligible by the conventions of genre is often less interesting than that which resists or escapes generic understanding."

10. Cf. Rawson's reference, in *Gulliver and the Gentle Reader,* p. 56, to "overspilling" in Swift's texts.

11. See pp. 21, 31, 36, 46, 47, 65, 85, 88, 89, 93, 103, 107, 117 (twice), 122, 132, 159, 160 (twice), 205, 225, 237, 282 (twice), and 285. Cf. "gentle," pp. 72, 96, 241, 285, and 291, and "gentleness," p. 38.

12. Culler, *Structuralist Poetics,* p. 151. Cf. Frederick Jameson, "Magical Narratives: Romance as Genre," *New Literary History* 7 (Autumn 1975): "The discovery of an apparently contradictory set of affiliations of Stendhal's novels to different generic traditions is no reason to abandon the categories of generic thinking entirely, but rather the occasion for widening the critical inquiry and raising a new theoretical issue, namely, that of the relationship of the various genres among themselves" (p. 152).

13. *Validity in Interpretation* (New Haven: Yale University Press, 1967), p. 78.

14. "The Styles of *Gulliver's Travels,*" in *Literary Meaning and Augustan Values* (Charlottesville: University Press of Virginia, 1974), p. 94.

Index